the IDENTITY TRINITY

BY GLENDA SHASHO JONES

A **CATALOG AGE** BOOK

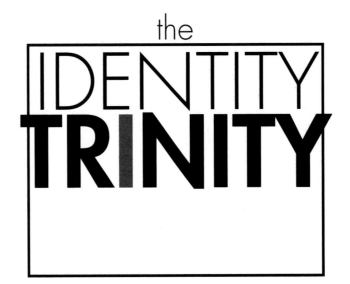

the IDENTITY TRINITY

BY GLENDA SHASHO JONES

Editor: Diane Cyr
Copy Director: Melanie Zimmerman
Production Coordinator: Kate Hanratty
Publisher: Laura Christiana-Beaudry

Front cover design: Claudia Ossa
Text design: Dana Maksin
Front cover photographer: Mark Melendez
Back cover photographer: Matthew Jordan Smith

ISBN 0-918110-25-4

Cowles Business Media, Inc.
11 River Bend Drive South, Box 4232
Stamford, CT 06907-0232

Printed in the United States of America

A **CATALOG AGE** BOOK

DEDICATION

This book is dedicated to my parents, Rhodalie and Donald Fishman, and to Andy Jones who each give me unconditional support and encouragement in every area of my life.

SPECIAL THANKS

When half of this book had been written, the demands and priorities of running Shasho Jones Direct took over. This book would not have been completed (at least, not before the year 2000!) had it not been for the help of Diane Cyr. Not only is she one of the best writers in our industry, Diane is a delightfully smart and insightful woman. While I don't miss the long hours we put in, I do miss the fun we had and the time we spent on the floor in my office showing each other different exercise techniques.

From the start, Terri Bartlett, our Marketing Director at SJD, threw herself into this project wholeheartedly. No one could be more dedicated and precise. It is Terri who contributed a clarity of details that might otherwise have been passed over.

The first section of this book could not have been written as it appears without the help and guidance of Andy Jones, executive vice president, director of strategic planning at Rapp Collins Worldwide. He is the most brilliant strategist I know, which I say without the prejudice that he is also my husband. He has taught me more than any single person about marketing and strategy.

My sincere gratitude, as well, goes to Laura Christiana-Beaudry, who has enthusiastically supported this book from the start. Melanie Zimmerman added an expert polish to the text, while Dana Maksin and Kate Hanratty kept us on schedule (somehow) and brought the pages to life.

The support of the entire staff at SJD has been inspirational. Our senior officers, Donna Wood, Claudia Ossa and Bob Frankel gave me the time to do this book...without inflicting an ounce of guilt. The calm and capable hands of my senior management assistant, Paulette Celestin, managed the project through some turbulent times!

Of course, anyone who has ever written a book knows the important role a friend can play during the process. No one could be more supportive or a better friend than Joyce Kole, whose thoughtful advise I seek on a regular basis.

I also owe many thanks to peers and friends who helped with and supported this project. Bill Michel, Sydney Klevatt, Gordon Cooke, Harry Rosenthal and Erv Magram all deserve applause for their willingness to participate in the book's case studies. Erard Moore generously loaned his time and expertise to our research chapters.

Finally, I am grateful to those in the catalog industry who inspire me every day. Whether they knew it or not, those at Lands' End, J. Peterman, Levenger, L.L. Bean, J. Crew, Chadwick's of Boston, Jos. A. Bank, Lew Magram and countless other catalog companies have gifted me with their brilliant examples of marketing-based creative. They are truly the ones who make this book possible.

INTRODUCTION

I've been around the direct marketing business a while, and I've known lots of brilliant catalogers. I've handled model selections, location shoots, marketing research studies, focus groups, creative brainstorming and business plans for more catalogs than I can sit down and count.

But when I really want marketing inspiration, I think of my grandfather.

Years ago he had a locksmith business on New York City's Lower East Side. I used to watch him at his desk, cutting out pictures of keys and pasting them onto pages for his customers. Sometimes I'd help out, creating my first catalog "layouts" with paste and scissors.

It wasn't glamorous work. No art directors, location shots, or even copywriters. This "catalog" was nothing much more than a price sheet. But what it had, I've learned, is what every catalog needs to survive and profit.

Identity.

Identity meant that my grandfather's "catalog" was recognized by his customers. When they saw his name on it, they kept it around. They knew from experience that they could expect great service, reliable product and prompt attention. Even today, when I visit a locksmith or hardware store in Manhattan, I like to ask whether they remember D. Silver Hardware. They always do.

I know, I know. Cataloging is a lot more complicated today. We've got databases to contend with, electronic pagination, merge-purging, square-inch analysis, you name it. We scrutinize concepts, positioning, merchandising, pacing. We mail our books to hundreds of thousands, or millions, of men, women, urbanites, suburbanites, people from every walk of life.

But it all comes down to the same thing. We need our customers to know us, trust us and buy from us. The way to achieve this is through creating a recognizable *identity.*

No catalog is merely the sum of its products, just as no person is the sum of his body parts. Open any Lands' End catalog, or J. Crew, or Sharper Image. You don't see an assortment of shirts, socks and luggage. You see a unique sense of life and movement, playfulness, moods and feelings. In other words, you see a recognizable personality. You could tear the covers off those books and you'd still know whose catalog you had.

How those catalogs get that way is no mystery. Along with entrepreneurial gut instinct, they use *marketing-driven creative.* They research the marketplace and customer base. They establish a consistent, *likable* brand and positioning within that marketplace. And then they choose the photography, design, layouts, order form, service and copy that support that positioning.

It sounds simple, but it's not easy. We all know beautiful catalogs that just don't speak to customers, and we all know catalogs with great offers that are just plain hard to get through. Those catalogs don't work because they don't merge looks and brains. They aren't warm, friendly, engaging. They don't have an identity, a personality.

Catalog identity is truly a fusion of the emotional and the rational. It merges the hard, plain facts about what consumers want with the intuitive, indefinable qualities of great copy and design. In short, it's a bonding of two worlds that rarely come together, *research* and *creative.*

I've learned a lot about those two worlds in my 20 years in the business. I spent the first six years of my career handling research for a packaged-goods firm. I then spent six years creating and heading the Direct Marketing Association's research, information and publications division.

After applying my direct marketing skills at Wunderman Worldwide, I joined catalog agency AGA and something clicked. Like the kid at my grandfather's desk, I was again drawn to the world of product layouts and presentations. But what I liked best was the knowledge that cataloging was both creative and *measurable.* My experience in three worlds—research, creative and direct marketing—showed that *profits* resulted directly from smart application of marketing-driven creative.

This book lays out the tools of marketing, research and creative to help you focus your own catalog's identity. You can learn to recognize your catalog's own unique merits and strengths—which, by the way, may not be what you think they are—and to build on them. You can learn to capture the likes (and avoid the dislikes) of your target audience and reflect them in your catalog's own personality. (After all, if your customers are going to spend money with you, they have to like *you,* as well as like what you're selling.)

More critically, you'll learn to recognize and solve your catalog's own unique *problems*—which again, may not be what you think they are. Does your catalog need a repositioning, or just a shape-up? Is response flat because of your product—or your creative? Is your targeting misdirected? Are you turning on the right customers? Are you drawing in the wrong ones? Should you try a spin-off? I'll help you find out.

What you'll find, in the end, is that no matter what your product line or customer base, no matter how long or short your catalog has been around, a strong, proactive, selling identity will help your bottom line. People buy from catalogs they like and trust. They buy from catalogs they identify with. Through marketing-driven creative, you can learn to create the kind of identity your own unique catalog was always meant to have.

You won't even need a paste pot.

THE IDENTITY TRINITY

Introduction 4

SECTION ONE
Positioning

Chapter 1: Why You Should Care About Brand Identity 9

Chapter 2: The Identity Trinity: Brand, Image, Positioning 15

Chapter 3: Secrets of Positioning:
What Makes Your Catalog Stand Out 21

SECTION TWO
Setting Up the Marketing Plan of Action

Chapter 4: Marketing Objectives: Strategies and Tactics 35

Chapter 5: The Art of Strategic Thinking 41

Chapter 6: Tactical Warfare...51

Chapter 7: Final Strategy: Boosting Your Numbers 59

SECTION THREE
Diagnostics and Research

Chapter 8: Diagnosing Your Marketing Problems 69

Chapter 9: The Use of Research...77

Chapter 10: The Tools of Research..85

SECTION FOUR
Executing the Brand Identity

Chapter 11: Secrets of marketing-Based Creative 95

Chapter 12: Getting the Front Cover Right 103

Chapter 13: The Inside-Out of Your Catalog..113

Chapter 14: Inserts and Order Blanks 123

Chapter 15: Adding up the Elements:
　　　　　　　Hoe to Put Pacing and Energy Into Your Book.................133

Chapter 16: The Supporting Role of Good Design 145

Chapter 17: Secrets of Photographs that Sell..151

Chapter 18: Choosing Models that Make Sense....................................159

Chapter 19: Finding Your Catalogs Selling Voice 165

Chapter 20: Putting it Together: Positioning and Copy 175

SECTION FIVE
Solving Your Catalogs Identity Crisis

Chapter 21: Meeting the Marketing Challenge 189

Chapter 22: The Challenge of Start-ups...191

Chapter 23: The Spin-off Catalog..199

Chapter 24: Should Your Reposition? 205

Chapter 25: The Catalog Face-lift..215

Chapter 26: Bringing Back Your Inactives..221

Chapter 27: Prospecting Catalogs 229

Chapter 28: Sale catalogs 233

Chapter 29: Identity: The Foundation of Your Catalog.........................239

section one

POSITIONING

CHAPTER 1

*Why You Should Care
About Brand Identity*

CHAPTER 2

*The Identity Trinity:
Brand, Image, Positioning*

CHAPTER 3

*Secrets Of Positioning:
What Makes Your Catalog Stand Out?*

CHAPTER 1

WHY YOU SHOULD CARE ABOUT BRAND IDENTITY

OK. You're in the catalog business. You're not selling hamburgers, cans of soda, or boxes of macaroni and cheese.

So what do you need to know about brand-building? Maybe "Where's the beef?" means millions of dollars to Wendy's—but what possible difference does it make whether you change your catalog logo, switch your models, or add a little catchphrase to your name?

Well, a catalog is a brand, too. More important, a catalog that's a *recognizable* brand immediately triggers a reaction in your customer. One glance at your logo or masthead, and your customer spontaneously associates a host of positive (or negative) thoughts with your catalog. In a heartbeat, she decides whether to wander into your catalog "store" or assign it to the trash can.

Brand identity, however, is more than a logo. Brand identity means your catalog is recognized *symbolically.* It means that all the elements of your book—logo, copy, design, model selection—immediately trigger in your customers the associations, values and ideas that belong to your catalog alone.

Done right, your catalog's brand identity signifies the trust and reassurance customers need to place an order. Customers know the book's value system and can "see" themselves in it. They can identify with the unique look and feel of the catalog, and they feel more confident buying from it than they would from some generic book.

Brand identity inspires confidence and trust. Here's how:

A few years ago, one very successful women's apparel catalog, which I won't name, took in approximately $100 million in annual sales. The name was well-known among young career women interested in fashionable, well-priced career and casual wear.

At a certain point, the catalog manager decided to follow the dictates of recent fashion trends. The catalog began "updating" certain clothing items. It started to feature grittier, more urban location shots. Its models stopped smiling for the camera and started assuming hip, serious attitudes.

Within a year or two, the catalog lost *40%* of its business. At that point, it came to us for help.

What happened? The cataloger had *misjudged the catalog's brand identity.* To its audience, the catalog's very name evoked certain expectations. Customers knew they could rely on this catalog for well-priced clothing that

NICOLE SUMMERS

TO CREATE BRAND AWARENESS FOR THE NICOLE SUMMERS CATALOG, DM MANAGEMENT OVERHAULED THE COVER CREATIVE. "THE COVER HAD TO MAKE THE STATEMENT IN THE MAILBOX," SAYS CEO GORDON COOKE.

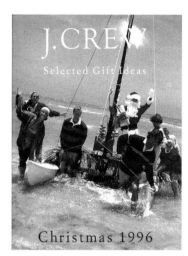

J.CREW

Selected Gift Ideas

Christmas 1996

BRAND IDENTITY HAS BECOME J. CREW'S
KEY ASSET, EXPRESSED THROUGH ITS FRESH,
UNIQUE IMAGERY.

suited their needs and lifestyles. When the catalog out-and-out changed its imagery and positioning, it turned its back on what made it appealing and relevant to customers. It lost business—which didn't come back until the cataloger began re-nurturing its original identity.

Now let's take a different apparel catalog that's also metamorphosed over the years. Look at J. Crew.

J. Crew, in its 13-year history, has established a strong brand identity. Through consistent, meaningful *imagery* and *positioning*, it has created a selling proposition that is *special, unique and different* from its competition. Through careful selection of merchandise, copy, models and photography, it has created an entire lifestyle associated with its brand.

This catalog brand identity means that no matter how J. Crew's product changes from year to year, no matter whether the catalog features urban streets or ski slopes or studio shots in its creative, customers know when they buy a Crew product, they're getting three things:

1) Classic clothing with a contemporary edge

2) A sense of belonging to a hip, assured lifestyle

3) A promise of quality

Brand identity, in short, has become J. Crew's *key* asset. Try putting J. Crew's product in any other catalog—without the J. Crew name. Try using even the exact photograph and copy. I guarantee it wouldn't sell one-half as well as it would just by having the J. Crew name attached.

Now, I'm not advocating that every cataloger immediately hire a brand manager or try to develop a private label. That's not the point.

The point is, understanding what goes into a good catalog brand can help you establish and strengthen your catalog's identity. That, in turn, will bring in more loyal customers, attract more prospects, and strengthen your bottom line.

Just picture for a moment the glut of catalogs hitting mailboxes these days—hundreds of books with similar merchandising and offers. Now consider the fact that consumers today have less time to shop than ever and are looking for ways to simplify their lives and use of time. Think of your own life experience, and how you find it easier and more reassuring to order (and reorder) from catalogs that you "know," trust and can relate to.

That's the whole point behind strong brand identity. A catalog with a strong brand automatically breaks through mailbox clutter. It grabs attention and immediately signals to busy prospects and customers that they're making a safe buying choice.

In fact, catalogers are pretty lucky when it comes to brand-building. Pepsi may spend hundreds of millions of dollars on image ads, but that's because at the critical moment of purchase, the consumer faces a mere can of soda. If she hasn't been saturated with Pepsi imagery, a can of Pepsi would be indistinguishable from a can of Coke or Royal Crown.

A consumer looking at a catalog, on the other hand, gets the whole she-bang: product, copy, logos, photographs. Anything we *want* to say to the customer we *can,* right there, at the point of purchase. No packaged-goods firm can do that!

Moreover, in a world where sixteen competing catalogs may land in a mailbox on a single October day, *brand identity is essential.* You can't get the sale if the customer doesn't pick up your book. A typical customer decides within two seconds whether to keep or toss a piece of mail. Which will she keep? The one that's familiar to her; the one that evokes a smile, a recognition, a sense of belonging and being understood. A brand identity does that. It takes the guesswork out of her decision. It separates *this* catalog from every other catalog.

NEED MORE CONVINCING?

Consider other advantages of developing a strong brand identity.

"Brand-name" catalogs are differentiated. We all know that in a catalog glut, catalogers need to stand out. Simple. But catalogs that look different for difference's sake just won't cut it with their audiences.

It's not enough for catalogers simply to try a gigantic format, or to put Madonna on the cover. New customers are drawn to those catalogs that possess unique *spirit* and *personality*—particularly when that personality resonates with their own. I still recall, for instance, how I felt when I first saw an early Banana Republic catalog, or the first Tweeds. Both times I felt newly and intuitively "understood."

Brand-name catalogs create loyalty. You know the marketing maxim (initially cited in the 1990 *Harvard Business Review*): The value of a current customer is about five times greater than that of a new buyer. That's why brand-name catalogs have a financial edge. They're familiar. Consumers know what the catalog stands for, and—so long as that image remains favorable—consumers are predisposed to buy from it, as opposed to buying from a catalog they've never seen.

Just watch customers in your local grocery stores. Often, they won't try no-name macaroni and cheese when they can pick Kraft. They won't chance scratchy toilet paper when they "know" Charmin is squeezably soft. (And as you can see, strong brands command higher prices as well. Just think of Ralph Lauren.)

In the same way, brand catalogs not only attract new customers—what college student hasn't heard of J. Crew?—but engender loyal ones. Once customers like and identify with a brand's values, they're more likely to keep coming back.

Brand-name catalogs can expand the business. If a catalog develops a strong brand, it's essentially created its own franchise position. Consider, for instance, "Crewcuts," the J. Crew children's apparel niche. Or "Lilly's Kids," the Lillian Vernon spin-off catalog for children. Or "Orvis Travel," "Green Mountain Mercantile" (spun off from Vermont Country Store) or scores of other expanded brands.

Credibility is a rich asset. Once a cataloger has worked hard to establish its own "name," that name automatically bestows credibility on just about every product it touches. (Provided, of course, the products make sense for the brand's target market and positioning. L.L. Bean, for instance, might successfully branch into baby gear, but it would have a tougher time with high fashion.)

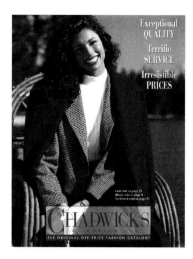

CHADWICK'S HAS BUILT ITS BRAND IDENTITY AS "THE ORIGINAL OFF-PRICE FASHION CATALOG." FEW CAN MATCH ITS QUALITY AND PRICE POSITIONING.

WHY CARE ABOUT BRAND IDENTITY?

- Strong brands inspire confidence and trust
- Strong brands stand out
- Strong brands deter knockoffs
- Strong brands justify premium pricing
- Strong brands help consumers choose among competitors

Brand-name catalogs deter knockoffs. Let's consider Ben & Jerry's. It's possible—if remotely—that yes, another ice cream chain could somehow swipe the Cherry Garcia recipe and create an impressive substitute. It's even possible they could give it a duly hip name, like Big Pink or Keep on Chunkin. But it stretches credibility to think an upstart could also swipe Ben & Jerry's social consciousness, environmental efforts, '60s sensibility and hirsute duo. In other words, the ice cream's brand position is so rich and clear in consumers' minds, it would be extremely difficult to churn out an imitator.

That's not been true of many catalogs. Consider Domestications, a Hanover House catalog once very successful with its then-unique format of selling value-priced bed linens. It grew from small to huge in a short amount of time, and created an audience comfortable with the catalog's dense presentation and photographs of room settings.

Trouble was, the company didn't protect the catalog with strong identity. The dense, generic image was easy to knock off, and before long, scores of linens catalogs flooded the market and cannibalized the business. If the catalog had created a unique lifestyle positioning, or established itself as the only source for certain merchandise (the way Lillian Vernon has), it might have discouraged others from settling on its turf.

Catalogs—particularly those selling mass-market goods, like gifts and apparel—need a unique selling position to thwart encroachers. Many catalogs, for instance, swarmed into the value-priced apparel turf occupied by Chadwick's—but few could match its look and quality positioning. Many tried the "preppy" or "outdoorsy" look started by Bean, and they certainly took some business. But in the end, no one could match the strength of Bean's reputation or brand. Bean had so completely forged merchandising to brand that upstarts could only capitalize on certain Bean-like elements, such as khakis.

(More fundamentally, Bean had established itself as the *leading* brand in the category. Its merchandise was the authentic original. That meant customers who bought khakis from a Bean imitator would have to contend with the nagging feeling that they weren't wearing the real thing. *That's* the power of strong catalog branding.)

Catalogers can always copy certain catalog elements. If one catalog succeeds because of good pricing, others will copy price. If another has inspired copy or funky typefaces, imitators will horn in. In fact, many catalogers start their businesses *in order* to knock off another's success—and in a very hot market, that attempt may certainly work for a while. Knockoff businesses, though, are driven largely on product or borrowed imagery. Those catalogs have no *raison d'être*. Sooner or later, without unique positioning to support them, they run out of gas. Customers stop buying because they're not offered any compelling reason to keep shopping.

Unique catalogs with strong position defy imitation. A Peterman knockoff would be ridiculous. No one could match the Pleasant Company package. For that reason, none try, which leaves those catalogs with one less business worry.

REBUILDING BRANDS UNDER DM MANAGEMENT

By the early '90s, catalog company DM Management had found its niche: upscale, classic women's apparel. Unfortunately, the company's mode of fulfilling that niche proved an unprofitable one.

Essentially, the company at the time consisted of four catalog brands: Nicole Summers, The Very Thing, J. Jill and Carroll Reed. Creatively, almost no one could tell the "brands" apart. Nichole Summers and The Very Thing, in particular, seemed almost interchangeable, with their competent, familiar, but unexceptional depictions of thirtyish models wearing classic clothes. Page layouts—standard compilations of backgrounded, evenly lit shots—looked exactly the same, spread to spread, book to book.

Moreover, each catalog visited essentially the same audience. Result: Few customers could tell the catalogs apart, and response began to drop off.

"By cross-circulating the lists of each book, we cannibalized ourselves, and eliminated the ability to make [brand] distinctions," says Gordon Cooke, who came on as CEO in 1996. "We were getting four books to the same customers with no product differentiation and no consumer differentiation."

According to Cooke, the old motto for the company was list-building. The new motto, under his direction, would be brand-building. "The catalogs have to have reason for being."

Step one of the new plan: eliminate Carroll Reed, the book with the weakest brand-building potential. Step two: fold The Very Thing into the Nicole Summers catalog. Step three: give each remaining book distinct personality.

As Cooke puts it, the Nicole Summers customer was older and affluent; the J. Jill shopper was a younger (but also affluent) wage-earner. "The needs of the two were significantly different," he says. "The older group was looking for more traditional suitings and more structured clothing. The J. Jill customer was looking for something versatile to go from day to evening."

Once the two targets were established, "it then got very easy to brand-build through different creative," he says. For its first holiday book, the redesigned Nicole Summers would sport a fresh, illustrated front cover, reminiscent of a classic *Harper's Bazaar*, rather than a standard product shot. Inside, classic suits, dresses and separates would mingle with accessories and gifts. J. Jill, on the other hand, would feature a new tag line, "uncomplicated style," accompanied by pages of younger, unfussy models in earthier, natural-toned layouts.

For both books, wide-open, lightly merchandised pages would feature hero spreads, location shots, themed apparel and color-grouped layouts. The books would contain more pages as well, ranging from 96 to 112. The sales increases, Cooke reasoned, would outweigh the increased expenses.

"Since we had no brand names of any awareness, the cover had to make the statement in the mailbox," says Cooke. "We had to differentiate from the competition. My whole thing was differentiation of merchandise and creative, with theme spreads so we look like fashion arbiters."

Result: After the first holiday mailing, DM Management's sales rose 34%, and earnings increased by more than $1 million. By spring 1997, Nicole Summers was gaining an average $70 million in annual revenues; J. Jill was at about $50 million. "I would say," notes Cooke, "that both businesses have the potential to be of a good magnitude."

CHAPTER 2

THE IDENTITY TRINITY: BRAND, IMAGE, POSITIONING

Good brands aren't born. They evolve. They hammer away at a consumer's consciousness until they become part of her subconscious, guiding her automatically in choosing whom to trust and what to buy.

To get to that point in a customer's psyche, a strong brand, with a recognizable identity, relies on three elements:

1) *The values associated with the brand itself*

2) *Imagery and voice*

3) *Positioning*

Let's consider Pepsi.

First, as a *brand,* Pepsi can be identified as a sweet carbonated drink that not only tastes great, but contributes to a youthful, fun-filled lifestyle.

Second, Pepsi's advertising *imagery and voice* plays off the brand promise by showing people having fun when they drink Pepsi. It also plays up taste benefits by showing people choosing Pepsi (sometimes at great physical risk) over Coke.

Third, Pepsi's *positioning* is summed up in its pithy marketing phrases: "The Choice of a New Generation" and "Pepsi People." The company has positioned itself to appeal to all consumers seeking youth and fun. Since most Americans want to identify with youthfulness, Pepsi ensures that if you're a cola drinker, you can't outright reject the Pepsi message without denying (at least subconsciously) your own desire to be perceived as youthful.

What's the point? Why does Pepsi spend hundreds of millions of dollars each year doing this?

Simple. So that the customer, at that crucial moment in the store, staring at 120 different brands of cold drinks, will have no trouble deciding where to reach. If she thinks of herself as youthful and fun, or if she's just convinced that "her" brand tastes best, she'll go for the Pepsi.

The same is true in catalog marketing. Let's take some well-known brands:

L.L. Bean

BRAND VALUES: Rugged, practical products for outdoors/country lifestyle, backed with honesty, tradition and great service.

IMAGERY: Down East, outdoors lifestyle photography; conservative stylings; recognizable, timeless logo and unique typeface.

IMAGE AND VOICE MAKE UP A CATALOG'S UNIQUE IDENTITY. LANDS' END'S "REAL WORLD" VOICE EXPRESSES ITSELF IN THE CATALOG'S CHOICE OF DRAMATIC, ALMOST JOURNALISTIC, COVER IMAGES.

THE EMOTIONAL CONNOTATIONS OF "BRAND" FEEDS INTO THE CUSTOMER'S OWN SENSE OF SELF AND ASPIRATIONS. L.L. BEAN CUSTOMERS EQUATE THE CATALOG'S BRAND WITH A HEALTHY, FAMILY-ORIENTED, OUTDOORS NEW ENGLAND LIFESTYLE.

POSITIONING: Old Yankee-style service, practicality and quality.

Lillian Vernon

BRAND VALUES: Convenient, wide-ranging array of fun, practical and well-priced items. Lillian finds for you the stuff you didn't know you needed.

IMAGERY: Lighthearted, bright, uncomplicated, overflowing choice, simple communication.

POSITIONING: Lillian Vernon herself knows where to find the best merchandise you need at the best price.

Each one of these brands seems easy to define now. But consider how each has evolved. Lillian Vernon started off selling leather accessories in the back pages of magazines; the original L.L. Bean was a boot manufacturer. How did they manage, over time, to get customers to "know" them, to have a clear picture of them, to choose to buy from them every time they heard the name?

The process wasn't easy, but for any cataloger, brand-building is worth doing. Let's take a look at what goes into the making of each of these elements.

1) BRAND

Sometimes, the way consumers think about brands is very hard to put into words. More often, it's a gut-level thing. Hearing a brand name, seeing it on a store shelf, or finding it while leafing through the mail, produces a distinct emotional reaction within the consumer. What's more, that emotional connotation feeds into the customer's own sense of self and aspirations.

Think about it. "Volvo" conjures a sense of safety. "Mercedes" stands for engineering. "Hallmark" triggers feelings of caring. So, if you buy a Volvo, you demonstrate to yourself that you care about your family, your passengers. If you buy a Mercedes, you show yourself to be sophisticated and educated enough to appreciate the finest engineering. If you write a message on a Hallmark card, you satisfy your need to make the intended recipient feel nurtured and loved. Plus, you will have alleviated your own insecurity about what kind of card to choose for the occasion.

All those emotional connotations spring from the three building blocks of a brand: *Attributes, benefits, and values.*

1) Attributes are simply what the product *is*. Pepsi, for instance, is a sugary, brown carbonated beverage. Mercedes is a car. J. Peterman is a catalog of upper-priced apparel, home items and accessories.

2) Benefits make up the perceived positives consumers get from the product. With Pepsi, for instance, the perceived benefits are good taste and good times. For Kraft, benefits might include the sense of wholesome product; of tastes you can trust. And J. Peterman offers the opportunity to be authentically American with unique and beautiful items that make the customer feel one-of-a-kind.

3) Values are those qualities that come to be associated with a brand. These are the thoughts and ideas people associate with the brand and that give them "permission" to seek one brand over another. Said another way, Wonder Bread stands for all-American. Peterman stands for unique, eccentric quality. The Sharper Image stands for innovation.

Of all the qualities of brand, *values* are most critical. Values are often what make people reach for that box of cereal, that brand of car, that catalog. If you doubt it, consider any BMW owner. She may *say* she loves how the car performs, and she may point out sixteen different and valid driving advantages the car gives her over, say, an Oldsmobile. Chances are, though, there was quite a different motivation at work when she wrote out that hefty check. She wanted to be associated with the free-spirited, sophisticated values of the brand.

As catalogers, it's easy to imagine the kinds of values we *want* customers to have about our catalog and our product. We want them to feel that we're reliable, fun, best-priced, unique, homespun, esoteric, important, or a hundred other wonderful qualities.

That's why brand management is critical. Catalogers need to establish at the outset which values they want associated with their own brand. They need to look for the values that will set them apart from the competition and create an emotional frame of reference in the customer's mind. To do that, catalogers not only need to establish their own unique offer or set of values, they also need to understand which hot buttons cause their customers to buy their product.

Once the brand is established, then catalogers can proceed on to *positioning* and *imagery and voice*.

IMAGERY IS THE VISUAL PRESENTATION THAT SUPPORTS A CATALOG'S POSITIONING. LEVENGER'S HIGH-QUALITY, "SERIOUS READER" POSITIONING COMES THROUGH IN ITS ELEGANT, WARM-TONED, STILL-LIFE COVERS.

2) POSITIONING

"You deserve a break today."

"It's Miller time."

"We're number two, so we try harder."

It doesn't sound like much, but worlds turn on those little phrases. Jingles, mottoes, catchphrases and the like are the literal distillation of *positioning*. They are statements that capture *why* consumers should use the brand, based on a motivating consumer insight.

Positioning, in other words, is really a statement about a brand that:

1) Is unique

2) Resonates for the consumer

3) Is "ownable"

In other words, positioning takes on a consumer need and addresses it. McDonald's addressed everybody's need for leisure with "You deserve a break today." United took on everybody's need for comfort with "Fly the friendly skies."

Catalogs, of course, don't rely much on pithy phrases. They don't need to. Granted, a few, like Norm Thompson ("Escape from the ordinary") rely on tag lines and mottoes to get across a certain meaning or identity. But consumers don't choose which catalog they prefer the way they choose their toilet paper. They don't have to remember "squeezably soft" at the moment of purchase.

A WELL-POSITIONED CATALOG HAS A
UNIQUE POINT OF VIEW THAT RESONATES
WITH THE TARGET CUSTOMER.

For catalogers, positioning is really summed up in the *whole presentation of the book*. It's in the photography, logo, copy, typeface and service. All those elements should play into one, clear-cut goal: *presenting something unique about the catalog, in a consistent manner, that also meets a consumer want or need*. Catalogs that are well-positioned don't need to "tell" their positioning statements; they already "show" it from front cover to back.

For that reason, it's easy to tell a well-positioned catalog from one that isn't. A poorly positioned catalog doesn't have a sense of its audience. It lacks individualism and personality. It relies on generic models, styling and photography. It carries generic copy. Its product offers may be all over the place, without any coherent thought to price range or audience need. If you tore off the cover, you would have no idea whose catalog it was.

A well-positioned catalog, on the other hand, has a point of view. The clearly defined target consumer—whether teenage girls or middle-aged executives—can look at the catalog and say, "That's me," or "That's the way I want to be." Customers can feel the copy "speaks" to them; that the product addresses their needs; that the models look the way they'd like to look and—*most importantly*—that the offer is unique, one they won't find anywhere else.

In these days of catalog glut, it's not easy to find good positioning. It involves sitting down and crystallizing your ideas about the catalog, and what makes it unique. It's not simply a matter of saying, "Oh, we offer the best service," or "We have a wide selection." It means focusing on the particular, unique attributes that differentiate your catalog from all others, *and* that have special meaning to the consumer.

Not easy. You can't position yourself on two-day shipping if fourteen of your competitors offer the same service. You can't position yourself on low prices if everyone else in your category has low prices as well.

Today, unique positioning depends on *owning the idea that resonates with the consumer*. Two catalogs may have exactly the same products, pricing and service, but the one that has a *perceptual* advantage—the one that customers identify with or perceive as superior—will be the one that gets the business.

If you doubt it, try this quick catalog personality test. Close your eyes and picture the following catalogs:

—L.L. Bean
—J. Crew
—The Sharper Image
—Acme Catalog

What comes to mind with that last book? *Nothing*. Which means if customers can't instantly picture *your* catalog when they think of its name, you're in trouble.

How to resolve it? That's where *imagery and voice* come in.

3) IMAGERY AND VOICE

Catalogs are a visual selling medium. We know consumers can't hear, taste, smell or touch what they're buying. All they can do is see it on the page and read about it.

That's why imagery is critical. I'm not talking here about the need for crystal-clear product shots (after all, J. Peterman sells thousands of products without a single photograph). Rather, I'm talking about tying together all your visual and creative elements to create a crystal-clear *brand identity*.

In a well-positioned catalog, every element harmonizes, as in a carefully crafted melody. Let's consider, for instance, Levenger and L.L. Bean. Assume both catalogs sold the same lap desk. Can you picture how the product would appear in each catalog?

It's not hard, since both catalogs have very different, and very clear, positions. Levenger's position is one of beautiful, hard-to-find products that enhance quiet reading and work. L.L. Bean's position is one of practical, unfussy goods for people who appreciate tradition and craftsmanship.

So, Levenger would show the desk, say, in leather wing chair, surrounded by library bookshelves. The copy would emphasize elegance, craftsmanship, practicality. Bean would likely show the desk in a comfortable student's room or den chair. The copy would speak of durability, pragmatism and quality.

Any switch in these creative elements would likely hit a wrong note in the consumer's mind, given each catalog's positioning. You could not, for instance, insert L.L. Bean's bluntly pragmatic serif typeface in a Levenger catalog without making it look clumsy and off-balance. At the same time, Levenger's burnished, elegant photography would make Bean look pretentious and awkward. Each catalog uses the perfect imagery for its own positioning, from logo and typeface to models and locations.

In both cases, too, each catalog's imagery has the following:

1) *It's consistent.* We know that Bean's typeface won't suddenly turn into Geneva one day. And we expect a certain polish in the Levenger book; that it won't be populated by executives one month and grunge teenagers the next. In a well-positioned catalog, any changes in imagery are made gently, thoughtfully, with care to make new elements fit with the catalog's clear brand identity.

2) *It's familiar.* Few logos are more recognizable than Bean's. That sense of recognition, of dependability, keeps customers from saying, "Who's catalog is this, anyway?" People like to repeat good experiences, and they use familiar imagery as a touchstone for knowing that they're in the right place.

3) *It's a mirror image of its customer.* Customers like to see themselves in a catalog—or at least, see themselves as they would like to be. A well-positioned catalog understands this. Its imagery reflects its customers. Two women's apparel catalogs might show the same blouse, but in Talbots, it might appear with pearls and a jacket. In Lew Magram, it might be shown open-necked with tossed hair. Each catalog knows its customers expects to see the blouse as *they* would like to wear it.

THE ELEMENTS OF BRAND

ATTRIBUTES
What the product is or does.

BENEFITS
What the product means to the consumer.

VALUES
What consumers associate with the brand.

VOICE
The unique personality of the brand.

IMAGERY
The unique visualization system that plays off the brand.

IT'S ABOUT IDENTITY

Put together, imagery and voice make up a catalog's unique *identity*. Just like a person's identity, a catalog's identity, as long as it's managed consistently, is its core, unshakable foundation.

We've all known people with strong identities. With these people, we always know what they stand for. They attract loyal friends (even followers) of like minds.

It's the same with catalogs. Those without strong identities drift from style to style, never sure what to offer or how to offer it. They can't hold onto a loyal customer base, and they never attract prospects for long.

Catalogs with stong identity, on both an overt and subtle level, tell customers why *this* book meets their wants and needs. A catalog that is merely an array of products will be treated that way by the customer. But a catalog with identity communicates specialness, uniqueness, identity. The catalog's brand identity gives the consumer a context in which to view the merchandise. It makes the customer feel she's buying more than great product—she's buying an attitude, lifestyle, personality.

Almost all catalog problems stem from a lack of brand identity. If customers stop buying, it's often because a catalog no longer means anything special to its target audience. If competitors are grabbing market share, it's because a catalog lacks the armor of a strong identity. If prospects aren't responding, it's due to a catalog's failure to say anything distinctive.

On the other hand, most catalogs that fix their identity problems find that most of their other problems get fixed as well.

PRICE AND POSITIONING

Here's a tricky question. If your customers are price-sensitive, how important is brand?

We all know, for instance, that there are those who would rather buy the generic macaroni and cheese if buying Kraft means spending an extra 20 cents. In the same way, there are those who would rather seek out the very lowest-priced sleeping bag even if they could get a great value from Bean.

The fact is, a strong brand will never sway the price-sensitive. These folks will always go where they can get their goods cheaper, or they'll only buy your brand when they see it on sale.

That doesn't mean, however, that you shouldn't build your brand. Brand-loyal customers are the mainstay of almost any business, far more reliable than fickle price-sensitive customers who flit from brand to brand. Brand loyalists, in fact, will always buy *in spite* of price.

What about those shoppers in the middle, between price-sensitive and brand-loyal? These customers might prefer your brand but need to be reassured on your price. For them, wording and imagery make the sale. To buy at your price point, these people need to know what makes your brand worthwhile. They also need to feel they'll be missing out on the authentic original if they settle for a cheaper alternative.

So while a strong brand can insulate against price concerns, it can't do the whole job. You need to show, in a consistent, believable way, why your brand is the best value.

CHAPTER 3

SECRETS OF POSITIONING: WHAT MAKES YOUR CATALOG STAND OUT?

If your catalog's identity is its personality, *positioning* is how you bare it to the public. It represents the single most motivating reason for a customer to buy from your catalog. It's the strongest side of your catalog's personality, the one you want your audience to know and see.

You can't build a brand without positioning. You may *know* that your catalog is the top source for solar-powered disk drives, or offers the widest selection of suede chukka boots, or is unbeaten in its expertise in picture frames. But unless you communicate the importance of this to your target market (in a consistent, compelling way), you're underleveraging your assets.

Recently, for instance, a clothing cataloger found that its market share had been dropping after many profitable years of selling business and casual men's clothing. The president was asked to state his catalog's position. His response: "We can outfit a man seven days a week." Our response: "How is that *different* from what scores of other men's catalogs can do? How is it even different from what hundreds of men's clothing stores can do?" This cataloger had to unearth its catalog's unique marketplace position (and yes, it had one) to bring its customers back.

Positioning requires you to crystallize your thinking about your catalog's selling proposition. Good positioning captures what makes your catalog *special, unique and different* in the marketplace.

In other words, finding your catalog's positioning isn't simply a matter of asking, "Who am I?" Positioning asks: *What do I offer to customers that is both valuable to them and different from what they might find elsewhere?*

ESSENTIALS

EVOCATIVE, DRAMATIC IMAGES FOCUS ON THE WISHES AND NEEDS OF THE CATALOG'S CORE BUYERS.

FIXING YOUR POSITION

To start off, think of the first words or associations that come to mind when you picture your catalog.

Chances are, you're nowhere near your actual positioning. Consider the above men's clothing cataloger. His initial statement—"We can outfit a man seven days a week"—was his first *association* with his catalog, but it's not a positioning statement. Neither is "We're number one in the market" or "Sales were up 15%" or "Our customer is educated and sophisticated."

All of these may be facts about your catalog. But to position, you must first do the following:

1) Take stock of your catalog's strengths and assets (service, quality merchandise, strong guarantee and so on)

2) Take stock of what's important to your customer

3) Determine how your assets fit with your customer

In brand management, this is called a SWOT analysis. You take measurement of your company's *strengths, weaknesses, opportunities* and *threats*. Naturally, positioning plays to a catalog's strengths (such as Bean's old-fashioned Yankee heritage) in order to compensate for any weaknesses (lack of fashion-forward merchandise).

Most important, however, effective positioning is built on a motivating insight into the customer. Bean's positioning, for instance, assumes customers want to have an authentic outdoors experience. They associate the right clothing and right equipment with making that experience complete.

Other strong brands work from their own consumer insights. Consider these (hypothetical) examples:

LANDS' END: Prospects want to feel confident that their style of dress has a timeless, all-American quality that reflects how they perceive themselves.

J. PETERMAN: Prospects are proud of their sense of individualism and look to express it in the lifestyles they lead and the clothes they wear.

CHADWICK'S OF BOSTON: Prospects enjoy shopping for clothing, especially when they can find the fashion styles that reflect their tastes, and at price points they perceive to be better than what they can find elsewhere.

THE CASE OF "TUSCANY GIFTS"

So let's say an entrepreneur named Sheila Smith is creating a catalog called "Tuscany Gifts." Here's how she might start working toward her positioning:

1) The catalog's history

How long has the catalog existed?

Clearly, the older or more historic the catalog, the more it can connote a sense of heritage and trust. Brooks Brothers and L.L. Bean, for instance, play up their longevity to reassure customers of a solid reputation.

Tuscany Gifts, however, is a start-up. Conclusion: *Longevity is not an asset.*

Does the catalog have a story? Is it family-owned? A kitchen-table start-up? An entrepreneur's dream?

Tales about launches, family history, product knowledge and so on makes a catalog human and familiar. Everyone loves an underdog. (That's from the old adage, "People don't buy from companies. They buy from people.")

In this case, Tuscany Gifts emerged because of Smith's love of Italy. In fact, Smith had bought so many wonderful Tuscan objects for her home that she quit her practice as a successful veterinarian to start the catalog. Conclusion: *Smith's catalog "story" is a possible asset.*

What is the catalog's country or region of origin?

For some catalogers, precision Swiss engineering or Italian design connotes quality and style. Hanna Andersson, for instance, positioned itself well as the quality Swedish resource for baby clothes.

FEBRUARY 1997

Thank you for your recent order. Save 10% on your next order of $50 or more. See page 6 for details.

EDDIE BAUER POSITIONED ITSELF AS THE ANSWER TO STRESSED-OUT, AGING BOOMERS.

Unfortunately, Smith can't call on long Italian family connections for her Tuscany Gifts book. But she can play up the beauty and wonder of Tuscany. Conclusion: *Regionality is a definite asset.*

2) The catalog's audience

Who is the customer? What are her values? What are her characteristics?

Most catalogers "know" that their typical customer is, say, married, 40 years old and has 1.2 children. But in truth, demographics are not the whole customer story. Well-positioned catalogers know their audiences inside and out, and their catalogs "tell" their customers' story.

At Chadwick's of Boston, for instance, the company might say its customer is wholesome, someone who prefers to be attractive rather than exhibitionist. She doesn't wear low-cut blouses or high-cut slits, but she takes pride in way she dresses. A Lew Magram customer, on the other hand, likes to stand out. She's the one who wears red to a party; she likes to flirt, to wear lots of makeup, perfume and sexy hair.

Smith decides to get to "know" her customers by personally acquainting herself with others she's met in Tuscany. She pores over data cards from similar gift books, and even leafs through magazines, like *Gourmet*, to cut out photographs of people who "look" like her customer. Conclusion: *Her audience is sophisticated, college-educated, urbane, world-traveled, mostly female and nearing retirement age. This customer would rather buy a sumptuous old textile than an Armani suit. She values beauty and quality over price and quantity.*

What customer trends—societal, economic, familial—are apparent?

A catalog's positioning must always relate to the customer's needs and wants *right now*. A positioning built on snob appeal or opulent luxury, for instance, works best in a robust economy when consumers feel societally competitive and financially secure. A value-oriented, price-sensitive positioning works best in an uncertain economy when consumers feel less secure. Through the decades, catalogers have seen consumers face everything from stressed-out yuppiness to new parenting to couch-potatoing. A well-positioned cataloger understands what their customers face in their day-to-day lives, and how those trends inform their purchase decisions.

At Tuscany Gifts, Smith finds her customers are capitalizing on their newly empty nests by spending more on travel and home decor. Conclusion: *Customer trends work in favor of her catalog's merchandising offer.*

What motivates the customer to buy?

Are customers looking for price? Are they pragmatic, or do they look for style over function? Do they want status or escape? Do they buy because they need to—or because they want to?

People don't buy products: They buy solutions to their problems. Catalogers must step into their customer's shoes and know what the customer wants to *gain* from her purchase. They also need to know what a customer needs to *feel* in order to buy. You can see, for instance, that a Smith & Hawken customer wants a sense of peace and serenity; that a Hammacher Schlemmer buyer needs to be cutting-edge.

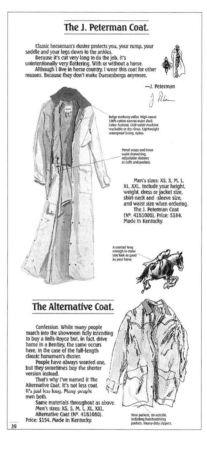

J. Peterman's signature product, The Peterman Coat, conjures images of romance and adventure.

Smith decides that Tuscany Gifts customers want to preserve the warmth and memories of an Italian experience, whether real or imagined. Conclusion: *The catalog's positioning must hit an emotional chord.*

How is the audience segmented?

A catalog audience may contain everyone from aspirational young professionals to upscale homemakers to well-to-do executives, all seeking the same set of matching lamps. To position well, catalogers must focus on the wishes and needs of their *core* buyers, or risk the folly of trying to be all things to all shoppers.

For Tuscany Gifts, Smith knows that her book appeals to aspirational young apartment-dwellers as much as to world-traveled sophisticates. But it's the latter audience that makes up most of her profits. Conclusion: *The catalog must position itself to the tastes and interests of older, wealthier buyers. The less-well-off in the audience will "follow the leaders."*

What are the audience's needs? Does it have unmet needs?

Many catalogs—particularly upstarts—position themselves primarily to focus on unmet needs. Omaha Steaks, for instance, long ago capitalized on the need for corporate gift-givers to send something more inspired than flowers or candy. More recently, the launch of The Voyager Collection, a hotel-traveler catalog, addressed the customer need to buy an emergency shirt at 11:30 p.m. in a strange town.

Smith realizes Tuscany Gifts focuses more on customer "wants" than "needs." Her customers feel strongly about creating beauty in their lives and in enhancing their surroundings. They're not looking to her catalog to find solutions for day-to-day problems. Conclusion: *Positioning must be more emotional than rational.*

3) The catalog's market:

Does the catalog address a vertical, or niche, market—or a horizontal, or mass, market?

The Nature Company catalog, for instance, positions itself to a market of nature lovers, regardless of whether the customers are old, young, computer programmers or garbage collectors. It addresses a *vertical* market, as does Gardeners Eden (gardening), Williams-Sonoma (gourmet cooking) or Early Winters (camping).

Most apparel and gift catalogs, however, offer a wide variety of product and style to a wide variety of buyers. In these *horizontal* markets, these catalogs must often position either with unique product, pricing and selection, or with service, attitude or personality. Hold Everything, for example, positions itself as the one source for unique merchandise for organizing the home. MicroWarehouse positions itself as the fastest, most inexpensive method for buying computer product.

Tuscany Gifts falls somewhere between vertical and horizontal. It appeals both to lovers of Italian product (vertical) and sophisticated acquirers of beautiful home decor (horizontal). Conclusion: *Tuscany Gifts can embrace both markets while maintaining a strong identity. Its positioning can*

VERTICAL POSITIONING MUST ADDRESS A COMMON INTEREST AREA FOR A VARIETY OF AGE AND DEMOGRAPHIC GROUPS.

establish the catalog's unique Italian merchandise as the sophisticated choice for home decor.

Is the catalog's market young and on the rise? Is it mature and peaking? Has it passed its peak?

Growing markets, naturally, offer the best positioning opportunities—provided a catalog can get in early, position well and stay ahead of the fray. That's what The Sharper Image did during the 1980s era of conspicuous consumption.

But when a market matures and peaks, the catalog must be ready to evolve positions in order to hold on. When the yuppie toy market declined, for instance, The Sharper Image repositioned to address a market more interested in value and function than glitz. Omaha Steaks, in the midst of health-consciousness, positioned itself with a greater emphasis on low-fat products, lean cuts and seafood.

Fortunately, the market for Tuscany Gifts appears in a growth mode. Smith believes aging baby-boomers and increasing European travel will continue to drive the market for Italian decor. Conclusion: *Any positioning created now will likely remain valid for some time to come.*

What are the market trends?

Catalogers that can sense trends can grab first place in the hearts and minds of customers. Chadwick's, for instance, launched when apparel buyers were just becoming more interested in price than fashion. It sensed the coming wave of price-consciousness and rode that wave after the higher-price catalogs, like Honeybee, had crested and folded.

Trend-watching also keeps catalogers in touch with their marketplace. During the '80s, for instance, J. Crew positioned itself as highly aspirational, with copy touting clothes that went "from stable yard to drawing room." In the '90s, Crew became far more accessible, and offered imagery with just enough slouching and stringy hair (but always on beautiful faces) to satisfy both young boomers and Generation X. The catalog modified its positioning without losing sight of its core values.

Obviously, Smith sees a budding trend of traveling empty-nesters. Conclusion: *Tuscany Gifts can capitalize on the market as long as it creates a decisive, resonant positioning.*

What other buying channels are in the market?

In this shopping climate, it's tough to find an exclusive channel for distributing a product. That means positioning is key in seizing market share.

Take, for instance, Wolferman's, a muffin catalog. Obviously, customers can find baked good everywhere, so to distinguish itself, Wolferman's not only offers unusual product (high-quality English muffins), but adds on gift-wrapping and "reminder" services that let customers know when it's time to reorder. This elevates the act of buying muffins from an everyday experience to a special occasion.

Smith recognizes that Tuscany Gifts will compete with hundreds of specialty stores, particularly in large cities. Conclusion: *The catalog's positioning should embrace unique, authentic product and possibly unique service, such as breakage insurance or decorative assistance.*

WHEN A MARKET MATURES AND PEAKS—AS HAPPENED WITH THE SHARPER IMAGE—THE CATALOG MUST EVOLVE WITH THE CUSTOMER.

4) The catalog's competitors

Who are the competitors? What do they offer? What is their market share?

Catalogers that know their competitors automatically can assess their own position in the marketplace. A *competitive analysis* (which I'll discuss further in Chapter 4), can address the following: How many catalogs sell similar merchandise? How many sell to the same target audience? What are their price points? What are their average order sizes? How dense are the layouts? How many products appear per page? What kind of type and copy do they use? What kind of space do they devote to mission statements and services? How large is their business? What are their customer demographics? How long have they been in business? The better catalogers understand *the competitors* unique strengths, the better they can formulate their own.

Even non-competitors offer comparison opportunity. Hold Everything customers, for instance, are likely the same demographic profile as J. Crew customers. Someone who orders from Hammacher Schlemmer may order from The Sharper Image and Brooks Brothers.

In her research, Smith finds that most of her catalog competitors offer Italian gift product as part of a larger gift offering. Similarly, most have a younger, less-monied audience, and a smaller order size. On the other hand, she finds that adventure catalogs, certain book and music catalogs and gourmet books have an audience similar to her own. Conclusion: *Tuscany Gifts can position itself with a more sophisticated, adventuring presentation than its gift competitors.*

What is the competitor's brand image and position?

A *competitive positioning analysis* tells how competitors create their own unique selling positions, and how they carry them out. Customer focus groups (which I'll talk about in Chapter 10), can determine how audiences perceive each competitor in the marketplace. With that knowledge, you can find out whether your book is perceived as a leader, follower or unique offer in the marketplace. You can also discover how you can position your catalog to play to the strengths and weaknesses of your competitors.

That's especially important in today's catalog glut. When so many consumers spread purchases across similar catalogs, the name of the game, often, is "share-shifting"—getting customers to spend more with your catalog than with your competitor. To take market share, you need to offer a superior reason to buy—which means that you need compelling positioning (not to mention the merchandise that plays off that positioning).

Not surprisingly, most competitors with well-defined positioning (*and* the right product and healthy market) often perform much better than those without a clear position or brand. Well-positioned catalogs offer the greatest challenge to any upstart in the marketplace.

Fortunately, Tuscany Gifts has no direct competitors in its marketplace—yet. Conclusion: *Unless a well-positioned catalog muscles into the market, Tuscany Gifts will have the advantage of being "first" in its customers' minds.*

What are the competitor's strengths and vulnerabilities? What advantages does the catalog demonstrate over competitors?

THE TERRITORY AHEAD
San Juan Islands, Washington
Indian Summer 1996

NO OTHER CATALOGER EMPLOYS THIS OUTDOOR IMAGERY OF ALMOST SURREAL SHARPNESS. THE MORE A CATALOGER CAN DIFFERENTIATE FROM THE COMPETITION, THE BETTER.

Any strong positioning statement presents unique advantages over competitors. Where is the competitor vulnerable? Does it lack unique product? Is its audience aging? Does it have an outdated image? Are prices out of line with the target market?

Clearly, the more a catalog differentiates itself from the competition, the better. But a word of caution: Well-positioned catalogs do not position themselves *against* the competition so much as *in favor* of their own target market. In the end, good positioning comes from a catalog's own strengths, not from the benefit of comparison to others.

5) The final analysis

With that assessment, Smith feels ready to tackle a positioning attempt. Here's her SWOT analysis:

STRENGTHS
—Unique merchandising offer with regional flavor
—No direct catalog competitors
—Growing market, with favorable market trends (aging boomers becoming seasoned travelers)

WEAKNESSES
—Start-up position in crowded catalog market
—Much specialty-store competition
—Aging audience (where will new buyers come from?)
—Catalog does not meet an "unmet need"

OPPORTUNITIES
—Capitalize on trend for sophisticated travel
—Empty-nesters have income, opportunity to buy home decor
—The number of competitive choices means consumers have to work too hard to find the styles and quality they want

THREATS
—Other, more well-heeled catalogs may enter marketplace
—Economic concerns could limit market for luxury goods

CONCLUSION
—Plenty of consumer demand exists for Tuscany Gifts' merchandise. Consumers, however, lack confidence in knowing how to select just the *right* merchandise that offers they quality and authenticity they want.

POSITIONING STATEMENT:
Tuscany Gifts offers a rare opportunity to discover authentic, hand-crafted product, imported exclusively for us and selected for the discriminating homeowner. Rediscover the warmth, colors and vibrancy of the Tuscan countryside through our catalog.

TRAITS OF GOOD POSITIONING

Now that Smith has analyzed her competitors, checked out her customers and market trends and examined her strengths and vulnerabilities—just how well-positioned is her catalog?

That's a matter of consulting the following positioning checklist:

Positioning should look to the future. It should anticipate trends and market shifts. Catalogs that get caught behind a trend risk losing ground to upstart competitors.

EFFECTIVE POSITIONING IS BUILT ON A MOTIVATING INSIGHT INTO THE CUSTOMER. WITH ITS CHARTS AND INFORMATIONAL COPY, L.L. BEAN ACKNOWLEDGES ITS CUSTOMERS' NEED TO BUY THE BEST PRODUCT FOR THEIR SPECIFIC, PRACTICAL NEEDS.

POSITIONING V. IDENTITY

It's not hard to confuse the concepts "positioning" and "identity." Here's how to differentiate:

Identity is the image your catalog brand projects to its target audience. The central element for establishing that identity is *positioning*. Positioning crystallizes your selling proposition; what you promise to your customers.

L.L. Bean's *identity*, for instance, is that of a catalog of authentic, top-quality outdoor gear and home products that fit a causal oriented lifestyle...and you can depend on them for great service. Its *positioning*—the central element of its identity—is a New England based company, committed to offering quality products at a fair price, providing only the highest level of service possible.

Good positioning works when it is based on *differentiation* and *consumer insight*. In other words, a well-positioned catalog addresses a specific consumer need, want, preference or motivational hot button. It also differentiates by putting a unique spin on that customer's need.

So in Bean's case, target consumers want an authentic outdoor experience with the best clothing and equipment available. Bean's unique spin is to deliver and guarantee quality with top-notch service.

Notice that without a strong core identity as a top outdoors merchant, Bean's positioning would be just an empty promise. Moreover, without its positioning of warmth and service, Bean would be nothing more than a well-kept secret among a cult of outdoor-products buyers.

Positioning shores up what the cataloger is. Just as people express their identities through their clothing, hairstyles and grooming, so too must catalogers express their identities through the elements of positioning.

Positioning (for a non start-up) should also look to the past. It must adhere closely enough to the catalog's core identity so that it doesn't lose longtime customers. (Think New Coke.) Tweeds learned this the hard way when it slipped an entirely new bright look into one of its spring catalogs. Old customers, used to the earthy introspection of the old Tweeds, left in droves before the catalog swung back to its core identity.

Positioning should be attainable. In his book, *Building Strong Brands,* David Aakers states, "There is nothing more wasteful than trying to achieve a position that's out of reach." Lillian Vernon doesn't try to do Horchow, and Neiman Marcus won't go value-priced. Their brand identities are simply too strong in their respective categories. Any switch would mean losing core buyers.

Positioning should coordinate with image. A catalog positioned one way should not undermine that position with the wrong imagery. That's why J. Crew promotes sale prices with a simple sticker on the cover. It refuses to risk its rich, lifestyle imagery with a price positioning.

One gift catalog began, for example, losing customers because its low-end imagery did not communicate its high-end position. It's important to make sure all catalog elements—price, typeface, photography, product mix—support the catalog's core identity.

Positioning is more than a tag line. Sometimes catalogers emphasize a a concept, gimmick or phrase when conceiving a position. While a tag line or symbol can be useful shorthand for bringing a cataloger to a customer's mind (the Bean boot), such a concept means nothing without positioning to back it up. The symbol must create a unifying theme for the catalog, both visually and conceptually. The Peterman "horseman," for instance, works almost as a full positioning statement within itself. It represents the catalog's history (the original Peterman coat) and conjures images of romance and adventure.

Positioning is more than product attributes. Yes, a Lands' End turtleneck has all the flat seams and tough fabric we care about, and a Hanna Andersson baby blanket will last for generations. Those attributes are certainly part of how those catalogs position themselves. But the products, in the customer's mind, are part of a larger package. People buy Lands' End because it represents quality, comfort and value; customers love their "Hannas" because of the cozy Swedish connotations.

Positioning is not easy to copy. Good positioning represents a complex assortment of associations. Customers wishing to knock off Smith & Hawken, for instance, would be challenged not only by the unique merchandising of casual apparel, decorative items and gardening supplies, but also by the catalog's serene mood, park-like imagery and ecological associations. Well-positioned catalogs speak in a particular voice that is not easy to emulate.

Positioning is carried out internally as well as communicated externally. Catalog employees—particularly creative staff—need to know and understand the catalog's position in order to carry it out. Catalogs filled with customer service benefits must maintain excellent service. Catalogs that emphasize quality must not deal with shoddy vendors. Positioning that rings false only alienates buyers.

THE SEVEN "LAWS" OF POSITIONING

Why do some catalogs make it in a category, and others flop? To a large degree, it can all be a matter of positioning. Consider these seven "laws" presented by Ries and Trout in their book *The 22 Immutable Laws of Marketing* (1993, Harper Business). Although these "laws" apply to product marketing, they apply equally well to catalogs.

1. The Law of Leadership:

It's best to be first than it is to be better.

In many categories, "first" products become legendary. When you want a copy of a report, you ask for a "Xerox." When you blow your nose, you reach for "Kleenex." When you want a soda, you ask for a "Coke."

Likewise, "first" catalogs in a category often dominate a market—even if they attract copycats. The Sharper Image, for instance, remains the market leader in electronic gizmos, while imitators have mostly shriveled. Chadwick's has remained ahead in off-price clothing, despite legions of competitors.

2. The Law of the Category:

If you can't be first in a category, set up a new category.

J. Peterman could have been yet another purveyor of high-end apparel, swallowed into the masses. Instead, it carved out an almost inimitable position of selling off-center styles with historic and romantic associations. Niche marketing, clearly, is one way to establish a unique position.

3. The Law of the Mind:

It's better to be first in the mind than to be first in the marketplace.

This may sound contradictory to Law No. 1—but it's not. Consider, for instance, *People* magazine. Before its launch, the magazine industry had plenty of movie and gossip titles. But *People* launched not only with a new take on celebrity gossip, but with the knock-out resources of Time Inc. Because of its heavy marketing, it became first in consumer minds, and no copycats have stolen its market.

In cataloging, it may well be true that there were cooking catalogs before Williams-Sonoma, or funky home-furnishings books before Pottery Barn—but no one remembers them now. Once a catalog captures minds and imaginations, it captures the market as well.

4. The Law of Perception:

Marketing is not a battle of products. It's a battle of perceptions.

It may be possible that I could find the same Smith & Hawken digging fork in some other lower-price gardening catalog. But when I *buy* from Smith & Hawken, I feel I'm getting the best product, chosen especially for a thoughtful, serious gardener like myself.

As David Aakers points out in his book, *Building Strong Brands,* marketers take a risk when they assume that customers care more about *function* than they do about style, status, reassurance and a whole host of other buying motivators.

5. The Law of Focus:

The most powerful concept in marketing is owning a word in the prospect's mind.

When positioning, it helps to tie your catalog to just a single word. Consider these following word associations for popular brands:

       Crest...cavities
       Volvo...safety
       Domino's...delivery
       Pepsi-Cola...youth
   Now try it with catalogs—but in reverse:
       electronics...The Sharper Image
       gadgets...Brookstone
       New York...Bloomingdale's
       gourmet...Williams-Sonoma

The most established and successful catalogs are ones that have a rock-hard identity within their category.

6. The Law of Exclusivity:

Two companies can't win the same word in the prospect's mind.

It wouldn't help Burger King, for instance, to tell customers "You deserve a break today." And only one beer gets to be "The king of beers." So it is among catalogs. The best ones may have imitators, but it's not likely that any other outdoor cataloger, for instance, could assume the word "Maine" the way Bean does. Catalogers that "own" their positioning have the best chance of success.

7. The Law of the Ladder:

The strategy to use depends on which rung of the ladder you occupy.

Number-one catalogers in a category, for instance, must remain consistent and continually reinforce their core positioning. (What would become of Lands' End if it stopped explaining the virtues of its turtlenecks?) But number-two catalogers have to ensure that they create a unique personality; a genuine buying option within the category. Lands' End might be first in quality turtlenecks, for instance, but Eddie Bauer might offer a slightly hipper option for the style-conscious.

WHAT'S MY LINE?
TIPS FOR THINKING ABOUT IDENTITY

Working through your catalog's identity fortunately requires no Freudian thinking.
Instead, you can play with a simple three-part analysis:

1) What's the ABV?

In other words:

Attributes:

What does the catalog offer?

What's the price range?

Who's the target audience?

Benefits:

What does the catalog offer that is unique, special and different—and meets the needs of the target audience?

Values:

What emotional connotation should the catalog have with its customers? Should customers feel warmly toward the catalog? Excited? Stimulated? Reassured? Inspired? Envious?

2) What's the POPS?

In other words, David Aakers, author of *Building Strong Brands,* recommends you look at your brand identity in four ways:

As Product:

What are your merchandise strengths and weaknesses?

Is your product unique?

Is is functional or stylish?

Is it exclusive to you alone?

Does it meet an unmet need?

Does it have special properties: durability, fashion, reliability, status-making?

As Organization:

What is your company's culture?

Its values and assets?

Is the company trustworthy?

Is it seen as an expert?

Is it friendly?

Does it have a social consciousness or unusual reputation? (Think Ben & Jerry's, Seventh Generation)

As Person:

If your catalog were a person, what would be its personality? Friendly? Aloof? Part of an exclusive club? Helpful? Considerate? Empathetic? Authoritative? Expert?

As Symbol:

What image would sum up your catalog?

What phrase or visual would communicate its values and culture?

3) And what about the following:

If the catalog spoke, what would it say to customers?

Consider these possibilities:

"Who's your investment banker?"
  (Brooks Brothers)

"Take off your coat and stay a while."
  (Norm Thompson)

"Where did I leave Dad's Land Rover?"
  (J. Crew)

"Too sexy for my cat."
  (Victoria's Secret)

"See you at the Mensa meeting."
  (Levenger's)

"Let's have a bottle of Montrachet."
  (Williams-Sonoma)

What word would describe the catalog's personality?

Try these:

Easy-going...Orvis

Funny...Oriental Trading Company

Sympathetic...Self-Care

Sexy...Lew Magram

Warm...Chadwick's

Tough...Patagonia

Can you picture your customer?

How about:

The Hanna baby v. the Lands' End baby

The Cabela's sportsman v. the Orvis sportsman

The Levenger's professional v.

The Sharper Image professional

The Frederick's of Hollywood woman v.

the Chadwick's woman

The Hearthsong kid v. Lilly's kid

What do your customers say about themselves?

How about:

"I enjoy the fine things."
  (Neiman Marcus)

"Money is tight, but we like to have fun."
  (Lillian Vernon)

"I feel empowered."
  (Talbots)

"My life is in order."
  (Hold Everything)

"Don't call me 'babe.'"
  (Tweeds)

THE NEXT STEP:
WHAT DO YOU WANT TO GAIN?

Once you've started to work out your catalog's identity and positioning, the next step is critical. That's figuring out how to put it into action.

Positioning is not an abstract process. You can't decide on a position because it sounds good, or because the competition doesn't have it. Positioning must have purpose.

In other words, your catalog's positioning must be backed up by concrete, thought-out *marketing objectives, strategies and tactics.* That's the topic of the next section.

CASE STUDY

▼

Eddie Bauer and the dawn of the Middle-Aged Slacker

Back in 1996, Eddie Bauer was primed for big growth. It had opened more than 300 stores nationwide. It annually mailed tens of millions of catalogs, both for retail traffic-building and for mail order selling. It had 5 million customers buying from its catalogs and stores.

But at the same time, it saw that it was missing a big chunk of potential consumers. Research showed a full 20 million Americans lived near an Eddie Bauer store and had the demographics of an Eddie Bauer buyer: a "classic" or "update" clothes buyer aged 25-54, income $40,000-plus. The question: How to attract those remaining 15 million prospects?

The answer: positioning. Through a spring 1997 national advertising campaign, the company set out to demonstrate just what was *special, unique and different* about Eddie Bauer. "We aren't just another casual lifestyle retailer," says Bill Michel, vice president, direct marketing.

For its campaign, the company first researched the characteristics of its prime customers, who are, in fact, baby boomers. Psychographically, Eddie Bauer found, boomers were worn out. A Gallup survey, for instance, showed 33% of Americans were willing to take a big cut in pay for fewer hours of work. IBM found 60% of its workers (32,000) were willing to take up an early-departure package. A trend toward "voluntary simplicity" had seized boomers' imagination. Eddie Bauer's conclusion? "It's as if people are waking up to a new reality and realizing they should get a life. It's what we have been referring to as the 'middle-aged slacker movement.'"

That was good news for Eddie Bauer, a business long defined by "an obsession with comfort and leisure." Boomers want substance: "Eddie Bauer has a long history, a home, a tradition." Boomers want balance: "Eddie Bauer has always had a healthy outlook on the role of work and play." Boomers want brands with timeless, enduring values: "Eddie Bauer has stood for quality and craftsmanship since 1920."

In short, Eddie Bauer's positioning dovetailed perfectly with the latest tick in boomer trends. With the core theme of "balance," The company set out a series of print ads, window displays and catalog designs.

"With our 76 years of experience with this lifestyle," says Michel, "who better to talk to all those tired baby boomers than Eddie Bauer?"

section two

SETTING UP THE MARKETING PLAN OF ACTION

CHAPTER 4

Marketing Objectives, Strategies and Tactics

CHAPTER 5

The Art of Strategic Thinking

CHAPTER 6

Tactical Warfare

CHAPTER 7

Final Strategy: Boosting Your Numbers

CHAPTER 4

MARKETING OBJECTIVES, STRATEGIES AND TACTICS

It takes two good mind-sets to create a strong catalog identity. And it's a lucky cataloger that has them both in the same head!

The first mind-set is *theoretical.* This is the creative, right-brain process that goes into positioning and brand-building.

The other mind-set is *strategic.* This ensures that your well-positioned catalog has a chance to thrive and grow.

That's the challenge. We all know about genius catalog concepts that went nowhere because of poor business planning. And we probably know about great business minds who went nowhere because of poor catalog concepts. The two notions are bound together: You can't have a great business plan without great positioning, and you can't position your catalog without a good plan of action.

In this chapter, I'll introduce you to the three elements of business planning: *marketing objectives, strategies* and *tactics.* You can't profit from your great brand identity, after all, unless you plan for it.

OBJECTIVES, STRATEGIES, TACTICS

In a sense, "growing" a catalog is much like growing plants. The first step—positioning—is determining *what* to plant. That means figuring out what will grow best in the soil, climate, space and environmental conditions available.

The next step is determining how much your "garden" will yield, and how to get the most from the "harvest." That's where marketing objectives, strategies and tactics come into play.

Look at it this way:

1) *Marketing objectives* are like crop predictions. They indicate how large you can expect your business to grow, and how soon.

Like crop yields, too, marketing objectives are based on experience, climate and resources. It may be that your objective is fairly modest: say, $2 million in sales, with break-even profit, within five years. Or, if you've got more capital and a hot product line, you might shoot for $50 million in sales and $2 million in earnings in five years.

The point is, you need *some* objective, some measurable goal, when growing your catalog business. Moreover, to keep the goal clear, it's critical that you state your objective in terms of *money over time.*

2) *Strategies,* in a sense, resemble marketing objectives. They're smaller, specific goals that enable you to meet your ultimate marketing objective.

So in farming, a strategy might be "increase yield per stalk by 10%" or "increase output per acre by 20 bushels." In cataloging, that might translate to "increase prospect response by 20%" or "reach $100 average order size." By setting up these goals, you lead the catalog down the path of meeting its overall growth objective, say, $5 million in sales, with break-even profit, in five years.

3) *Tactics* are the methods you use to deploy your strategies. If you want more output per acre, you might need to plant more thickly and better prepare the soil. And if you want to increase prospect response by 20%, you need specific tactics—such as free shipping and handling—that can help you get there.

MARKETING OBJECTIVES:
THE WISDOM OF PLANNING AHEAD

Why have a marketing objective at all? Plenty of catalogers, particularly new ones, are often tempted to simply put their catalog in the mail and see what happens. In their minds, they're out to "test" the marketplace, fine-tune their concept and figure out their viability.

What they usually get, though, is chaos. Catalogers without a measurable goal can be swamped with backorders, or worse, stuck with a backload of unwanted product and no cash flow to keep going. They have no clue as to what kind of overhead they'll need, what mailing strategies they'll require, or even how much product to keep on hand. They're flying blind and hoping not to run into trees.

A focused marketing objective, on the other hand, is like a homing signal. It keeps catalogers moving forward. With a clear goal in mind, catalogers can look realistically at their market, audience, strengths and weaknesses, as well as their own resources. They can map out the best flight and sail along. For them, a marketing objective is a kind of personal finish line—after they've determined the length and course of their race.

STRATEGIES AND TACTICS:
THE WAY TO BEAT YOUR PLAN

I have a friend who's a bicycle racer. Ask him about his last race, and his response is usually one of three: "I beat my best time"; "I was 30 seconds behind my best time"; "I was right on my best time."

Catalogers are the same way. Ask about their last mailing: "It's way above plan." "It's right on plan." "It's 10% below plan."

Like racers working from their best time, successful catalogers are always working a plan—which means they're constantly looking for ways to meet or beat their marketing objectives. To do so, they turn to *marketing strategies* and *tactics*.

My biking friend, for instance, calls on a whole host of strategies and tactics for beating his time. Sometimes he takes a strategy of building his endurance. In that case, he lifts weights and runs between races. Other times he takes a strategy of improving his equipment. So he might lower his seat by an eighth of an inch, or switch to a more aerodynamic helmet, or attach some fancy clip to his pedals.

As a cataloger, you've got just as many choices in meeting and beating your profit objectives. As a strategy, you might choose to emphasize service, to build average order size, to promote price, or to demonstrate quality. For those goals, you might want to introduce such tactics as mailing more sale catalogs, changing copy, strengthening the guarantee, offering 20% off orders of $200, you name it.

Notice the differences between *strategies* and *tactics*. Strategies are the business options you can choose to reach a marketing objective while maintaining your positioning. Tactics are the specific methods that support the strategy.

BRAND IDENTITY: THE GUIDING HAND

It all comes back to brand identity. Once again, *any strategy or tactic really depends on the catalog's brand identity and positioning.*

Let's say, for instance, that your apparel catalog has a marketing objective of reaching $2 million in profits in its fifth year. Currently, your four-year-old catalog is 5% behind plan. Your catalog's brand identity is elite maternity apparel for upscale women, with a heavy service orientation.

To build profitability, you probably wouldn't slash prices or switch to cheaper paper. Both tactics would likely undercut your brand identity. Instead you might choose to offer free returns as an exclusive convenience. Or you might try to increase order size by offering more accessories.

So, here's how your objectives, strategies and tactics might break down.

Objective: To reach $2 million in profits within five years. Currently, the catalog is 5% behind its business plan to meet the objective.

Strategies: Elevating awareness of service. Creating programs to build customer loyalty. Increasing order size.

Tactics: Offering free returns, conducting more customer surveys, rewarding frequent shoppers with discounts and adding accessories to the product mix.

Now let's take another apparel catalog with the same marketing objective. This time, though, assume this cataloger takes a position based on value, price and assortment. Here's how his strategies and tactics might look:

Objective: To reach $2 million in profit within five years. Catalog is currently 5% behind business plan.

Strategies: Increase response. Emphasize price and promotion. Demonstrate value.

Tactics: More callouts for specially priced items. More information on special sizing and colors available. Wider merchandise mix.

Changing your positioning and creative presentation dramatically can alienate your customer base.

Getting back to visuals that reflect the core audience worked for Clifford & Wills.

In each case, notice that *strategy really reflects brand identity.* If you position your catalog on customer commitment, for instance, you might choose growth strategies focused on, say, lifetime value or relationship marketing. Your tactics might include improved guarantees or regular customer surveys.

But if your position is product selection and pricing, you might want to try strategies to build average order size or to increase response rates. As tactics, building product lines, changing creative or extending offerings might work.

It can get complicated. But bear in mind that no matter which strategies and tactics are used, the ultimate goal is always simple: improving profit and reaching growth objectives.

CASE STUDY
▼

CLIFFORD & WILLS
Repositioning Strategies

Women's apparel cataloger Clifford & Wills made a serious positioning error back in 1993-1994. At the time, the cataloger decided to scuttle its old positioning as a value-priced mainstream fashion book. Its "new" positioning and creative became urban, edgy, niche-oriented, fashion-forward.

But while the creative had changed, the customers hadn't. The suburban buyers, the bread-and-butter of the business, found the new look cold and unapproachable. They weren't buying.

As a strategy to rebuilding its profits, Clifford & Wills decided to reactivate old buyers. It tried mailing back into its old lists, offering free shipping and handling and testing new offers to win back those core customers.

But the tactic wasn't enough to support the strategy. What Clifford & Wills really needed was to reposition itself closer to its original positioning. That called for new creative execution. Once again, the catalog began using models who were friendly and approachable; who looked straight into the camera and walked across sunlit beaches rather than city streets. The catalog's trendy styling was cut back; it took on a warmer, more familiar look.

Now, combined with such response-building tactics as free shipping, the strategy—reactivating customers—began to gel. Core customers started coming back, and the catalog's growth plan turned back on track.

In the end, Clifford & Wills found that while its objective was clear-cut, its strategies and tactics needed to evolve more slowly.

THE BUSINESS PLAN

It's one thing to have a marketing objective that tells you how many dollars you would like from your catalog over the next, say, five years. But to make it work, you need a business plan. All successful catalogers work from a goal-oriented business plan—preferably from one that looks at least three years into the future. (For most new catalogers, breakeven is at least two to three years down the road.)

A business plan tells you the specific actions you'll need to take to meet your objective. It paints a realistic picture of your audience, marketplace, competition and sales opportunities. It lets you know whether your marketing objective is realistic, and if not, how to make it that way.

Business plans differ for every cataloger. After all, if you're planning $2 million in sales in five years, you'll need far different fulfillment planning, prospecting goals, inventory control and overhead than a cataloger planning 20 times that growth.

Since business plans deal with financial, not creative, strategies, I won't tackle the subject in detail here. But I can show you the basic ingredients of a business plan, and how each contributes to a catalog's marketing objective.

Plus, you'll see how each part of the plan helps you crystallize your catalog's positioning. If you're unsure of your catalog's ability to "speak" to its market, filling out a business plan will help you work it through.

Let's say an established gift catalog—call it Gifts Unlimited—is debating whether to spin off a jewelry book. Essentially, this cataloger's business plan would address the following:

1) *A business assessment and point of view.*

Here, Gifts Unlimited would explore how to make its spin-off financially viable. It might point out, for instance, that the catalog would need to reach a target market of style-conscious, affluent young consumers who are already mail order friendly, and that it must offer jewelry unlike any currently available by catalog.

2) *A background statement of the marketing problem or opportunity.*

The cataloger would state why the time is right to launch a new book. It may note that jewelry is the catalog's best-selling category; that the market for jewelry is growing faster than the overall gift market, and that its particular jewelry offering is unduplicated by other books in the market.

3) *A situation analysis.*

Gifts Unlimited would then detail its current strategies and marketing issues. It might state that since the main gift catalog's audience is aging, a spin-off could bring in younger consumers. It might also note that the main catalog needs to broaden its product line in order to tap higher-margin categories, and that the company is also exploring other spin-off opportunities in separate product areas.

4) *A competitive analysis.*

At this point, Gifts Unlimited would list the different levels of jewelry offerings in the market, ranging from Tiffany and Black, Starr & Frost to costume earring catalogs. Its principal competition might be mid-range casual jewelry catalogs, such as Sundance's.

In a full competitive analysis, Gifts Unlimited would explore the average number of pages per catalog among its competitors, the number of products per page, the average price points, average order sizes, payment methods, number of items per order and estimated profitability—as well as layout densities, styling, photography techniques, use of models and so on.

5) *A look at the target audience.*

The cataloger would then explore the primary, secondary and tertiary audiences for its proposed spin-off. Target buyers, for instance, might be young, affluent professionals who currently buy from the gift catalog. Secondary audiences might include older gift buyers, less affluent, young customers, and prospects from other gift books.

6) *An assessment of marketing and creative strategies.*

Based on its research, Gifts Unlimited would detail the look and positioning of its proposed spin-off. The spin-off, for instance, might be designed as a "slim-jim" to differentiate it from the gift book, and it might play down the Gifts Unlimited logo in order to appeal to a different customer group. Other strategies might include a more stylized, product-focused presentation than the current gift book, higher average price points, an emphasis on jewelry collections in order to maximize average order size, and a lower page density than the parent book.

7) *An assessment of merchandising strategies.*
Next, Gifts Unlimited would outline its proposed product mix, along with the gross margins for each category and the percentage of the book occupied by each. Rings, for instance, with a margin of 52%, might take about 15% of the catalog; necklaces, with a 45% margin, might consume another 32%. At a later time, the catalog might include leather goods or scarves to broaden the line.

8) *A circulation strategy.*
Gifts Unlimited would then look at which lists it might rent for its new spin-off, and determine how much of the proposed circulation should go to the parent file and how much to prospects.

9) *Fulfillment and backend strategies.*
Gifts Unlimited would outline how it intends to separate the order-taking and fulfillment of the spin-off catalog in order to provide the quickest service. A complete analysis would detail the cost of setting up the fulfillment operation, and the proposed financial or service benefits/problems of doing so.

10) *An outline of catalog development costs.*
Next, the cataloger would note what it expects to spend on creating a concept, acquiring lists, retaining consultants and all other services needed to pull the spin-off together. It would also note expected costs for printing, production, merchandising, fulfillment, postage, creative and operations.

11) *A financial pro forma.*
At this point, Gifts Unlimited would outline all the costs, expected revenue and expected performance of the spin-off. It might assume, for instance, a 10% return rate, a 43% gross margin, catalog costs of 75 cents per book and list rental costs of $125 per thousand, as well as all operating and fulfillment costs, shipping and handling income, and general and administrative cost. The cataloger might also note that it expects to drop three times a year, achieve a $100 average order size, and mail to a 2% overall response rate. Finally, a profit-and-loss statement would indicate the catalog's ultimate marketing objective: say, $10 million in sales, with break-even profitability, in three years.

12) *Long-term opportunities.*
Finally, Gifts Unlimited might look at other potential audiences and spin-off ideas, such as a watch and accessories catalog, or a catalog of fine jewelry. It might list future promotions to test, such as free shipping and handling or dollars-off coupons. It might also suggest testing ordering sites on the World Wide Web.

REALISTIC FLEXIBILITY

In the end, of course, Gifts Unlimited's business plan is grounded in a clear marketing objective: $10 million in sales in three years. But the intent is not simply to state a plan and objective and stick it in a drawer. For any cataloger, marketing objectives and business plans need to be flexible and ongoing, receiving constant attention and evaluation.

Gifts Unlimited, for instance, might choose to scale up its growth goals after watching a competitor fold, or after finding a cheaper source for supplies. Or the cataloger may find the market isn't supporting the spin-off, or that wholesale jewelry costs have skyrocketed, or that the warehouse plans endanger spotted owls. Whatever happens, the marketing objectives—along with the business plans that support them—can be adjusted to suit the new reality.

CHAPTER 5

THE ART OF STRATEGIC THINKING

When times are tough for catalogers (and frankly, when aren't they?), it's very tempting to look at your catalog business and think, "Well, why not try improving *everything?*"

In other words, why not try improving the response rate...attempting customer loyalty programs...demonstrating more value...promoting better service...and on and on and on. After all, this book demonstrates dozens of ways you can improve your catalog's brand identity, and its business. Why not call on them all?

The truth is, though, you can't give all strategies equal weight. That would be like trying to build the perfect catalog by combining signature styles from anyone worth swiping from—L.L. Bean's service, Lillian Vernon's merchandising, Lands' End's value. Try it, and you'll end up with an empty-handed, dull, homogenized book—direct marketing oatmeal.

So, when you are launching a catalog, or trying to solve a marketing problem, it pays to simply identify one or two *clear* strategies that will help you reach your business goal.

In this chapter you'll learn how to identify those strategies and how to determine which work best for you.

STRATEGIES ARE NOT CREATED EQUAL

We all know how service is top priority at L.L. Bean. I remember once debating whether to order a size six or size eight coat. The L.L. Bean operator offered to send both coats with a return sticker so I could send one back, no charge. Someone else I know called and said she wanted a new garment bag, since her five-year-old bag was too large. L.L. Bean not only took back the old bag and sent the customer a new one, it even sent along a refund check, since the new bag cost less than the old one!

Now that's a great positioning tactic. Bean's strategy, obviously, was improving customer loyalty through exemplary service. Did it work? You bet.

But what about a different cataloger—one whose profitability strategy is to hold down return rates? Maybe it's a company selling swimsuits, or maternity apparel. Should that company employ the tactic of sending free-return stickers?

Not necessarily. L.L. Bean obviously wants to be financially successful—but it's not willing to compromise service for financial goals. Other catalogers may not be willing or able to afford such a strategy. Expensive service tactics probably wouldn't help their company's positioning, or bottom line. Instead, they might rely on such tactics as improving the catalog's sizing chart, or offering "fashion counselors" to dispense advice.

PICKING WHAT WORKS

So how do you determine your own catalog's growth strategies?

1) *Know your marketing objective.* If you've got aggressive growth goals, you likely need numbers-oriented strategies, such as increasing response rates. If you want time to build brand and positioning, you might focus on such strategies as creating customer loyalty. In other words, your growth goals will dictate which strategies you can afford, and which might just hold your business back.

2) *Know your brand identity.* You'll be hearing this a lot from me. Strategies and tactics must be in line with your catalog's core values and identities. Service-oriented catalogs, like Lands' End, are guided by strategies that promote that ethic. Upscale catalogs generally want strategies that preserve their quality appearance while numbers-oriented books may take more of a promotional tack.

3) *Identify the strategies and tactics that support your positioning and marketing objective.* (See below and in the next chapter.)

4) *Prioritize your strategies,* keeping in mind your category of business. Consider, for instance, how your customers currently feel about your catalog, or what tactics your competitors use, or the service and product expectations of your target market. One cataloger's key strategy—say, improving order size—may simply not work for another cataloger whose price points are high but whose response is low.

Now, let's look in detail at how to pick strategies that work for you.

TOP STRATEGIES THAT WORK

When you come right down to it, good marketing strategies are pretty simple to define. Basically, they boil down to the following:

1) *Capitalizing on brand*
2) *Creating customer loyalty*
3) *Promoting perceived quality*
4) *Promoting price*
5) *Demonstrating value*
6) *Promoting service*

Keep in mind, though, that these strategies are not generic. You won't find any one-size-fits-all marketing strategy here. Instead, as you'll soon see, each strategy works best for particular types of catalogs.

Strategy #1:
CAPITALIZING ON BRAND

We all know how "brand" works in the packaged-goods world—especially when one product is pretty much like another. Brand creates an association in the consumer's mind that seldom has to do with the actual taste of carbonated sugar water, or with the merits of grease-cutting soap. Mountain Dew is "hip," Coke is "it." Marlboro is "manly," Virginia Slims is "sexy." Brand images like these, once established, stay lodged in a consumer's mind forever.

It's the same with catalogs. For some, the name alone becomes almost an emotional shorthand. "Disney," for instance, may be a media conglomerate, but it still means mouse ears and wholesome entertainment to those who page through its bright and chipper catalog. Likewise, Coach and Tiffany capitalize on their well-crafted brands with cleanly elegant (and, in Tiffany's case, traditional sky blue) creative, reminiscent of the exclusiveness of their stores.

MORE THAN MOST CATALOGERS, THE DISNEY CATALOG HAS THE WHEREWITHALL TO CAPITALIZE ON BRAND.

Which catalogers benefit from brand strategies?

Any catalog with an established brand name should capitalize on it. Take Sundance, a catalog synonomous with Robert Redford. Every issue captures both his rugged handsomeness (there's a photo and letter in every issue) and the image of the ruggedly handsome Sundance Institute. The product mix, heavy on Western motifs, is carefully chosen to reflect this image, and the models, dressed in Western chic, wander through rustic ranch settings.

Some catalogs, on the other hand, ought to cultivate a brand strategy, even if they're not yet brand names. Such catalogs include the following:

—*Catalogs with mass audiences.* Niche audiences expect a catalog to meet their particular needs, whether it's for sky diving outfits or Corvette accessories. When they look at a favorite catalog, they're not as concerned with "brand," with an emotional connotation, as they are with product selection and service.

Mass audiences, on the other hand, deal with many similar-looking catalogs. They need a reason to buy kids' clothing from *this* catalog as opposed to *that* one. In many cases, brand makes the qualitative difference. A brand name matters a lot more to the consumer seeking bed linens than to the consumer looking for candle-making supplies.

—*Catalogs whose products are attacked by or compared with a competitor.* Such catalogs can use brand imagery to bring positive associations to consumers. Customers who have to choose between Eddie Bauer boots and no-name boots at the same price will most likely pick the name they know.

—*Catalogs that are not clearly differentiated from the competition.* By capitalizing on brand, look-alike catalogs can establish a name, a point of leverage, in the consumer's mind. Two gift catalogs may appear similar, but the one that carries, say, the Horchow or Smithsonian name is the one that most likely gets opened first.

INSIDER'S CLUB

Join now and get a 10% discount on this and all future purchases! Own everything the pros wear. And get exclusive benefits.

As a charter member you'll be able to own the same exact apparel your favorite pros and teams are issued. Plus, we offer signed collectibles and official videos—all at Club discounts. Join today, become an insider and receive these benefits:

• **10% Discount.** Members get 10% off any purchase for one full year when they order through SI's Insider Authentics Club.

• **A Free Surprise Video.** Receive an action-packed video from our inventory.

• **Exclusive "Insider" Sales.** Insider mailings alert members to any special sales on apparel, videos and other authentic merchandise.

• **Express Delivery on all Purchases.** All your orders will be shipped via Air Express delivery. With this special member benefit, you will receive in-stock orders paid by credit card in 3 business days at no extra charge above regular shipping and handling.

• **Membership Card and Customer Hot Line.** Exclusive toll free number offers customer assistance 24 hours a day, 7 days a week.

• **Money Back Guarantee.** If you're not completely satisfied, cancel your membership and receive a full refund. The free video and Authentics catalog are yours to keep.

• **33% Off Membership Fee.** As a charter member, your fee will be a low $19.95. That's 33% off the regular yearly membership of $29.95.

• **Receive Sports Illustrated Insider® Authentic Catalog for a Year.** This is the exciting new and easy way to see what the pros are wearing and to order it right from your own home.

Call toll-free **1-800-274-5200** and tell the operator you want to become a member. You'll receive the 10% discount automatically on all your purchases.

TO BUILD LOYALTY TO ITS CATALOG, SPORTS ILLUSTRATED BEGAN AN "INSIDER'S CLUB" FEATURING DISCOUNTS, EXPRESS DELIVERY AND FREEBIES.

REAL GOODS' MEMBERSHIP PROGRAM INCLUDES LOW-COST PROMOTIONS, SUCH AS NEWSLETTERS AND SOURCEBOOKS, DESIGNED TO APPEAL TO ENVIRONMENTALLY CONSCIOUS CUSTOMERS.

Strategy #2:
CREATING CUSTOMER LOYALTY

We all know the old 80/20 rule: how catalogers gain 80% of their profits from the top 20% of their customers. Less known is this fact: Most catalogers spend about 80% of their marketing dollars trying to find new customers.

Obviously, new customers are the one source of catalog growth. But catalogers must remember that *good* customers, established customers, are the source of its *profits*. Loyal customers generally spend more per order than new ones, and they order more frequently. That means earning customer loyalty can be a lot less expensive than finding new customers.

Customer loyalty programs, then, make sense for many catalogers. La Costa Spa, Plow & Hearth, Saks Fifth Avenue and Neiman Marcus, to name a few, have all created programs in which customers—who sometimes join for a small amount of money—earn benefits each time they make a purchase. Often, these customers also receive advance sale notices, special offers and discounts, newsletters or even T-shirts.

The value-added benefits for customers are obvious. The benefits for catalogers, though perhaps not so obvious, are often even better. Such programs create an ongoing dialogue and relationship with customers, making them feel nurtured by an exclusive club. The customer repays with loyalty, usually in the form of bigger orders and higher response.

Which catalogers benefit from loyalty strategies?

Catalog loyalty programs aren't for everybody. Because they're labor-intensive, they require a serious administrative commitment. Catalogers can't simply decide to "test" a program and pull it if it doesn't pay off. Customers who join a catalog program, after all, *expect* to continue receiving newsletters, or special mailings and discounts. If they're accumulating points toward future purchases, they're going to expect regular updates and statements. That means catalogers that ask for loyalty from their customers have to be willing to give back in return.

So which catalogers gain most from this strategy?

—Catalogs with new and younger customers. It's easy to imagine that catalogs with older, established customers are naturals for loyalty programs—and in fact, many are. But older customers also like to shop around. They're savvier than younger consumers, and are far more easily swayed by the competition.

Young consumers, on the other hand, are generally looking for roots. They've yet to experiment with a number of brands, and through their buying habits they hope to find meaning, reliability and identity. Because security matters to them, they often look for it in labels and brands. (Consider Nike and Tommy Hilfiger's grip on the market.)

Catalogs that provide a meaningful experience for young consumers usually earn their ongoing loyalty. Just consider what one 26-year-old professional I know says of J. Crew: "If I'm going on vacation and need a pair of shorts, I just call them. I know what they'll deliver and I know what to expect." It's likely this customer, who got hooked on Crew in college, will remain hooked for many years to come.

—*Catalogs that emphasize a high level of service.* Catalogs that can and do provide a high level of customer service usually have what it takes to create loyalty programs. For them, creating special services or offers may simply be a matter of fine-tuning the customer service they already provide. Moreover, since they've already acclimated consumers to expect good service, their customers might be more willing to hand their loyalty to them.

—*Catalogs with a strong brand identity.* It's tough for new or unestablished catalogs to create loyalty among customers. After all, customers in loyalty programs rightly expect to have a relationship with the catalog, and it's a lot easier to have a relationship with a known friend—like a DKNY or Lands' End—than an unknown entity.

—*Catalogs with customer niches.* Most apparel catalogs have fickle customers. These consumers aren't so much brand-influenced as they are style-influenced: If they see what they like, they buy it, regardless of whether the catalog offers them a buying club or loyalty program. Such catalogers may find customer loyalty programs a waste of money and time.

On the other hand, loyalty programs work well for catalogs that already have a loyal customer base. Customers who identify with, say, J. Peterman's upscale fashion eccentricities, would likely take advantage of programs that reward their loyalty.

—*Catalogs with continuity products.* We're all familiar with the good success of book and CD clubs. Sure, books and CDs can be purchased just about anywhere. What makes the club concept work is that buyers receive convenience, service and terrific offers on products they would buy anyway on an ongoing basis.

It's human nature to stick to routine, and many catalogers are in a good position to take advantage of that. Seventh Generation, for instance, offers consumers a restocking service for their laundry detergent, paper towels and other ecology-friendly replaceable goods. Omaha Steaks similarly offers product that combines raves and repeat buying with a short shelf life. That gives Omaha Steaks an ideal platform for creating loyalty.

—*Catalogs with specialized product.* The more unusual or hard-to-find the catalog product, the more likely that customers will be loyal to it. It's easy, for instance, to buy bagels just about anywhere, so a bagel catalog could probably do little to engender loyalty. On the other hand, consider Wolferman's, a catalog of unique English muffins and bakery products. Because customers can't get the product or service anywhere else (each muffin is flash-frozen out of the oven), consumers who get hooked on Wolferman's have no choice but to keep giving the the catalog their business!

TYROL INTERNATIONAL'S LOYALTY CLUB FEATURES DISCOUNTS AND SERVICES.

TO ILLUSTRATE THE STRENGTH OF ITS CLUB PROGRAM, PLOW & HEARTH INDICATES THAT 70,000 CUSTOMERS HAVE ALREADY JOINED.

RUE DE FRANCE CAPITALIZES ON A QUALITY POSITIONING THROUGH EVERY DETAIL OF ITS CATALOG, FROM THE EXQUISITE COVER IMAGE TO THE LUXURIOUS PHOTOGRAPHY AND PROPPING THROUGHOUT.

Strategy #3: IMPROVING PERCEIVED QUALITY

Of all catalog strategies, improving perceived quality may be the biggest contributor to a healthy long-term bottom line. As David Aakers notes in his book, *Building Strong Brands*, "Perceived quality is usually at the heart of what customers are buying."

No customer wants to waste money. Customers who feel they're getting true value for their money, or some long-term benefit, are far more willing to buy on a regular basis than customers who feel they're simply getting a deal or a bargain. Bargain prices may stimulate short-term loyalty, but quality brings customers back for more.

Which catalogers benefit from a quality strategy?

Not all catalogers need or benefit from "quality" positioning. For many apparel customers, for instance, fashion is far more of a key selling point than craftsmanship. Likewise, customers who shop for price, whether for office furniture or cereal, are often more motivated by price than quality. For those reasons, low priced books like Newport News make no pretense that the quality of their apparel is up to Land's End standard. Newport News positioning is price and fashion, not double-stitching and durability.

Some catalogers, though, are better off following a quality position. They usually include these characteristics:

—*Catalogs with unique product.* Hanna Andersson, when launched in the early '80s, was the only choice for mothers seeking high-quality baby clothing. Likewise, Rue de France has become unique in offering high-end continental linens and gifts, and Garnet Hill has perfected sumptuous bedding and bath products.

Most of these catalogs discourage competitors because of the difficulty and expense of developing and marketing quality product. Their presentations help establish the perception that their products are uniquely sourced by caring merchandisers and are created as a labor of love.

—*Catalogs with expensive goods.* Catalogs of high-priced products, of course, need to emphasize quality in order to justify the price tag. They must anticipate the customer dilemma: "Why should I pay $225 for a blanket in one catalog that looks similar to a $165 blanket in another?" Simply put, if a catalog expects customers to pay more, it has to give them reasons why they should. Expensive products deserve adequate copy and appealing photography.

—*Catalogs with a mandate for the best.* Quality positioning helps sell even value-priced products—provided, of course, that the value-priced cataloger has a quality mandate.

Not long ago, for instance, a well-known men's apparel catalog found that its business was in decline. The decline wasn't surprising, given the number of menswear outlets and catalogs that had lately flooded the market. What was surprising was that the catalog had traditionally emphasized a price positioning, which, by then, had been completely undermined by such stores as Today's Man and Syms.

Fortunately, the catalog had kept an eye on its product quality. Focus group research, in fact, showed customers were far more impressed by the catalog's craftsmanship and care than by its price. Because the cataloger had already mandated the best merchandise, it was now free to abandon its old positioning in favor of a new focus on quality.

—*Catalogs with educated consumers.* Catalogs with quality merchandise generally cater to customers who not only can afford the goods, but can appreciate them as well. These informed, careful shoppers are willing to read about, study and appreciate the effort, fabrication or craftsmanship that go into quality products.

Less-educated consumers are often stimulated by price, convenience or fashion. They may prefer to hear about $40 washable sheets, while a Garnet Hill customer searches copy for references to thread counts and all-natural cotton.

Strategy #4: PROMOTING PRICE

Most customers, of course, are sensitive to price—today, more than ever. But price positioning can be risky. It can imply poor quality, or invite comparison with other catalogs or shopping outlets. It can lead to short-term buying as opposed to long-term loyalty.

Still, for certain customers, such as software or CD buyers, price can become the primary obstacle—or incentive—in purchasing decisions. For them, the catalog that communicates the right product at the right price makes the sale.

Which catalogers benefit from price promotion?

Not every cataloger needs to communicate good price, even if its customers are price-sensitive. Catalogs with unique or necessary product, for instance, tend to attract buyers, not bargain-hunters. The same is true of catalogs that emphasize perceived quality, or that present some other unique draw, like high fashion or niche marketing. If a collector falls in love with, say, a Native American goatskin drum, it's not price (usually!) that brings in the sale.

Catalogs that tend to promote price, then, include the following:

—*Catalogs with mass audiences.* Mass-market catalogs tend to carry commodity products, like kitchen utensils and funny T-shirts, that one can often find at the local department store. They also attract audiences who tend to buy wherever the price is best. For that reason, mass-market catalogs often do well to promote the best deal around.

—*Catalogs with easily-attained product.* Catalogs like MicroWarehouse yell their prices like a circus ringmaster. Since their merchandise is hardly

POSITIONING ITSELF ON SERVICE, VIKING CATALOG OFFERS NO LESS THAN FIVE SERVICE PROMOTIONS ON ITS COVER (NOTICE "1-800-SNAP-FAX" FOR FAX ORDERS).

HOLY PRICE POINTS! MACWAREHOUSE CLEARLY TAKES A PRICE POSITION, AS SEEN THROUGH ITS 40 COVER EXCLAMATION POINTS (MORE OR LESS) AND ITS LIBERAL USE OF THE TERMS "SLASH," "FREE" AND "AS LOW AS."

unique—and available through a dozen other channels—these catalogs have become locked in a shouting match for attention. Price promotion is one of the few strategies that helps them gain an ear.

—*Catalogs not positioned on quality.* Quality products are difficult to source and expensive to promote. They're not likely to attract price-sensitive customers, and so they gain little from price-promotion strategies.

—*Catalogs not positioned on lifestyle.* Price-positioned catalogs also tend to be product-positioned catalogs. Catalogs that take a lifestyle position, like J. Crew, cannot afford to undermine their hard-won image with heavy price promotions. Given too much deal-making, the customer loses touch with the emotional sell of the catalog.

Strategy #5: DEMONSTRATING VALUE

Between price and quality lies the concept of value. It's my belief, in fact, that "value" is probably the most familiar, if overused, catalog term today.

Years ago, customers who bought on price were considered "cheap." These days, they're "smart shoppers." What makes them smart is that, given the stampede of retail outlets and superstores, they know if they *want* deals, they can find them almost anywhere. As a result, shoppers today want both price and quality, and most catalogers have to assure them of both.

Which catalogers benefit from value promotions?

Value-positioned catalogs are mostly those that fall between mass-market and niche-oriented books. Generally speaking, mass-market books have plenty of customers and price competition, but little customer loyalty. Niche books, on the other hand, may have fewer, but loyal, customers, and little price competition. In between are those catalogs that have a mass-market direction—say, well-priced women's apparel—but require the differentiation and customer loyalty associated with quality.

Strategy #6: PROMOTING SERVICES

I'm convinced: Service is going to drive the catalog business of the next millenium. Even five years ago, few catalogers offered free shipping and handling, overnight delivery, unconditional guarantees or same-day shipping. Now customers can order on December 22 to have gifts in time for Christmas, and catalogs like MicroWarehouse deliver overnight for a few dollars. In the future, we'll see even higher service standards as catalogers struggle for parity. Catalogers that fall down in service will also fall down quickly in customer expectations.

LANDS' END'S VALUE POSITIONING EMERGES IN ITS PROMINENT USE OF CLOSE-UP SHOTS, CALL-OUTS, PROMINENT LABEL AND HISTORIC PRODUCT REFERENCES ("1994—ADDED THINSULATE TO SLEEVES; WARMS ARMS TWICE AS WELL").

Which catalogers benefit from service promotion?

Though all catalogers need to offer great service, not all need to *position* themselves that way. Those that do, tend to fall into the following categories:

—*Higher-end catalogs.* The more upscale the catalog, the more service its customers will expect. After all, these customers believe that one of the premiums they pay for is the right to good service.

At apparel cataloger Barrie Pace, for instance, managers actually encourage order-takers to spend time with customers on the phone, an action considered treasonous among non-service-oriented books. Likewise, some catalogs send clothing on hangers or packed in elegant boxes; others offer free gift wrapping, gift cards and other service touches.

—*High-competition catalogs.* There's a good reason why MicroWarehouse offers overnight shipping: It knows customers have the alternative of driving three miles to the nearest computer superstore. Service, although increasingly important for all catalogers, is a particular pressure for catalogers in heavy retail competition, or for those that compete with other catalogers that can ship faster and for less money.

When customers have a choice in where to purchase product, price and service usually make the sale.

NEXT STEP: TACTICS

Each of these strategies works through its own set of tactics. After marketing objectives and strategies, think of tactics as the third, supporting leg holding up your catalog's business and brand identity. Tactics, the subject of the next chapter, make up the actual actions you need to take to get your catalog rolling.

CASE STUDY

▼

CHADWICK'S BRAND IDENTITY

Capitalizing on brand is an easy call for catalogs started by such companies as Sundance, Disney or Pepsi.

But what happens when your catalog is started by a company whose brand you would rather forget?

That was the case with Chadwick's of Boston. The catalog's parent was TJX Corp., which owns the off-price apparel chains TJ Maxx and Hit or Miss. A TJ Maxx catalog, or Hit or Miss Direct just wouldn't convey the higher-quality image the company wanted for its new launch. So it invented a new "brand." Chadwick's of Boston was born.

The distinct breach with its parent helped Chadwick's develop its own identity as an off-price apparel book. Through repeated exposure, consistent imagery and time, Chadwick's developed on its own as a recognizable brand, synonymous with women's clothing at a good price.

The separation is so complete, in fact, that it's not likely one customer in 100 would know the relationship between the off-price book and its off-price parent.

BY INVENTING ITS OWN CATALOG "BRAND," THE TJX CORP. DISTANCED CHADWICK'S FROM THE BRAND IMAGERY OF ITS RETAIL CHAINS, HIT OR MISS AND T.J. MAXX.

CHAPTER 6

TACTICAL WARFARE

"Buy a million dollars' worth of merchandise, and we'll deliver it free in your new car!"

You may not remember this terrific promotion from the old Archie McPhee novelty catalog—but I loved it. To me, it was the perfect Archie McPhee tactic: goofy, funny, out-there. It was completely in keeping with the catalog's brand identity as a hip novelty book.

Of course, most of us need more pragmatic ideas when it comes to boosting business. That includes all of the more common tactics listed in this chapter.

At first, you might be tempted to skip over some of these tactics. If your catalog positions itself on price, for instance, why read about tactics for building service? Here's why: All of us need to ramp up on ideas for creating loyalty, emphasizing value, building brand identity. So while your catalog may emphasize one particular strategy over another, never neglect a good idea. I guarantee you'll get a lot out of looking through all the tactics listed below.

Tactics for
CAPITALIZING ON BRAND

If you've got a brand catalog, or intend to create one, Job #1 is to communicate that identity to customers. Your customers must have an *emotional association* with your name, and, of course, you want that association to be positive. Moreover, you need the association to be consistent, fresh and long-lasting as well. You don't want your customers to feel one way about your catalog this fall, and another way about it next spring.

Much of this book, of course, addresses just that issue. But here's a shorthand list of the tactics you'll need to employ:

Make sure creative and imagery suits the brand's position. Sundance would quickly lose its allure, for instance, if it switched to urban settings. Likewise, Coach supports its wealthy suburban aura through its restrained imagery, and Victoria's Secret hypes its glamour through the use of supermodels. All strong brands support their identity with specific, well-chosen models, copy, typeface and design.

COTTURA CATALOG'S LOGO RESEMBLES A SHARD OF FINE CERAMICS, PERFECTLY IN KEEPING WITH ITS FINE-ART IMAGE.

TO CAPITALIZE ON ITS WELL-KNOWN RETAIL BRAND, NEIMAN MARCUS EMPLOYS THE SIMPLE TACTIC OF TRANSFERRING ITS RETAIL LOGO TO ITS CATALOG.

EDDIE BAUER'S DISTINCT, BOLD LOGO SPEAKS TO THE CATALOG'S OUTDOORS HERITAGE, AS WELL AS TO ITS RELAXED FASHION SENSE.

Coach products are unique. Handmade of the finest natural materials, they have distinct characteristics all their own. They are beautifully crafted and designed to be lifetime companions. Our leather is like no other. It burnishes over time, acquiring a rich, lustrous patina that is the wearer's individual imprint. Our products are not frivolous. Each one is conceived to suit a purpose, to conform to the user, to enhance everyday experience. Like true friendship, a gift from Coach is special and enduring.

COACH USES ITS CATALOG TO TELL THE PRODUCT'S STORY, ENHANCING ITS QUALITY POSITION WITH WORDS SUCH AS "RICH, LUSTROUS PATINA" AND "OUR PRODUCTS ARE NOT FRIVOLOUS."

AS A TACTIC TO MOTIVATE FENCE-SITTERS, LEW MAGRAM OFFERS 10% OFF PURCHASES MADE WITHIN A TIME DEADLINE.

Tell the brand's story. Coach continually uses catalog space to show the craftsmanship behind its brand. J. Peterman repeats its famous "cowboy duster" tale from catalog to catalog, and Sundance speaks of the goings-on at the Institute. Nearly every good brand has a history worth repeating, and worth reinforcing in the customer's mind.

Establish a logo and use it heavily. Brand catalogers, like Williams-Sonoma, not only sprinkle their logos liberally throughout their books, but they also frequently denote product exclusivity through the use of symbols.

Tactics for
CREATING CUSTOMER LOYALTY

Creating customer loyalty demands commitment to service, research and relationship-building. It's not easy, but it's worth it to catalogs that rely on repeat business. Here's a list of suggested actions:

Survey customers. Catalogers that talk to customers regularly through the catalog, or survey them by phone, mail or e-mail, can find out what matters to them in terms of service and product. If you've got an auto-parts catalog, for instance, your customers might tell you they'd like mechanics tips inserted in your book, or sent to them in a newsletter. If you've got a beauty-products book, your customers might say they'd like to receive occasional samples. Such suggestions can help you custom-build a program that creates a bond with your buyers.

Some catalogs, like apparel book Lerner, also benefit from feedback from *consumer panels.* These are groups of customers contacted continuously every three or six months. Consumer panelists, not surprisingly, are super loyal. They not only report enjoying a relationship with the catalog, they feel they have an "investment" in it as well. That tends to make them very committed shoppers! (I'll talk more about surveys and panels in Chapter 9.)

Offer rewards. Most of us, of course, like to think of rewarding our good customers—those who buy, say, $100 worth of product, or who have ordered from the last three catalogs. But how about rewarding customers who do nothing at all?

Believe me, it can work. Customers who are surprised by a $20 coupon or free shipping are psychologically encouraged to do business with their benefactor. They feel that if the company extends an effort, they can (or even *should*) extend their loyalty.

Prove worthy of a customer's business. Remember, loyalty is a voluntary commitment that a customer makes for a variety of reasons. Some, like environmental catalog Seventh Generation's customers, may simply feel good about what the company represents. Others may brag about Hanna Andersson's durability, or Neiman Marcus' prestige, or Lands' End's service.

The point is, consumers give their loyalty to catalogs that *mean* something to them. So to earn loyalty, it's your job to create that meaningful experience, whether through service, prestige or quality.

Create a relationship. Sometimes, overdoing discounts and rewards defeats the purpose. Instead of creating loyalty, they only teach customers to expect deals. You can avoid the problem by creating relationships with your customers instead.

There's a difference between relationship and loyalty programs. Loyalty is gained through service; through offering something the customer values, such as gift wrapping, free shipping, unique product and so on. Relationships, on the other hand, essentially have to do with transactions. Like any other "friendship," that means ongoing contact between you and your customer.

Customers, of course, establish their side of the relationship through sales and feedback. For your part, you can use newsletters, letters or special mailings, in addition to catalog mailings. Tactics might even include mugs and T-shirts—whatever it takes to keep your catalog name in front of the customer.

Naturally, brand-name catalogs have the easiest time doing this. In fact, the Coca-Cola catalog, with its Coke-labeled products, came into being simply because of Coke's ability to capitalize on its bond with customers!

But even less-established catalogs can bond, provided they possess the kind of unique product line or company identity that engenders loyalty. Seventh Generation, for instance, gives T-shirts to customers who support the company's environmental stand. A steak knife would make sense for Omaha Steaks shoppers. Cat lovers loyal to a kitty products catalog would likely enjoy a free cat dish with logo.

The point is, creating relationships can be simple, provided your catalog has an established identity. Customers drawn to a particular personality will stick with it, as long as it keeps making a place in their lives. As one marketer puts it, "Transactions do not build relationships—but relationships yield transactions."

Tactics for
ENHANCING PERCEIVED QUALITY

If your catalog emphasizes quality, you have a special mission to prove it. You can't assume that "everyone" knows the value of a Mont Blanc pen. Nor can you assume that a customer in a high-income zip code knows more about, say, high-thread-count sheets than a customer in the boonies.

When you sell expensive, quality product, you must take the appropriate space in your catalog to emphasize its specialness. Ignorance, in this case, is a lost sale.

Some tactics:

Symbols and visuals. When Williams-Sonoma stamps its exclusive products with "Grande Cuisine," it's not simply evoking gourmet sophistication with an elegant name. It's showing customers that the cataloger cares enough to find unique and important merchandise.

Symbols are critical for showing customers, in a neat, shorthand way, that your catalog delivers quality. Hanna Andersson, for instance, refers to its clothing as "hannas," summing up in a warm, friendly word the kind of

EXPOSURES EMPLOYS SPECIAL POSTCARD MAILINGS AS A RELATIONSHIP-BUILDING TACTIC.

CALLOUTS, SUCH AS THESE IN LANDS' END, ARE AN EFFECTIVE TACTIC FOR SPELLING OUT QUALITY AND VALUE.

Our Grande Cuisine Symbol denotes a Williams-Sonoma exclusive.

BECAUSE WILLIAMS-SONOMA'S GRAND CUISINE SYMBOL INDICATES EXCLUSIVE PRODUCT, IT'S A GREAT, SUBTLE TACTIC FOR ASSURING QUALITY.

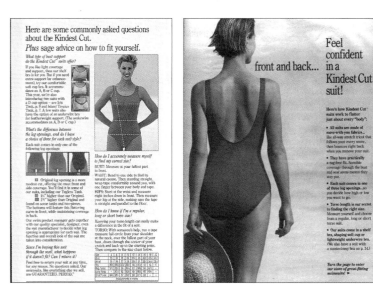

ABOVE: INFORMATIONAL TEXT IS A FIRST-RATE TACTIC FOR PROMOTING SERVICE AND QUALITY. IN LANDS' END, THIS QUESTION-AND-ANSWER COPY ASSURES ANY SIZE CUSTOMER THAT SHE CAN FIND THE RIGHT SUIT, WITH CONFIDENCE OF A GOOD FIT.

RIGHT: EXPLANATORY, NON-SELLING TEXT ALSO PRESENTS AN OPPORTUNITY TO REINFORCE A CATALOG'S POSITION.

EXTREME CLOSEUPS, PARTICULARLY WITH UNUSUAL CROPPING, NOT ONLY STRESS "QUALITY," BUT PROVIDE GREAT STOPPING POINTS IN THE CATALOG.

apparel customers won't find anywhere else. If a cataloger cares enough about a product to give it its stamp of approval, its customers will more likely approve it as well.

Informational text. I love paging through Coming Home for tips on how to buy a comforter, match bedding to wallpaper, or fit a swimsuit. Any catalog that takes precious space to educate customers makes the implicit case that both the products and the customers are worth the time and effort.

That says a lot about quality. For that reason, Coach, in the past, has inserted text and photographs about how its bags are constructed. L.L. Bean tells tales of taking new sneakers on a canoeing expedition. Because the text is informational, rather than hype or promotional, it generates a level of trust in the quality of the offer.

Closeups and samples. It's one thing to talk about the wonderful texture of a knit, or the hand-turned detail of a table leg. It's another to actually see or feel it. Some catalogs, like Peruvian Connection, enclose fabric samples to create a sense of quality; others rely on sharp closeups to display the grain of wood or the gleam of gold. Garden Botanika, a catalog of bath products, includes scent strips to let customers sample fragrances.

Either way, these catalogs invite customers to pay attention and study craftsmanship at a level that most competitors cannot offer. Such expense and effort speaks to the pride they take in the fineness of their merchandise.

Low density. In high-density spreads, products mingle and hide, much as they do on grocery store shelves. Low-density spreads, on the other hand, act like showcases or display windows. They allow customers to "settle" into the page and examine the product with full attention. Although few catalogers can afford page after page of white space, keep in mind that a relaxed use of space shows confidence. It tells customers that your products deserve their full attention.

Tactics for PRICE PROMOTION

For some catalogs, price promotion seems like little more than a scream-fest carried out in red ink and slash marks. While that may work in some markets—like office supplies—it's wise to be careful. Screaming type can become an obvious, lazy way of promoting a bargain. In some catalogs, it can even distract from the merchandise.

The key to good price promotion is to make sure the message is clear, but not overwhelming. Some suggestions:

Use design. If you've got a busy, high-density catalog anyway, starbursts, boxes, stickers and other elements can often call attention to a special price without smothering the product itself.

On the other hand, you might also find that a more discreet approach can work better. You can, for instance, simply draw a line through the old price and announce a new, lower price right next to it. That slight design disruption on the page is usually enough to focus a customer's eye right where you want it.

Draw comparisons. If you've got a service- or value-oriented catalog, communicating price can become a kind of customer service. Words like "Compare at . . .," "Elsewhere at . . .," or "Retail price at . . ." imply that your customers get both the quality of a higher-priced product and the price of a bargain.

Even high-end catalogs use this technique for price promotion. The Saks Folio Outlet, for instance, shows designer styles in low-density, elegant layouts, but makes it clear, both from the "outlet" name and from its "compare at" price promotions, that shoppers actually receive special deals. Catalogers that won't go near a starburst with a 10-foot pole can always use a price comparison to make their point.

ALTHOUGH SAKS DOESN'T SELL WITH A PRICE POSITION, IT CAN STILL CALL ON UNFUSSY PRESENTATION AND A "COMPARE AT" PRICE TACTIC FOR ITS "FOLIO" CATALOG OUTLET. RESULT: CUSTOMERS GET THE PRESTIGE OF SAKS AND THE SATISFACTION OF A GOOD DEAL.

Tactics for PROMOTING VALUE

Since value is overhyped these days, most value promotions are hard to make credible. Here's how to best play up the price and quality of a product, and win your customer's trust:

Unique product, unique price. For value-oriented catalogs like Lands' End, it's not unusual to see price promoted hand-in-hand with quality. "100% cotton at the lowest price this season," for instance, shows how one benefit rarely gets mention without the other.

So the best way to drive the value message is to equate price with quality. One of my favorite value statements appeared at the end of long copy promoting a silk jacket in the J. Peterman catalog. After extolling the fashionable and adventuresome pedigree of the garment, the copy quoted a mere $135 price tag. Stated the catalog: "The silkworms know us."

Callouts. Open any Lands' End catalog, and you'll find page upon page of headlines attesting to quality. Double stitching! The softest cotton! Fit to flatter! "We searched everywhere!"

Liberal callouts don't work in all quality-positioned books. But they make perfect sense for this catalog's value positioning, convincing customers not only of a great price, but of unbeatable quality.

Low density. It's tough to convince customers of high quality when products are jammed together on a page. To assess value, customers need to examine product details, to see multiple colors clearly and to investigate size and appearance.

STARBURSTS, BANNERS, EXCLAMATION POINTS, TYPE VARIATIONS AND SCREAMING HEADLINE SIZES ARE ALL TRADEMARK TACTICS OF PRICE PROMOTION. THEY WORK ESPECIALLY WELL FOR COMMODITY OR BUSINESS ITEMS, WHERE CUSTOMERS NEED TO BE SOLD MORE ON THE PRICE THAN THE PRODUCT.

High density and clutter invite doubt, leaving the customer wondering about what she *can't* see. Low density invites confidence. Granted, white space is expensive, but it makes product seem important.

Explanatory text. The word *value* implies a contradiction: If a product is priced well, it can't be good quality; if it's good quality, it can't be cheap. So if you've got a great product at a great price, just picture your skeptical customer in front of you, asking: "So how did the price get so low?"

To answer, take some time and space in your catalog. Consider, for instance, how Lands' End (the reigning value champ) uses ample text to explain how it wins wholesaling discounts through its buying power and marketing clout.

Explanations don't have to be long (as in Peterman's "The silkworms know us"), but they have to be convincing enough to win your customer's confidence.

Tactics for PROMOTING SERVICE

If you've got great service, you can't hide the fact on your order form, or on page 47. Service today often means the difference between winning a sale and losing it. The more catalogs compete on service, the more you have to reflect on what makes your catalog's service different and better.

Consider the following ideas:

Emphasize trained personnel. Many customers, particularly high-end shoppers, want to know they'll be taken care of. So if you've got a service-oriented book, it pays for your order-takers to not only know the product line, but also company history and policies. They could even be empowered to solve customer problems on the phone.

Take a risk. Encourage your order-takers to spend as much time with customers as they do processing orders. I recall how a customer once called Lands' End's Coming Home catalog in search of linens that matched her bedroom wallpaper. The order-taker, it turned out, had the same wallpaper in her home, and recommended a precise match. (The story, of course, made great catalog copy.)

Is this kind of service expensive? Yes. But if your customers demand service, it's essential for your repeat business.

Talk to your customers—and order reps. Naturally, focus groups and surveys (which I'll take up in Chapter 9) can let you know exactly what customers expect in terms of service. In fact, a bind-in card is always a good idea for generating customer information and feedback.

But order-takers themselves can prove a great resource as well. It's a smart idea to gather them together periodically in an anything-goes meeting to hash over ideas, complaints and problems. After all, those on the front lines of service every day can tell you a lot about expectations and service quality.

Lands' End and Coming Home offer different products. But both offer above-and-beyond services.

TO STRESS ITS SERVICE POSITIONING, LANDS' END'S COMING HOME USES A FULL PAGE TO INTRODUCE ITS OPERATORS AND SPECIALTY SHOPPERS.

At some catalogs, order-takers even ask customers directly about their experiences with shipping, gift-wrapping and other services. Novelty catalog Oriental Trading Company, for instance, gathers order-takers during light work periods to phone and survey customers—not to upsell shoppers, but simply to ask how the catalog can do a better job. Consequently, the catalog has improved both its offerings and service. I wouldn't be surprised if it improved business as well.

Go an extra mile—and don't advertise it. Catalogs like L.L. Bean, Jos. A. Bank and others send fabric swatches or color samples on request. L.L. Bean sends its best customers a card with a special 800 service number. Other catalogs delight customers with beautiful wrapping, wooden hangers, gift cards, a free set of batteries or a variety of other small packaging touches.

What's especially nice about each of these efforts is that they're not expected. Most customers figure they'll get an order packed in styrofoam peanuts and crushed bags, and most of the time, they're right. That's why unearned treats can't help but leave customers with a great impression and, naturally, a desire to repeat the experience.

Mind your manners. If a shipment is going to be late, you need to notify customers quickly. If an item is returned, you ought to issue credit right away. If a customer is unhappy, you should write to say "I'm sorry." If a customer is happy, you should write to say "Thank you." If a product is complex or unique, you ought to enclose information.

It all sounds basic, but you can't afford to forget good manners if you've got a service-oriented book. Most catalogs choose to focus on what they *have to* do (such as adhere to the Federal Trade Commission's 30-Day rule) rather than on what they *can* do.

Does your catalog enclose a UPS return shipping label? Do you have in-house 24-hour order-taking? If you position your catalog with service, you must back it up with appropriate action. Even the smallest of service efforts, like a "thank you," can do a lot for your credibility. That, I'm willing to bet, will pay off in sales.

PUTTING IT TOGETHER

By now, you've probably identified at least a handful of strategies and tactics that can start you up your growth track. Bear in mind, though, that there's still one more strategy you *must* pay attention to, regardless of your brand identity or positioning.

That strategy involves *enhancing your numbers.* All catalogers must pay attention to the tactics that have a direct impact on their bottom line. Because that issue is so critical, I've taken it up in the next chapter.

CHAPTER 7

FINAL STRATEGY: BOOSTING YOUR NUMBERS

You know the scenario. It doesn't matter how long your catalog's been around, how solid its brand identity, or how inspired its positioning. At some point, sales start to flatten. Response rates dip. Earnings fall off. There's financial trouble brewing, and it's time to take action.

The question is, what action do you take?

That's where "numbers" strategies come into play. When financial numbers need a boost, the best ways to do it include the following:

1) Improving response rates

2) Increasing average order size

3) Increasing the number of items per order

4) Boosting frequency of purchase

We all know financial problems rarely exist in a vacuum. If you've got good response rates, for instance, you may find your average order is low. If you've got high average orders, you may discover that core customers are buying less frequently.

Likewise, these numbers strategies don't exist in a vacuum either. They work together to solve problems and boost the whole business plan. Rather than apply each strategy like a Band-Aid, you can learn to deploy them in tandem, in the right time and place.

The challenge, then, is figuring out when and how to apply each strategy. Let's look at each in turn.

Numbers Strategy #1: IMPROVING RESPONSE RATES

Response rate is the litmus test for determining the strength of your catalog. If customers aren't responding, your catalog isn't growing, no matter how large the average order size.

But improving response rates isn't a generic catch-all strategy. If your response is falling off, you have to ask some key questions to determine where the problems and opportunities lie. Those include:

—How does the response rate compare with previous books?

—How does it compare with the competition?

—How does response from house files compare with rented files?

—How do rented files compare with one another?

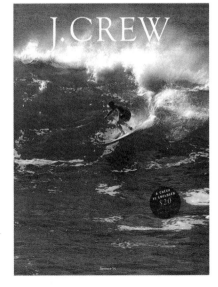

A $20 CHECK, PROMOTED ON THIS DOT WHACK, HELPS BOOST AVERAGE ORDER SIZE AND INCREASE RESPONSE.

SWEEPSTAKES, LIKE THIS BIG DOG VACATION
GIVEAWAY, BUILD RESPONSE RATES WHILE PRO-
MOTING THE CATALOG'S FLAGSHIP LOCATION.

FREE SHIPPING
CAN PROVE A
GOOD RESPONSE-
BUILDER FOR CAT-
ALOGS THAT
AREN'T POSI-
TIONED ON PRICE,
SUCH AS JOS. A.
BANK.

LEFT: FINGERHUT INDULGES IN SUCH RESPONSE-
BUILDING TACTICS AS "LAST CATALOG" THREATS AND
FREE GIFTS FOR ORDERING.

RIGHT: DEFERRED BILLING CAN BE A TERRIFIC TACTIC FOR
RESPONSE-BUILDING, PARTICULARLY IN OFF-SEASON BOOKS.

You should also look at response rates in tandem with other numbers. It may be that overall response is good, but that sections of the customer file are dying off. It may be that some surefire lists have run out of steam and need to be replaced.

Even if you've got a decent overall response rate, don't be placated. Keep asking questions! Overlooked problems in response rates can rend serious holes in the fabric of your business.

Which catalogers benefit from response-rate strategies?

All catalogers must examine their response rates continually. Like consumers themselves, lists are not static, generating the same numbers mailing after mailing. At some point, you've got to rejuvenate your house files with more responsive names, and you must examine prospect files to see where response challenges and opportunities lie.

Tactics for improving response rates

Just about any improvement you make to your catalog, naturally, can drive up response rates, whether it's better photography or a heavier paper. I'll address dozens of those ideas throughout the book. But in the meantime, pay close attention to the specific tactics below. All of them can push response rates in a hurry.

Testing free shipping and handling. Let's face it. These are times when customers *expect* top service and convenience. We all know, for instance, that Federal Express delivery used to be rare and expensive, limited to a few catalogers that could offer it to select customers. Now most catalog customers expect next-day delivery on demand.

So, instead of offering *faster*, try offering *free*. In my opinion, free shipping and handling can definitely drive a fence-sitting prospect into a sale. At this point, customers who consider faster shipping their right might also feel that free shipping is a *treat*. That can make the difference in luring response.

Creative executions. If prospects aren't responding to an offer, it may be that the offer simply doesn't speak to them. Experience shows that changing or improving the look and appeal of a catalog can make a big difference in a consumer's perception of the quality and value of the merchandise. A dense, generic layout can smother what could be a winning product.

Cover executions. Covers are key to response. A boring, been-there, seen-that cover won't even get a book opened, never mind generate response. Every mailing should offer something new on the cover. Familiarity can breed resentment. If customers whiff déjà vu on the outside, they won't bother exploring the inside of a catalog.

Price point executions. "Deals" drive response. There's no question that highlighting bargains or sales will crack catalogs open—particularly among house-file customers who may have been on the fence about a purchase.

It's important, though, to make sure that price point executions are in line with a catalog's positioning. J. Crew, for instance, highlights its sales with a simple sticker on the cover, never compromising the upscale portrayal of its models and product. J. Peterman also uses a sticker—and inside, adds the novel touch of enumerating just how many Moroccan necklaces or Girl from Ipanema vests are left in inventory. In keeping with its not-for-everybody personality, this catalog ably merges value with exclusivity.

Beware, however, that sale prices can be overdone. Just as many retailers have now "taught" their customers to buy on sale, so have many catalogers run the risk of overexposing bargains. If consumers know that a particular item will probably run in a sale book next month, why should they buy now at the higher price? "Deals" are response-building weapons that should be used responsibly and judiciously.

LEFT: BUILDING ORDER SIZE IS OFTEN A FUNCTION OF OFFERING DISCOUNTS FOR VOLUME ORDERS, AS IN THIS LEW MAGRAM SALE BOOK.

RIGHT: ANOTHER RESPONSE-BUILDER: PRE-APPROVED CREDIT AND DEFERRED BILLING.

Numbers Strategies #2 and #3: INCREASING AVERAGE ORDER SIZE/INCREASING NUMBER OF ITEMS PER ORDER

Both strategies are key for bringing up margins—particularly if you're paying for shipping and handling! Clearly, the more money customers spend per catalog, the less the cost of the sale.

Which catalogers benefit from order-size promotions?

If your catalog has low price points, you probably could use a lift in order size. Even if you've got good margins on your low-price products, chances are your catalog is a high-cost sales vehicle. Therefore, you need to build your order to cover your costs.

Generally speaking, all catalogers need at least a $50 average order size in order to cover overhead and make a profit. That can be tough to accomplish when the average price point is $15 or $20.

Tactics for increasing order size

Order-size tactics don't involve lots of thought about positioning and brand identity. They're specific, price-and-quantity promotions that can garner increased business on an order. Just about any cataloger, from computer marketer Insight Direct to high-fashion Neiman Marcus, can take up an idea or two to keep the average order high.

VICTORIA'S SECRET USES A TRIPLE WHAMMY FOR BUILDING RESPONSE FROM INACTIVE CUSTOMERS: $25 OFF, DEFERRED PAYMENT AND SALE OFFERS.

LEFT: BY OFFERING 20% OFF EVERYTHING IN
THE BOOK (WITH A TIME DEADLINE) CLIFFORD
& WILLS CAN TEST THIS PROMOTION AS AN
ORDER-BUILDING TACTIC.

RIGHT: CHADWICK'S OF BOSTON PRESENTS THE
SAME PRICE PROMOTIONAL TACTIC THREE WAYS:
"BUY 2, SAVE $10," "ONLY $19 EACH" AND
"COMPARE AT $38."

RESPONSE-BUILDING TECHNIQUES ARE ESPECIAL-
LY CRITICAL FOR PROSPECTING CATALOGS, SUCH
AS THIS PETALS CATALOG WITH A 20% OFF
INTRODUCTORY OFFER.

Bundling. If you're selling steak knives and cutting boards—both of which have a low price point—it makes sense to sell them together. Not only should two like products appear next to one another, or in use at the same time, but they should be priced together as well: "Save $5 when you buy both for $39.99."

As long as you keep a broad merchandise spread, there's no limit to the ways in which you can bundle merchandise. In fact, computer catalogs are expert at this. They keep an enormous variety of components on hand so they can anticipate customer needs. Is the customer buying more memory? Maybe he could use a zip drive as well. Is he interested in a laptop? He might need to get a modem.

Just about any other cataloger can do the same. Apparel catalogs, for instance, can add scarves or button covers to their blouse offerings; gift catalogs can package glassware with china or prints with frames; sports catalogs can sell walkmans with carrying packs. If any two items make sense purchased together, why not sell them together?

Twofers and threefers. I like how Chadwick's almost always sells certain items together, such as two tank tops for a special low price, or three T-shirts for the price of two. "Twofers" are a great way not only to build average order size, but to liquidate commodity items, like mugs, belts, CD-ROMs, stockings and more.

Percentage off. Like "twofers," percentage-off deals ensure that more items move off the pages. Victoria's Secret, for instance, sells bras and panties for about $18-$25 apiece—but it often advertises 10% off orders over $75. That's certainly incentive for consumers to add "just one more" to the shopping list and assure themselves they're getting a bargain.

Numbers Strategy #4:
INCREASING FREQUENCY OF PURCHASE

If you want your customers to buy more, why not try to get them to buy more often? Frequent purchasing strategies boost cash flow and improve cost of sales. Moreover, the strategies build customer loyalty. Once customers get in the habit of buying more often, they tend to keep buying.

Which catalogers benefit from frequency strategies?

Some catalogers are just naturally geared toward customers who make small (or large!) but frequent purchases. Business-to-business catalogers, for instance, often rely on top customers who place orders monthly, even weekly, for items ranging from software to spill rags. Since men in general are often shopping creatures of habit, many men's apparel catalogs also find their customers buying from them eight or 10 times a year.

But other catalogs can't count on that kind of customer behavior. A bathing suit catalog, for instance, may simply be seasonal in nature, and no strategy—short of mailing to beauty pageant contestants—can bump that frequency. Likewise, furniture catalogs may work great for new homeowners, but once the customer's home is furnished, it will likely stay that way for a while.

On the other hand, catalogs with continuity product, like food, books or records, lend themselves to frequent buys. So do sporting goods catalogs that mail to year-round enthusiasts, or catalogs of, say, underwear, office products or CDs. All of them can benefit from tactics that boost their visibility and appeal when shoppers are in the mood to buy.

Tactics for increasing frequent purchases

To boost buying frequency, you can't just rely on pricing tactics or fancy creative techniques. Instead, you have to think strategically about what you offer and to whom you offer it. Consider the following ideas:

Become predictive. Let's face it: Many catalogers keep mailing to their best buyers because the numbers generally tell them it's a good idea. But, rather than mail blindly to recent customers week after week, it's better to take advantage of technology to analyze customer buying patterns.

In other words, you need to find out which customers are buying, and when. It may be that one group of your "good" customers only buys seasonally while another group may buy only annually. Some customers may buy only on Mother's Day; others on every holiday. By using predictive and database modeling, you can learn to mail when your best customers are buying.

Predictive modeling can also determine which customers—even infrequent buyers—need frequent mailings in order to keep buying.

It may be that some of your customers simply need to page through three or four catalogs before placing an order. Modeling can help you decide whether those customers are worth the extra mailings.

Offer something new. Like old friends, familiar catalogs are always welcome to customers—but not if they show the same product issue after issue. Many catalogers try to stimulate new interest by slapping new covers on the same insides, but after a while, like the boy who cried wolf, these catalogs inspire skepticism rather than interest.

Catalogers don't necessarily have to change product book after book, although that practice would certainly pique curiousity. What they can do, however, is add one or two new products to each book, or remove one product from an earlier book and run it later. Catalogers can also run a different photograph of the same product, or try different layouts or design techniques to get customers paging through. J. Crew, for instance, often mixes old product with fresh, but updates the repeat product with different stylings, colors or models.

Repaginate. At the same time, of course, it's expensive to put out "new" catalogs month after month just to satisfy customer curiosity. For some catalogs, the best solution is simply to repaginate.

An apparel catalog, for instance, might try putting long-sleeved clothing in the front of its early summer book, and move the shorts and tank tops from back to front for early spring. An office products book might feature letterhead choices up front one month; workstation accessories up front the next.

Either way, the technique practically forces customers to keep looking through the book. To see familiar product in a new way is almost as satisfying as seeing totally new product.

Promote special offers. Nothing stimulates fresh interest like a price cut. Catalogs moving deeper into a season can perk up purchase behavior with bargain offers, either mailed separately from the main catalog, or inserted into the main book. (Combine those offers with repagination, or new merchandise, and you've got an even better chance of sales.) Sale catalogs, interspersed with regular catalogs, also work well for getting your best customers to buy more frequently.

THE FINAL ANALYSIS

By now, you've had a very broad-brush look at how to boost your catalog business. You've seen the advantages of establishing brand identity, and you know how to tackle general strategies for improving response.

At this point, it's time to delve into what really makes your catalog tick. How do you know whether you're really "speaking" to your customers? How do you know what your customers want to hear from you?

To address those issues, the next section will cover problem diagnosis. After all, you can't establish your catalog's brand identity, and you can't solve your catalog's problems, unless you perform diagnosis and research.

section three

DIAGNOSTICS
AND RESEARCH

CHAPTER 8

Diagnosing Your Marketing Problems

CHAPTER 9

The Use of Research

CHAPTER 10

The Tools of Research

CHAPTER 8

DIAGNOSING YOUR MARKETING PROBLEMS

Everyone remembers the Sears Big Book. For nearly a century it offered everything from scissors to pantyhose to car batteries. But when the end came in the early '90s, not many grieved. The catalog world had turned niche-oriented, the Big Book day passed, and consumers moved on.

Which goes to show that not even a century of doing things right can stop cataloging from going wrong. Even catalogers with unbeatable positioning, brilliant strategies and drop-dead creative may find their "day" can pass. The market may shift, audience trends may die out, consumers may spend less in the category, or a drop-dead creative may start looking dim, dated and dull. Dozens of potholes can litter the road to success.

Worse, many catalogers may not even see the pothole until they're up to their axles. They might see a dip in response rates, a flattening out in order size, or a lack of pull in a rental list. They might try to fix things by tweaking creative or throwing on more services. By doing so, they're addressing only symptoms, not the problem.

That's where marketing diagnosis comes into play. All catalogers, at some point, need to look closely at their symptoms in order to discover the root of a real problem. Only then can they get to the right marketing solution.

In this chapter, I'll introduce you to the concept of marketing diagnosis. You'll find the typical "symptoms" exhibited by sick catalogs, followed by questions you can ask to determine the range of the illness. Is your catalog on a slight slip, or is it in big trouble? Finding out the extent of the problem is the first step to curing it.

DIAGNOSING SYMPTOMS

As Freud once said, the human psyche doesn't exhibit all that many different types of problems—but the causes of those problems can be infinite.

So it is with cataloging. Most marketing symptoms fit one of two major categories:

1) Dwindling response rate

2) Falling average order size

The reasons they happen, however, differ for everyone. One catalog could be in a problematic category, like luxury electronics. Another could have an aging audience. A third could have stale creative. The symptoms may all be the same—poor response—but the causes are unique.

To unravel the causes of a problem, one needs diagnosis. And a diagnosis is made by asking questions and conducting research. Just as medical malpractice is prescribing medical solutions without a proper diagnosis, so too is marketing malpractice prescribing marketing solutions without any knowledge of the cause.

Consider, for instance, the case of one upscale gift book that had been mailing profitably to house files and prospects for years. After several decades of success, prospect response started to die off. The catalog took the logical step of testing different lists. No luck. It threw in geographic and demographic overlays. Nothing happened.

The first step in solving the problem was to diagnose it. The cataloger considered the following questions: What was its positioning? What were the characteristics of its audience? Were buyers suddenly price-wary? Were they sensitive to presentation and creative? Had the audience changed? Had the catalog changed—or failed to?

The cataloger then hired consultants, conducted telephone surveys and analyzed each response cell from its rental and house files. It then conducted a price-point analysis and evaluated its product selection. Finally it examined competitors and evaluated market trends.

In the end, the cataloger reached a diagnosis. It found it had lost touch with the currant market as its core audience died off. It had drifted from its original core identity of offering fine and unusual European gifts, and had cluttered its catalog with product that didn't fit. It had failed to address a new generation of gift buyers who preferred more sophisticated catalog presentations. Saving the business meant executing a whole host of merchandising and creative strategies to bring the catalog back to life.

We'll talk more about these marketing solutions in a later chapter. For now, consider some typical symptoms and see which questions will tell you what's gone wrong.

Symptom: House file no longer pulls

Questions:

—*Has your catalog changed its creative approach?* An extreme creative tack can turn off core buyers used to a certain presentation. On the other hand, unchanged creative can grow stale, which could drive bored customers into shopping elsewhere.

—*Has your catalog re-evaluated services?* Poor service, more than anything else, can keep customers from buying again. That's doubly true when competitors begin offering free returns or free shipping, both of which can steal your core buyers.

—*What's happening in your marketplace?* Perhaps a growing chain of off-price retail outlets has undermined your catalog's value-priced offering. Maybe competitors have sprung up in your niche category. Maybe customers are simply ready for a new offer.

Consider Vermont Teddy Bear, which conceived the brilliant idea of sending teddy bears for occasions that normally call for candy and flowers. The concept's only problem was that, unlike candy and flowers, one teddy bear lasts a long time. Without something new to offer customers, this cataloger ran into trouble keeping its market.

—*What's happening among consumers?* The Sharper Image and other luxury-toy books took a beating when consumers turned frugal in the '90s. Career apparel catalogers shrank when the "casual" trend hit the workplace. If your catalog fails to shift with the times and trends, you've got eroding response.

—*What are competitors up to?* Are they, like you, also offering unconditional guarantees, lower prices or broader selection? Are they duplicating or undermining your catalog's positioning? The more players in your category, the harder it is to stay at the top of the heap.

Symptom: Prospect files no longer pull

Questions:

—*Is there a list problem?* A good list broker can evaluate whether your catalog's prospects have the demographics, buying history, mail order affinity or even category affinity that you need. Sometimes, too, your catalog may be reaching the right prospects, but you may have worn out your universe of potential buyers. In that case you need to focus harder on getting your customers to buy more.

—*Is your catalog creatively eccentric?* Your house customers may love your catalog's quirks and eccentricities, but prospects may not understand it. Prospects who first receive, say, the Vermont Country Store catalog may certainly wonder at its homespun appearance, for better or worse.

—*Is your catalog speaking to the wrong buyers?* If your catalog reaches a mature audience, for instance, you might have trouble attracting young prospects. Likewise, your catalog of kids' clothing might appeal to gift-giving grandparents, but it might turn off practical-minded parents.

Rented lists, for the most part, need to parallel your house list. If you go fishing for new buyers, you need to know the exact characteristics of whom you'd like to catch.

—*Where's your competition?* Most likely, competitors would have trouble wooing your core buyers, but a much easier time courting your prospects. A sudden competitive onslaught in your catalog market could lead to poor response if everyone's hunting the same game.

—*Is your catalog prospecting creatively?* If you've hit the wall with list rentals, you might need to try space ads, television or the Internet for gathering prospect names. These sources may yield fewer names than rental lists, but the response can often be worth the effort.

Symptom: Average order size eroding

Questions:

—*Has your catalog analyzed price points?* Many catalogers respond to tough economic times by lowering price points. Lower prices, clearly, lead to lower average order sizes, unless you take steps to boost the number of items per order.

—*How does your competition look?* If competitors still have good average order size, then your catalog might be alone with its problem. But if every competitor complains of lower average order size, the entire category may be in trouble. That affects everyone's ability to find a solution.

—*Does your catalog offer multiples or complementary products?* Failing to group low-priced items, like scarves and blouses, represents a missed opportunity to boost average order size. So does failing to offer percentage discounts or dollars off for rewarding volume orders.

—*What are your consumer trends?* If your customers now prefer lower-priced apparel to "investment" clothing, that could signal trouble if you're in the high-end apparel marketplace. Or, if your debt-crunched consumers have reached their credit limits, that means less buying power to go around. Like any cataloger, you need to stay abreast of any trend that keeps your customers from shopping the way they have in the past.

Symptom:
Failure to reactivate older names

Questions:

—*Have customers moved out of your catalog's market?* If you're an apparel cataloger, you may find that your former customers have gravitated from nightclub wear to sweatpants over the past few years. Likewise, children's products catalogers inevitably lose core buyers, as do maternity catalogs and certain business books (eventually, customers get promoted!). Not every catalog can even afford to reactivate buyers—particularly when those buyers simply disappear.

—*Are customers transient?* Many customers change buying habits as their incomes increase (or drop), as they retire, have children, or as their marital status changes. Other customers simply relocate. Transients are often tough customers to find, let alone reactivate.

—*Have these customers had a bad experience?* Maybe a change in fulfillment operations or computer systems left orders stranded or backed up. Maybe a creative misfiring or merchandising snafu caused buyers to abandon a favorite catalog. Customers who've had bad experiences need more than a remailing before going back to their buying habits.

—*Is your customer aging?* Some catalogs, like Hanover House's former Mature Wisdom, have clearly positioned themselves to older audiences. But intentionally or not, catalogs that sell golf equipment, travel goods, health supplies or other items often court the same demographic.

Older customers can be problematic. Often, they're less loyal than younger ones, frequently have less disposable income, and can be lost through attrition, either by death or incapacity. And a creative presentation that appeals to older buyers risks losing out on younger prospects and customers.

Symptom: Promotions no longer pull

Questions:

—*How's the product?* If your merchandise isn't what people want, no amount of promotion will sell it. Or, if your promotions, like sweepstakes, *do* push reluctant fence-sitters into buying, you might find yourself stuck with unresponsive, one-time customers. Rule of thumb: The best products need little promotion to sell, and the best customers need little promotion to buy.

—*What's your competition up to?* If your competitor offers $20 coupons or 10% off large orders, that could affect your own promotion's pulling power. Or, if your competitor offers the same free shipping and special service as you do, that eliminates any promotional point of difference. Catalogs with promotional parity don't offer customers any compelling reason to order from one over the other.

—*Do customers understand the promotion?* Many promotions are so understated that buyers may not even see them. If customers don't get the promotion, they won't get the offer, either.

—*Are customers overpromoted?* If you're constantly pushing sale items, dollars-off coupons or sweepstakes, relax! You risk burning out the immediacy of your offer. Once customers stop feeling the urgency to order *now*, they often stop ordering altogether.

Symptom: Customers aren't loyal

Questions:

—*Can your catalog pass the logo test?* Think about it: Could your customers identify your catalog without looking at the logo? If not, you've got an image problem. Strong catalogs are instantly recognizable from their design, merchandise and overall creative, regardless of their name or logo. Weaker catalogs lacking brand identity can suffer everything from eroding response rate to infrequent ordering.

—*Does your creative support your positioning?* Every creative element in a catalog, from photography to copy to models, must support the catalog's overall positioning. A "Yankee" catalog like L.L. Bean cannot use big-haired models or elegant script type. Lew Magram, by contrast, can ill afford to put introspective Tweeds models inside its fitted and spangled dresses. Customers need creative cues to understand what the brand stands for.

—*Does your brand address the target audience?* Mailing a Lew Magram catalog to a diehard L.L. Bean preppie generally results in one more wasted mailing. To be loyal to a catalog, a customer must see herself in the catalog—or at least a part of herself. She must identify with the models and feel comfortable with the creative.

—*Does your catalog stand out in the mail?* Does your catalog differ enough to draw attention, both in typeface, creative, format and overall appearance? Catalogs without a unique look are like retail stores with curtains in the window. They don't advertise their offerings, and they don't let customers know what to expect inside.

—*Does your catalog have a merchandise niche?* The more niche-oriented your catalog, the stronger its potential customer loyalty. Catalogs facing lots of competitors, like those in women's apparel, have a much tougher time differentiating themselves than catalogers with few competitors and a strong niche.

NEXT STEP: RESEARCH

Asking questions is just the start of diagnosis. A doctor facing a patient, for instance, doesn't just ask about symptoms and stop there. She'll likely want to run lab tests, take X-rays, perform biopsies, check blood count or do any number of other projects that can help her reach an exact conclusion.

In short, the step after asking questions is *performing research*. In cataloging, it's the key step to solving a marketing dilemma.

CHAPTER 9

THE USE
OF RESEARCH

It's not hard to know when your catalog has a problem. All you need is a dip in response, or a downturn in order size, and you can be off to the races guessing at what went wrong.

The only way to *understand* your catalog's problem, however, is to do research.

Questioning can only narrow down the causes of a specific marketing problem. Beyond that, you need to confirm what's behind your catalog's symptoms. That's where research comes in. Through surveys, focus groups, customer panels and a host of other tools, you can begin to understand and solve what ails your catalog.

In this chapter, I'll talk about what research is and isn't (research, for instance, *isn't* testing). I'll also go over various types of catalog research, and indicate when it's best to use them. You'll find a host of options available for diagnosing and solving your marketing dilemmas.

USES OF RESEARCH

Research isn't just for problem solving. In fact, you'll probably need to use it throughout your catalog's lifecycle.

Through research, for instance, you can figure out whether to start up a new book, or simply reposition an old one. You can choose a new look or positioning statement, or decide whether to create a spin-off. You can stay in touch with your customers, and understand their demographics, buying histories, attitudes and product needs. And by getting continual feedback on merchandise, services and creative, you can even prevent marketing problems before they start.

But however else you use it, you'll find research key to diagnosing your problems. Say your catalog's response rate is down 10% from last season. You can use research to find out, for instance, whether core buyers have been turned off by a new design, or whether prospects don't understand a promotion or offer. You can discover whether a competitor is coaxing away core buyers, or whether you've done something to make your audience feel your catalog isn't trustworthy.

Conversely, you can also use research to point out unsuspected strengths. One apparel cataloger, for instance, used research to find out why core buyers weren't responding to its price position. It found that customers were actually attracted to the merchandise quality instead. Likewise, research might point out that your catalog attracts a more upscale demographic than you thought, or that it appeals to more men than you realized.

Whatever your reason for using it, catalog research can confirm what you may think you already know about your business—or it can find out what you don't know.

WHY TESTING ISN'T RESEARCH

Many catalogers believe testing takes care of their research needs. They're mistaken. These catalogers "research" a new format, for instance, by mailing it out and seeing what happens to response rates. They test new creative by sending it to core buyers; they test new lists by mailing smaller books; they test promotions on old lists or they test a new merchandise mix on core customers.

For these catalogers, whatever the tests "say" then becomes the new marketing directive. If prospects like a product cover better than a lifestyle cover, then roll out the product cover. If core buyers respond just as well to a lighter paper stock as to a heavier paper stock, then roll out the lighter stock.

Make no mistake: Testing is critical. You need testing to confirm the appeal of a new look, or the validity of new positioning. By testing, you can find out whether certain prospects are worth pursuing, or whether a higher-density look or new creative can still pull good response.

But in truth, testing is most valuable for just that: *confirming*. It's a way for you to throw something against the wall, like a new logo, and see if it sticks. Testing seldom indicates the *causes* of such symptoms as eroding response. To get to the root of a problem, you still need research.

In fact, the more competitive your marketplace, the more you need research to figure out your customers and markets. For that reason, most major catalogs have at least one full-time research staffer on board; others have entire departments devoted to surveying customers and crunching statistics. Smaller catalogs can choose from a number of competent outside firms for their survey and research needs.

WHEN TO USE RESEARCH

Research makes sense at almost every stage of your catalog's history. Properly used and interpreted, research can do the following:

1) Establish a catalog and confirm its positioning.

Even before a debut mailing, research can ensure that your catalog appeals to its target market, has unique positioning, differs from the competition and offers a compelling reason for customers to buy.

2) Better understand consumers.

Research can determine your customers' preferences, interests, attitudes and lifestyles, all of which help inform how you use creative, brand imagery and lists.

3) Find customer hot buttons.

Research helps you pinpoint what makes customers buy—or not. For instance, would parents buy adult clothing from a children's book? If not, is it because the presentation is wrong, the clothing is wrong, or the idea is wrong? Research fills in the answers.

4) Solve design issues.

If certain pages are poor sellers, research can identify where customers look on the page, how much time they spend with each page, or whether the page has good "eyeflow." On a more basic level, research can tell catalogers if their overall design is unreadable or turns off customers in the first place.

5) Straighten out emergencies.

If orders back up or customer service goes haywire, telephone research can find out how to best soothe upset customers. Or, if response suddenly falls off a cliff, research can tell whether customers even received the latest catalog, or whether three other competitors arrived the same day. Research can help you not only size up the seriousness of a problem, but figure out how to solve it.

TYPES OF RESEARCH

In practice, research methodology can take myriad forms. You can use the mail or phone for research, or you can hold focus groups, speak one-on-one to customers or simply lay out a bunch of list cards to determine how competitors are doing.

In the end, though, research essentially boils down to three problem-solving categories:

1) *Customer satisfaction research*
2) *Customer profiling*
3) *Positioning research*

According to catalog research maven Erard Moore of Riverside, CT, here's how each category works.

1) CUSTOMER SATISFACTION RESEARCH

When response erodes or order size falls off, this type of research can tell you whether your catalog has hit a wall in pleasing your customers. After all, customer satisfaction research measures exactly that: how happy customers are with the product mix, service and overall appeal of a catalog. If your buyers lose interest in product or grow discouraged with slow service and eroding quality, this research can point the way to the cause of the problem, as well as to the solution.

Methods to try:

—*The Direct Marketing Association cooperative survey.* Once a year, the DMA surveys customers of 10 to 15 different catalog companies to compare service and satisfaction. Customers rate catalogers on everything from quality of merchandise to arrival condition. Catalogs that participate, moreover, can compare their own scores with aggregate scores from other participants. (And no, Macy's doesn't tell Gimbels. Participants see only their own grades.)

Even non-participants can "benchmark" themselves against these surveyed catalogs. Say, for instance, the average cataloger in the survey takes four days to ship and scores well on shipping and handling costs. If your own catalog takes nine days to ship and charges high shipping and handling, you might have a problem. The DMA survey, in other words, can tell you whether your own service meets, beats or falls below the average.

—*Ongoing mail surveys.* Many large catalogers survey customers every six months or so, not only to collect demographic information, but to find out how pleased customers are with quality, pricing and service. Because it's ongoing, this research can track satisfaction over time. If 45% of customers this year say they are "very pleased" with quality, for instance, that would compare quite well to the 37% who responded that way the year before.

If you use mail surveys, you also have the freedom to query different customer segments, like first-time customers or reactivated old customers. You can also design your surveys to gauge reaction to new product categories or a new design.

A customer satisfaction survey will not necessarily predict whether a new blouse will become a best-seller, but it might determine how customers reacted to the blouse's quality and presentation. Typical questions, for instance, might include the following: *Did the product arrive in good condition? Was the product what you expected based on its picture? Was the fabric and size what you expected?*

—*Occasional telephone surveys.* As with mail surveys, telephone surveys can gauge customer satisfaction to a just-shipped order or just-mailed catalog. (At Oriental Trading Company, for instance, telephone operators, during "down" times, regularly call customers to measure satisfaction.) Order-takers can also engage customers in satisfaction feedback, but these casual encounters produce anecdotal results rather than statistical ones.

—*Customer panels.* Some catalogers, like apparel book Lerner, query groups of customers regularly to find out how they feel about merchandise, presentations and service. Because these customers are less "anonymous" than those in regular mail surveys, they can answer more in-depth questions, such as *How did this season's offering compare to last season's?*

How often to do customer satisfaction research: For consistent benchmarking, catalogers should survey customers every six months to a year.

Who should do it: Most mail questionnaires can easily be designed, mailed and tracked in-house. Telephone surveys may require the expertise of an outside firm.

Who should be surveyed: Generally, any segment of the house file, or the entire house file can be surveyed. Satisfaction surveys, however, are best done among fresh buyers (30 days is ideal) but should not be inserted as bouncebacks in packages. Bouncebacks generally have a low response rate, and usually reflect partiality toward the catalog.

2) CUSTOMER PROFILING

Like most catalogers, you're probably already familiar with customer list segmentation and modeling techniques. These are database techniques that involve "scoring" a list to see which customers are most likely to buy. "Scores" are generally based on the amount, recency and frequency of past purchases.

Customer profiling, however, is different. This research method details the *attitudes and behaviors* of your customers. It's useful in helping you understand who the customer is, not just what she buys.

By finding out your customers' behavior, you can also find out whether your brand identity fits your customer base, and whether certain consumer trends and market patterns are worth watching. If your catalog mainly serves conservative baby boomers, for instance, you might want to track political trends (will customers be in a buying mood after the election?) as well as social ones (what will customers buy as they age?).

Methods to try:

—*Lengthy questionnaires.* Customer profiling is quantitative research. It involves gathering reams of information on a good sampling of customers in order to project results across the whole customer base. (The results, incidentally, are useful not only to catalog management, but to circulation, creative and merchandise departments.)

Survey questionnaires frequently run six to eight pages. Questions can range from how often your customers take vacations to whether they shop in supermarkets or convenience stores. Mostly, questions address behavior and attitude, such as the following:

Demographics, including age, income, gender, number of children, education;

* *Competitive catalog purchase behavior*, including amount spent, categories purchased;

* *Competitive catalog attitudes*, including overall ratings and product ratings on price/value, quality, style and fit;

* *Customer psychographics*, to determine whether customers are bargain hunters, risk-averse, experimental, aspirational, status-conscious;

* *Merchandise attitudes*, including importance of price, quality, style, ease of use.

When to do customer profiling research: Some catalogs, like Coach, profile their customer base every year or two. Given the time and effort involved, customer profiling is difficult to do more frequently.

Who should do it: Because profile information is tough to gather and interpret, outside specialists often do a better job than catalog staffers. That's particularly true when conducting surveys by phone rather than mail.

Who should be surveyed: You can profile either your entire house file or a segment, such as frequently mailed core buyers. Surveyed customers should be fairly recent buyers (within 24 months), although you can sub-segment the results by three-month buyers, six-month buyers, long-term buyers and so on.

3) POSITIONING RESEARCH

Positioning research is qualitative. Unlike customer satisfaction and profiling research, positioning research doesn't ask for information, but for feedback.

For that reason, it's especially useful when your catalog business is in transition. If you're developing a new book, repositioning an old one, trying out new tag lines or changing format or creative, positioning research can help you decide what works best.

Essentially, positioning research gets straight, unfiltered customer reaction to new ideas. Sometimes that new design or typeface you have in mind—which already passed through six levels of bureaucracy—can stop dead with the customer who throws it aside, complaining that she just doesn't get it.

Methods to try:

It's critical to perform positioning research in person. Unlike, say, new cars or credit card products, catalog concepts and brands are difficult to grasp by description alone. Customers need to view the entire package—the catalog concept, design and copy—in order to give informed opinions. They must also be encouraged to comment freely. Ordinary, close-ended survey questions—*Would you buy this product? Does this logo appeal to you?*—simply won't generate the kind of open-ended feedback that you may need to hear.

Positioning research methods, then, include the following:

—*Focus groups.* For positioning research, you need to talk face-to-face with real prospects and buyers. In just a few hours, focus groups can help nail down a catalog's positioning strengths and problems far faster and better than weeks of extrapolating attitudinal data from customer satisfaction surveys.

Recently, for instance, a large communications company wanted to launch a general interest catalog tied to its well-known brand. This company wanted to know whether its brand positioning should be technological expertise, entertainment resource, or friends-and-family lifestyle.

The company submitted all three positions to a focus group of prospects. Conclusion? Customers preferred a lifestyle approach—a position this cataloger planned to confirm using customer profiles, satisfaction surveys, and of course, the response rate to the catalog itself.

—*One-on-one interviews.* Your researchers can interview customers individually to gauge honest reaction to new formats or positions. Away from the influence of others in a focus group, customers can talk freely about thoughts, opinions and ideas regarding the cataloger's proposal.

The communications company, for instance, performed one-on-one interviewing after deciding on a lifestyle positioning for its catalog. The individual interviews confirmed that potential customers understood and agreed with the new positioning, and that the cataloger had a potent niche worth testing.

When to do positioning research: Any time you want to make a substantive change in design, merchandising or position, or any time a launch or spin-off is in the works.

Who should do it: Positioning research not only requires research expertise, but objectivity as well. Catalogers that interview their own customers may (understandably!) tend to add bias, respond defensively, even argue. For that reason, positioning research is best done with outside help.

Who should be surveyed: Researchers should survey both catalog customers (if they exist) as well as prospects. It's important to ensure that a position simultaneously appeals to new or would-be customers, as well as to veteran buyers.

NEXT STEP: FIGURING OUT THE TOOLS

Once you know when to use research, you need specifics on how to do it. It's not enough to just send out questionnaires, or to get your order-takers on the phone asking questions. Gathering information without properly understanding the research methodology is just about as bad as gathering no information at all. The next chapter will examine the tools you need to get the best results from your research.

CHAPTER 10

THE TOOLS
OF RESEARCH

When you think about it, conducting research doesn't necessarily *have* to be scientific. Plenty of catalogers just plop mini-surveys in their package inserts and bill stuffers. Plenty of others ask for feedback when taking orders or fielding service questions. Not long ago, Bloomingdale's mailed an apparel survey to its best buyers, asking which styles they preferred.

After all, this isn't rocket science. This is cataloging! Why participate in a lot of expensive arcana?

The truth is, mini-surveys can yield plenty of anecdotal information about customer likes and dislikes. But if you're going to isolate the causes of a real marketing problem, or if you're going to launch a new book into an untested market, you're better off investing in real research.

No matter what kind of research you choose, you'll likely use one or more of the following standard tools:

Mail surveys
Telephone surveys
Focus groups
One-on-one interviews
Customer panels

Each has its own advantages and drawbacks, and requires the right use, at the right time, and in the right way.

Mail surveys

Best for: Generating *quantitative* statistics and staying in touch with customers. If you want to know how many buyers are Hispanic, or how many earn over $100,000, or how many were unhappy with their last order, you're best off using the mail.

Advantages: Generally, mail surveys are inexpensive and easily done in-house. (Detailed customer profile surveys, however, should be conducted by professional research firms.)

Surveys are also useful for benchmarking. You can find out, for instance, that the number of $100,000-income customers increased 6.5% over the past year, or that 14% of recent buyers gave a higher rating to customer service.

Drawbacks: Mail surveys generate statistics, not ideas or opinions. They also don't create feedback in a hurry. Surveys may require remailing (or a $1 incentive) in order to generate a 50% response rate, the minimum for statistical validity.

Usage tips: Mail surveys should use short, close-ended questions (answered by a yes or no) or multiple-choice questions (such as income $75,000-$100,000). For benchmarking, questions must be consistent year to year.

Sample size: A random selection of 500-1,500 customers usually fully represents a house file, regardless of the file size. Larger catalogers can divide that sample into subgroups, such as six-month buyers, but each subgroup should at least number in the hundreds.

Telephone surveys

Best for: Tapping immediately into customer response about, say, a recent mailing or service change. If you know that a UPS snafu delayed delivery on Christmas orders, you can phone customers to find out the extent of the problem. You can also use the telephone for conducting in-depth interviews or gathering statistical information, like household size.

Advantages: With the phone, you can address customer problems or issues before they get out of hand. Moreover, you can probe customers in phone surveys. If a customer says she likes golf, for instance, your interviewer can ask whether any of her friends golf.

The phone can even generate ideas. One gift cataloger, for instance, telephoned each customer who'd taken a catalog-sponsored trip. By asking questions about their experience and about the catalog in general, this cataloger picked up several ideas for incorporating the company's European heritage into its creative.

Disadvantages: Telephone calls are expensive and can be problematic. Inexperienced interviewers may lend their own "bias" to a call and skew results. Long telephone interviews also risk fatiguing—not to mention alienating—good customers.

Usage tips: To avoid caller fatigue and ensure statistically viable answers, interviewers must use short, consistent, close-ended questions for formal surveys. (Informal surveys can be more free-form.) Professional interviewers generally draw better results than a cataloger's own order-takers and customer service reps.

Sample size: For feedback on a problem, you can call as many customers as you wish. But for statistical validity, you need to maintain the same sample size and response rate as you would using a mail survey.

Focus groups

Best for: Soliciting direct feedback on new designs, tag lines or catalog ideas.

Advantages: Like any group that works well, focus groups can generate a rich mix of ideas and opinions, and can often provide you with fresh notions and tag lines. At one focus group we conducted, for instance, the words "unbelievable pricing" were used so often they became part of the catalog's positioning statement.

Disadvantages: As in any group, one member almost always threatens to dominate a focus group. For that reason, these groups require a skilled screener and moderator.

Also, like juries, focus groups tend to gravitate toward a single opinion, which could mask individual, and equally valid, opinions. Moreover, focus groups don't yield statistical or demographic data, and they can't predict how well a catalog will do in the mail.

For that reason, focus group research should be taken with a large dose of skepticism. Because they represent only a few people chosen in an unscientific way, focus groups are not gospel. They are qualitative and tentative.

Usage tips: An experienced moderator is a must. (Catalogers can view the proceedings from a two-way mirror.) The focus group "document," which outlines the topic of discussion, must be clear. Focus groups, after all, are not think tanks, and they must follow a proscribed formula of discussion.

Moreover, you must provide all the materials necessary for a good evaluation. If you want to try three new positioning statements, for instance, you can't just trot out the tag lines. You must first let the group decide which designs, logos, layouts and products they prefer. Only then can you ask whether those images fit the positioning statements. If your catalog's position is "quality," for instance, but all the group sees is "price," that shows you've got a positioning/image problem.

Sample size: Focus groups should comprise 8-12 people who meet for about two hours. Members should include past 24-month purchasers who intend to buy again, as well as mail order prospects who've bought from appropriate categories.

One-on-one interviews

Best for: A follow-up to focus-group research, and for getting reaction to a "test" catalog launch or positioning statement.

Advantages: Isolated from a focus group, participants can speak freely about their thoughts and ideas. The interviewer is equally free to lead the discussion wherever it needs to go. If a customer says she's a Christmas ornament collector, for instance, a skilled interviewer for a gift cataloger can gain a lot of insight about how collectors buy. Just as focus groups are good places to generate lots of ideas, one-on-one interviews are great for refining those ideas.

Disadvantages: One-on-one interviews are time-consuming. Each one can take up to half an hour, compared to two hours for a full focus group.

Usage tips: Clearly, you can't stand behind a two-way mirror for the duration of these interviews. (You'll fall asleep!) So you might want to attend at least a portion of them to gain a good sense of the dialogue. You can find out immediately whether someone is confused or thrilled about your presentation or positioning statement.

Sample size: About 10-20 people may be selected for one-on-one interviews, following the same criteria as for focus groups.

Customer panels

Best for: Informal surveys on customer satisfaction and service.

Advantages: Cheaper than regular mail surveys, since panelists are more likely to respond faster, and at a higher response rate, than random customer samples. Also, catalogers can ask more open-ended questions.

Disadvantages: Survey results are not statistically valid, since they're not obtained from random samples. Also, panelists can fatigue if mailed too frequently.

Usage tips: You can create customer panels by mailing invitations to customers, or by promoting the panels in the catalog. Just be sure to reward your panelists for their trouble. Special discounts or incentives are always appreciated.

Sample size: To prevent panelist burnout, you need to rotate surveys among a total of up to 5,000 participants. Smaller catalogers, obviously, can create far smaller panels, but risk wearing out their participants.

OTHER TYPES OF RESEARCH

For special problems or marketing snafus, you might want to consider one of the following less-generic research methods:

Eye-movement research
Appending psychographic information
Secondary research
Competitive analysis

Here's a look at each one in more detail.

Eye-movement research

Although fairly common in packaged-goods research (where manufacturers check customer eye movement on store shelves), eye-movement research is still relatively new to cataloging. As the name suggests, it measures precisely where a customer's eye falls on a catalog layout.

By attaching an infrared device to a customer's head, researchers can follow the customer's eye around the page, finding out where her attention catches, and for how long. This research also indicates how much time the customer spends per page, her overall eyeflow across a spread, and what she looks at last before flipping the page.

Best for: Deciding design and merchandise executions. Do customers spend more time with a geometric design or an open-ended design? Do they look at the model's physical features, or at what she's wearing? Do they spend less time with a more-dense page than with a less-dense page?

Advantages: Used correctly, eye-movement research ostensibly predicts which spreads will produce winners and which will produce losers. At the least, it could indicate which typefaces and designs are most customer-friendly and readable.

Disadvantages: According to some experts, eye-tracking results rarely correlate with real-life buying. In short, the amount of time customers spend on a page often has little to do with what's actually purchased—or not.

Appending psychographic information

If you're looking for specific details on your customer file, such as how many customers play tennis, or how many belong to civic groups, you need more than straight demographics. By running your customer list through a national database of demographic and lifestyle information, you can generate this kind of detail on your file. It may not yield the quality of a customer profile, but it's a good start.

One gift cataloger, for instance, appended demographic and psychographic data to its file to find out how many buyers were of European heritage and to which income groups they belonged. The results helped this client decide which product mixes, copy and creative would bump up response.

Best for: Obtaining a quick read on buyer characteristics for catalogers that haven't fully profiled their customers.

Advantages: Appended information can point up gaps and weak spots in a buyer file. One cataloger, for instance, found that most of the core customers for its upscale gift book were actually blue-collar shoppers—even though the catalog had a relatively high average order size. That explained why the catalog had had a problem with its upscale rental lists.

Disadvantages: Often, appended information discloses an incomplete picture. Usually gathered in packaged-goods surveys, this information often doesn't match a large portion of a cataloger's customer base. It also doesn't provide the necessary details—such as specific catalog purchase habits—to round out a full consumer portrait.

Secondary research

When you need information that *doesn't* come from your own customer base, you need secondary research. Although this information won't tell you who's buying from which catalog, or who's likely to buy, it can help you target potential markets and spot consumer trends.

One type of secondary research, *syndicated media research*, is gathered by such companies as Simmons Market Research Bureau and Mediamark Research Inc. Both companies conduct face-to-face interviews with a cross-section of adults to determine media and buying tendencies, including mail order buying habits. While syndicated research doesn't talk about a cataloger's specific customers (with some exceptions), it does indicate overall demographics of mail order buyers.

A second type of secondary research, *product-market research*, is gathered on behalf of product manufacturers to describe, say, the aspirin industry or skiwear industry. You can use this research to find out which companies are biggest in your marketplace, the overall dollar volume, and which items sell best.

Other types of secondary research include *Census Bureau* reports, or *DMA market studies,* or even *list cards* from catalogers. If it's research that doesn't come straight from customers, it's probably secondary research.

Best for: Catalogers starting up, repositioning or spinning off a new book.

Advantages: Relatively easy and inexpensive to gather, secondary research can home in on critical marketplace trends. If you want to launch a catalog of Irish imports, for instance, you can learn just how many Irish-Americans live in the Northeast, or how many own homes. Or if you want to start up a food catalog, you can gather data on food trends and eating habits.

Disadvantages: Secondary research does not predict buying habits. Although 400,000 Irish descendants may live in New England, no one can say how many are catalog shoppers. For that reason, secondary research is best used to supplement your own customer data.

Competitive analysis

Any decent market analysis naturally involves looking at the competition. By investigating list card data and the competing catalogs themselves, you can find out plenty about your competitor, including the following:

Price points

Design densities

Merchandise

Services

Growth of house file

Market share

Customer demographics

Average order size

You get the idea. Your competitor can be your most valuable source of business information!

Best for: Any catalog, but particularly a start-up or one in a hot marketplace. Competitive analysis is best performed any time a new competitor comes onto the scene.

Advantages: A good analysis can clearly show one catalog's strengths and weaknesses against another's. If a competitor seems to be gaining market share, or attracting younger buyers, or pulling a higher average order, a competitive analysis can explain why. Perhaps the competitor has a more up-to-date look, or better price points or product mix, or a stronger brand image. Just reading the catalog will often yield subtle clues about how a competitor draws in customers.

Disadvantages: Competitive analysis is often subjective. You may think your own book has the superior design, but customers may disagree! Moreover, a competitive analysis tells you little about the financial health of the competition. It may be that your competitor has a horsey look and so-so product mix—but it may also possess an extremely loyal customer base, high margins and a thick bottom line. Competitive analysis would reveal the former, but not the latter.

THE FINAL DIAGNOSIS

Between marketing questions and marketing research, you can untangle the causes behind just about any ailment that keeps your catalog off its growth track. Whether it's poor response, infrequent ordering or a drop-off in customer loyalty, the right diagnosis tells you where the faults lie.

Analysis can be painful. Nobody likes to hear about poor service, outdated design, confusing presentation, or lack of brand identity. But unless you're willing to look at your problems, you'll never solve them. You need to find the potholes that can crater the road to your success.

CASE STUDY

▼

LEW MAGRAM: THE LIMITS OF RESEARCH

Research does have its rewards—and its limitations, as Lew Magram's experience has borne out.

For this clothing cataloger, the good news was in eyeflow research. In a session with Perception Research, Magram's customers flipped through several versions of catalog spreads while researchers captured information on where their eyes landed, skimmed or hesitated.

Results? Magram rediscovered the value of hero pages. "We found out that it was important to stop customers in their tracks, as far as a headline is concerned, or a dramatic photo," says president Erv Magram. Since its 1995 research session, the cataloger has beefed up its use of low-density, high-impact spreads where practical. "We think that makes the book much more exciting," Magram says. "You're endorsing an item when you do that, or when you have a headline that pertains to the advantages of that item, or indicates that it's news this season." He does insist, though, that density must be such to produce an appropriate income per page and book.

Magram even used the research to come up with unique apparel groupings. In one instance, the cataloger took a best-selling dress and featured it in a hero spread in two different lengths, 19" and 36". "We called it 'The long and short of it,'" he says. "Putting that together really blew it away."

Research sessions for merchandise screenings, however, proved less successful. In this instance, customers looked at screenings of merchandise and rated them on their likelihood to buy. In one case, an item rated dead last turned out to be a number-one seller!

The lesson here: Look out for those who attend your research sessions. Even though all those attending the screening were Magram customers, "that told us we had many different kinds of customers out there." Those most likely to buy certain items, he notes, are often the working professionals who don't have the time or inclination to attend focus groups.

"You've got to be very careful with research," Magram concludes. "Sometimes you can wish [for certain results], or look for certain results." In many cases, he notes, "it may not be the Holy Grail" you're searching for.

section four

EXECUTING THE BRAND IDENTITY

CHAPTER 11
Diagnosing Your Marketing Problems

CHAPTER 12
Getting the Front Cover Right

CHAPTER 13
The Inside-Out of Your Catalog

CHAPTER 14
Inserts and Order Blanks

CHAPTER 15
*Adding Up the Elements: How to
Put Pacing and Energy Into Your Book*

CHAPTER 16
The Supporting Role of Good Design

CHAPTER 17
Secrets of Photographs That Sell

CHAPTER 18
Choosing Models That Make Sense

CHAPTER 19
Finding Your Catalog's Selling Voice

CHAPTER 20
Putting it Together: Positioning and Copy

SECRETS OF MARKETING-BASED CREATIVE

Like A students or prom queens, some catalogs just seem to be genetically blessed.

Lands' End, for instance, is definitely an industry pet, always coming up with some brilliant marketing innovation. Not long ago, I picked up one catalog that screamed the words "Inside Out" in huge type on the cover. Inside, every key item in the catalog was photographed *inside out* to show the phenomenal detail, flat seams and lack of loose threads in every Lands' End garment.

What other catalog would dare do this? When you realize that Lands' End, L.L. Bean and Eddie Bauer all pursue the same buyers with the same "basics" clothing lines, you can't help but admire Lands' End's quest to stand out, whatever it takes.

What Lands' End does, however, is no mystery. It accomplishes what any successful cataloger needs to do. *It finds the strategies and tactics that hold up its brand identity.* This is a catalog that knows its brand identity (quality, basic clothing at a great value) and understands its marketplace positioning (service, value, friendly, down-home humor) and finds the creative tactics that get its message across.

Lands' End, in short, employs *marketing-based creative.* So, too, do catalogs like J. Crew, J. Peterman, L.L. Bean, Chadwick's of Boston, Clifford & Wills, and scores of others. These catalogs don't merely employ nice looking creative, or paste up pretty photographs. Every design element, every piece of copy in their books speaks to their research, objectives, strategies, tactics and positioning.

These catalogs know how to achieve great marketing through great creative. That's something all catalogers can learn from.

WHAT MAKES GOOD CREATIVE

First of all, we all know creative alone doesn't make or break a catalog. A great typeface won't make up for shoddy merchandise, and fabulous models won't overcome lousy service. What drives any catalog's true success is a combination of merchandise, offer and audience.

What creative *can* do, though, is hold the rest of those elements together. More often than not, creative is what gets customers looking at a catalog in the first place. Shoppers can pick it up and sense immediately whether the catalog understands their needs and desires.

So what makes for good creative?

1) *Communication*
2) *Impact*
3) *Relevance*
4) *Consistency*

Let's look at each in turn, using Lands' End as an example.

ELEMENT #1: Communication

In real life, communication means getting a message across with clarity and precision. Not easy. Whether on the job or in relationships, miscommunication is common and troubling enough to put books like *Men Are From Mars, Women Are From Venus* on the best-seller list for years.

"REAL" MODELS, SNAPPY HEADLINES, CHATTY COPY AND GREAT PRODUCT SHOTS MAKE LANDS' END A MASTER OF COMMUNICATION.

Why is communication tough? Because it's not just about *words*. Up to 90% of personal communication is nonverbal. A tone of voice, crossed arms and a frown, for instance, can make the words "Nice to see you" relatively meaningless.

It's the same way in cataloging. Unsuccessful catalogs simply don't communicate, and their creative elements don't speak in the same language. The merchandise and models might say "elegance" or "prestige," but the dense layout, type treatment and cheap photography might say something else entirely.

Catalogs, then, must communicate two things clearly to customers.

1) Unique positioning
2) Ease of shopping

A unique look does no good if the catalog's message isn't clear, and a clear message gets pretty dull if the catalog's positioning isn't unique. If the customer doesn't know what the catalog stands for, or how to get to what she wants, she doesn't have any reason to buy.

So, let's look at Lands' End. You've got big, easy-to-read typeface. Friendly models having lots of fun. Plenty of copy about the terrificness of the product. Value-oriented headlines, with a heavy dose of zippiness. Logical product groupings, with best-sellers up front, accessories in the middle, expensive products in back. You've even got big, bright photographs and clothes that look freshly washed.

It all says that Lands' End is about quality, value and fun. The catalog's sharp presentation means there's no hemming and hawing about how things will fit, or what the colors will look like. Positioning, brand identity and ease of shopping are crystal-clear.

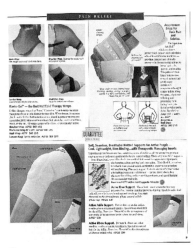

CALLOUTS, DIAGRAMS AND SIMPLE ILLUSTRATIONS—NOT TO MENTION CLEAR HEADLINES AND BANNERS—ENHANCE SELF CARE'S ABILITY TO COMMUNICATE TO ITS CUSTOMERS.

ELEMENT #2: Impact

As a concept, *impact* isn't hard to figure out. It's what makes a customer stop, linger, turn a page and want to see more. More often than not, it starts with what the customer sees first—the cover.

Impact, however, needs depth as well as wallop. A huge format might have a kind of impact, or an all-chartruese cover, or a photograph with lots of cleavage. All of those get people looking, but none of them get people buying. For real selling power, *impact must communicate brand identity.*

Lands' End is a master at this. Sometimes it tries all-type covers, or covers with cartoons, or sepia-toned images. I liked one recent Coming Home cover that didn't show any product at all—just a pair of scissors and piece of wallpaper. As explained inside, the cover introduced a new service to match bedding to any customer's wallpaper. Lands' End could have handled the introduction in any number of predictable ways, but the mysterious cover had impact.

With Lands' End, you never know whether a cover will convey value, yuks, hearth and home, sentiment or friendliness. What you *do* know, however, is that the cover will always convey the catalog's down-to-earth, smiling personality. More critically, it will do it with impact. It won't settle for just another happy-faced model when it knows customers need a real reason—or at least, real intrigue—to get inside that book.

ONLY PATAGONIA WOULD SHOW A BAT-WINGED SKIER TO COMMUNICATE THE AUTHENTICITY OF ITS OUTDOORS APPAREL.

ELEMENT #3: Relevance

Relevance is another one of those concepts that's simple to explain, tough to achieve. Relevance means a catalog has meaning to its audience. Customers can pick it up and feel, "That's me," or "That's the way I'd like to be."

Naturally, achieving relevance means knowing a customer inside-out—with emphasis on the *inside.* Relevance doesn't necessarily mean speaking to a customer's outside reality, by using row-house homes for backdrops, or middle-aged housewives for models. Relevance means understanding not just how your customer is, but *how she wants to see herself.* Successful catalogers know this, and speak to customers' hearts as well as their heads.

Lands' End does it beautifully. It knows its customers don't relate to the fantasy beauty of supermodels or Hawaiian beaches. So the catalog employs wholesome, good-looking folks in Anytown, U.S.A., settings. It's a happy, unsentimental picture of achievable American life.

More critically, Lands' End correctly assumes that its customers are less interested in fashion than in clothing that speaks to their intelligence and good sense. That means the catalog invites customers to "investigate" the construction of a polo shirt, to look closely at a detailed description of its cotton threads, or to welcome attention to proper fitting.

Not long ago, for instance, a friend told me how she saw three women at her health club all wearing the same Lands' End suit—and all bragging about the details that made it fit so well! *That's* relevance.

EDITORIAL COPY ON CITRUS LENDS RELEVANCE TO WILLIAMS-SONOMA'S SELLING PAGES OF COOKING PRODUCTS.

ELEMENT #4: Consistency

Like good friends, catalogs should be recognizable. Familiarity often breeds contentment! Customers feel they "know" a catalog when they keep getting consistent signals from it: that identifiable logo, that friendly model's face, that emphasis on free delivery or 12-hour shipping.

Consistency, however, does not mean using the same typeface or format again and again (after all, customers need variety, too). Good consistency evolves. It means taking familiar elements and stretching them to create freshness and interest.

Metaphorically speaking, consider Dick Clark and Madonna. The former is ageless, unchanging, boring. All predictability, no interest. The latter is all over the place, switching identities as if changing shoes. That's confusing. (Madonna, you might say, has lost her brand identity.) But now consider, say, Bette Davis. Strong identity, strong persona, able to shift roles and create interest without losing herself. *That's* true consistency!

Lands' End achieves consistency by identifying itself as "quality" in a hundred different ways. In one book, Lands' End may photograph its down parkas in the Arctic. In another, it may tell tales of Egyptian cotton or Shetland wool. In a third, it may talk about the history of blue jeans.

Lands' End, like a great friend, catalog by catalog becomes a model of trustworthy consistency, may change the elements of its design, but its creative personality happily remains the same.

THE IMPORTANCE OF DESIGN

You can't talk about creative, of course, without design. Design is to creative what makeup is to a model. Like shadow, blush and lipstick, design comprises the physical elements—typeface, photography, copy, layout, white space—that make up the catalog's appearance and communicate its image. In other words, creative is the concept, design is the execution.

The job of good design is this: *to make it easy for customers to shop.* In a hundred subtle ways—through symbols, well-lit photos, high-contrast type, a dynamic expression—good design takes customers by the elbow and leads them from page to page, product to product.

At the same time, good design also supports three critical marketing issues:

1) Supporting the brand image and positioning. As a catalog marketer, you know now that brand identity is critical to repeat sales. So it is that every design element you choose is critical to supporting brand identity. If you want customers to identify you with quality and high-tech, you can't print black-and-white on supercalendered paper. If you want to be known for low prices and value, you can't hide your prices in 8-point type.

Lands' End, as we know, chooses an easy-to-read serif type, exceptionally clear photography, friendly, fresh-faced models, and a clean layout with plenty of white space. The whole design speaks to the catalog's friendly brand image and value-oriented positioning.

Similarly, Victoria's Secret uses elegant script and luxurious settings to establish its position of indulgence and beauty. Williams-Sonoma supports its position with sumptuous photography and quiet design right out of *Gourmet* magazine. In each case, design elements support and enhance the catalog's established identity.

2) Addressing density issues. If you want to start a company battle, get an art director and financial manager arguing about density. The art director, no doubt, wants pages as airy as possible; the money guy wants them jammed to the edges. Each has a point—which is why merchandise and positioning, in the end, dictate the density of the catalog page.

If you're Saks Fifth Avenue, for instance, you need lots of white space and studio settings to convey the elegant look that's critical to your customer base. You simply can't sell fur jackets six to a page.

But if you're Lillian Vernon, you need high density to give your customers the opportunity to shop the page and find what they're looking for. High density conveys value and selection. Besides, Lillian probably carries 300 to 500 SKUs; all those products have to fit somewhere!

As a design issue, though, high density doesn't necessarily mean crowded. Through judicious use of composition, copy placement and color, plenty of dense catalogs can create good eyeflow and give space to the product. (See the old Williams-Sonoma digest-size catalogs for a great lesson in this.) Density is neither good nor bad; it's simply an issue catalogers need to address through their marketing plans.

3) Addressing budget issues. More often than we'd like, the catalog of our dreams collides with the budget of our reality. Dense pages, for instance, simply cost more to separate than those with just a few products, although they bring in more revenue. Special touches, like fifth colors, gold ink, die cuts or embossing, add production expenses. Celebrity models cost plenty, and so does heavier paper stock. Even advertising sale prices in red ink can add costs when you have to make up a new printing plate!

Good designers can find ways around budget problems while still holding true to their visions. Sometimes, for instance, a designer can simply photograph a gold color and strip it in instead up setting up a gold ink-jet on press. Some catalogs, like Levenger, print photographs of textured paper to give their lighter paper the illusion of heft. These budget considerations, when seen as a challenge instead of problem, can sometimes inspire creativity to a new level.

PUTTING IT TOGETHER

In some ways, putting a catalog together is like creating an Impressionist painting. Pick any Monet, and up close, all you see are tiny

To communicate "luxury," Victoria's Secret mixes the obvious (silken sheets, bouquets of roses, sumptuous indoor locations) with the subtle (British-style spellings, such as "glamour").

Dense pages can still communicate, thanks to Lillian Vernon's orderly presentation.

Two well-organized photographs can sell six objects: Proof that density doesn't have to mean disorder.

brushstrokes of color, each perfect, each distinguished on its own. Step back, and all the strokes and colors blend together into a whole. Only then do you see that each stroke and bit of color supports the entire image.

While I would hesitate to call any cataloger a Monet, I will say the analogy does hold up. To put together an effective selling vehicle, you need myriad elements to blend into a perfect whole. You need to examine typeface, photography, logo, format, models, order blanks, and a host of other elements to see how each can suit your overall design.

It's not aesthetics at stake, but marketing. How would this logo support your brand image? How would a large format speak to your positioning? Which models would your customers identify with and relate to? What callouts could you use to inspire trust?

Beyond that, you need to organize and pace your catalog. You need to group colors, styles and merchandise types not only for good eyeflow, but for maximum selling power. You need to find ways to keep customers moving through your catalog, and you need to know when, where and how to stop them in their tracks.

Further, you need to understand how each part of a catalog has its own issues and challenges to resolve. What makes a great selling cover? What should customers expect on your order blank? How can you make your back cover work harder?

We'll address all these issues, and lots more, in this section. To solve your marketing problems with creative, you need to understand not just what makes great creative, but how you can apply that to your own unique marketing needs.

CHAPTER 12

GETTING THE
FRONT COVER RIGHT

I've sat in many focus groups, and it's scary to listen to people talk about how they empty their mailbox. Usually they walk right to the garbage with their pile, sorting as they go. A catalog, poised above the trash, has only two seconds to make the cut. For the most part, the whole thumbs-up or down rests on one single page: the front cover.

Though it may not be the first thing customers see (given that many catalogs are stuck into mailboxes address-label-up), the front cover inevitably becomes the first place recipients start investigating what's inside your book. It must tell the whole selling story. It must clearly state your catalog's brand, image and positioning. It must relate aesthetically and stylistically to the rest of the catalog. It must look special, unique and different from the heaps of other catalog covers that may crowd the mail that day. Above all...

It must get the catalog opened.

So I'm going to spend this chapter talking about what makes a good cover, and what makes a bad one. You'll not only learn the general principles behind great covers, but the specific design elements that can make it or break it.

TWO WAYS TO BLOW IT

Most catalogers seem to suffer one of two ailments in planning their covers.

1) The "Our image: love it or leave it" syndrome. Basically, this results in the same kind of cover, month after month, issue after issue. It's the mark of short-sighted, long-published catalogs either too afraid or too arrogant to make changes to their image. They feel customers "know" them, so why fix what's not broken?

2) The "Who are we?" syndrome. This disease is marked by a lack of identifiable cover style. In these catalogs, logos are unmemorable or change month to month; merchandise, styling and product selection look pretty much like any of a dozen other catalogs. Alternatively, these catalogs may suffer from covers that simply have nothing to do with what's inside the book. Cover images simply reflect whatever's hot, new or promotional, with no reflection of the book's true purpose and audience.

In truth, customers are a lot more fickle than we may think. If a catalog doesn't change, customers either start to believe they've seen the catalog before,

SPRING SELECTIONS
1997

TIFFANY & CO.

USING ITS TRADEMARK LOGO AND SKY-BLUE COLOR, TIFFANY & CO. CREATES A COVER DESIGN THAT IS UNIQUELY ITS OWN.

LOVE THIS COVER! THIS SOLUTION-ORIENTED CATALOG CREATES A MESSAGE OF PERFECT **RELE-VANCE** FOR BUSY, STRESSED-OUT CUSTOMERS.

HOLD EVERYTHING CREATES VISUAL **DRAMA** FROM ORDINARY COAT HANGERS.

or they simply lose interest in seeing it again. If a catalog changes too much, or lacks an identity to grasp, customers can't figure out why it offers anything special. Either way, the catalog ends up in the trash.

Keeping a customer relationship healthy is like keeping any other relationship healthy. It's the cataloger's job to remain reliable (but not boring), and interesting and desirable (but not neurotic and scatterbrained).

What it comes down to is one simple rule. For effective covers, *you must make your customers see RED.*

What's that mean?

Keep reading.

THE BEAUTY OF RED

RED is the key acronym for getting a catalog opened. It stands for three things:

Relevance

Emotion

Drama

Here's what I mean by that:

THE "R" FACTOR: Relevance

Customers need to relate to your catalog cover. They need to know that you understand not only how they live, but how they *want* to live. Whether your catalog goes to a homemaker in Canton, Ohio, or a young executive in Los Angeles, it must say something that has meaning to the person picking it up.

That gets back, of course, to knowing your customer—as well as knowing your brand image and positioning. The right cover speaks to customer desires and aspirations, as well as to customer needs. It also establishes the catalog's identity, and cues customers as to what they'll find inside.

For that reason, lifestyle covers on L.L. Bean look very different from those on Smith & Hawken, or from Early Winters. Bean prefers casual, easygoing outdoorsy scenes, while Early Winters picks high-impact travel shots consistent with its more rough-and-tumble image. Smith & Hawken, meanwhile, prefers the silent, poetic landscapes and product shots that speak to a gardener's soul.

Relevance, of course, can also be captured in product shots. Take The Sharper Image covers, which speak of high-tech pragmatism, or Hold Everything covers, in which clothes hangers and trash cans become visual haiku. You can almost imagine the audiences for those books: busy briefcase-toters on the one hand, and neat perfectionists on the other.

Similarly, beautiful empty kitchen shots provide relevance for Pottery Barn customers, and close-ups of home libraries speak to the aspirations of Levenger's "serious readers." For any cataloger, in fact, the bottom line is this: As long as the image matches the audience, it's got relevance.

THE "E" FACTOR: Emotion

We all know Hallmark is ingenious at soliciting tears in its 60-second mini-dramas, and the old "Reach out and touch someone" ads didn't do a bad job either. Emotion, though, is a lot tougher for mere catalogers to capture. Making customers smile, laugh, warm up or glow is not easily done in a single image (which is probably why we pay top artists and photographers so handsomely!).

When it comes to creating emotions, most catalogers can turn to some of the following:

Kids and critters. Children, of course, can weaken anyone's knees. I've always treasured the early Hanna Andersson catalogs and their "little punkin heads." Animals, too, believe it or not, are right up there in generating smiles and coos. But you have to watch the sentiment factor. If your kids' cover turns too cutesy-poo, you've got a relevance problem (see "R" above).

Photographic outtakes. If you want to find an image that tingles, try looking through all your reject transparencies at the end of a shoot. Here's where you might find a model's off-guard asymmetrical smile, or a goofy laugh that came after a long day on location. That's genuine emotion, and that's contagious.

Actors and actresses. After all, their job is to convey emotion, right? Many catalogers sometimes turn to actors and actresses for certain shoots in order to create that elusive sense of real life.

"Snaphots." J. Crew is masterful at capturing "intimate" looks between models, or allowing us readers to "watch" these good-looking folks goof off on a beach or hillside. If you let models be real, they can often reward you with true emotion, not just smiles.

Humor. Lands' End, on the other hand, likes to prod readers with a tickle or a laugh, maybe using an off-beat photo or cartoon illustration. Using humor, though, can be a tricky task: You have to make sure customers will "get" your joke.

Warmth: Big family photos can create emotion for, say, Plow & Hearth customers. A Rockwellian table brings up nostalgia for Vermont Country Store shoppers. If a catalog's brand identity calls for warmth, home and family images, with appropriate sentiment, can make it happen.

The point is, customers will always pay attention to what they see, provided it generates something they also *feel.*

THE "D" FACTOR: Drama

It's not easy to define drama, but put it this way: You know it when you see it.

Take just about any Lands' End cover. One, I recall, showed nothing but the giant prow of an icebreaking ship, painted like the jaw of a ten-ton great white shark. Another showed the back of a bald man's head; another depicted a lion dressed in a polo shirt.

The point is, each cover created drama by taking a risk with the viewer. Each showed something unexpected; each created impact with a memorable image or illustration. Most of all, each one got the catalog opened!

Some catalogs lend themselves to obvious drama, like Patagonia with its mountain-trekking and river rafting. Others, like Bean, create a kind of outdoorsy drama with lifestyle images (canoes and picnic baskets), while catalogs like Garnet Hill create poetic drama out of sheets and sunsets. I love how Hold Everything can turn ordinary shoe trees or wastebaskets into beautifully composed images. When the round tops of garbage cans are

HUMOR, WARMTH, FAMILY *AND* PRODUCT PROMOTION...WIRELESS EFFORTLESSLY PACKS IT ALL INTO ONE COMPELLING COVER.

It may not say "apparel," but this surprising image definitely says "Lands' End." Pure drama gets a book opened, even by the most jaded customers.

Black type, used either in boxes or straight on the cover design, enables easy-to-see, easy-to-change promotional messages.

arranged like so many ostrich eggs, that, believe it or not, is drama.

It's not difficult to create drama for a cover. Lighting and texture can do the job, as can a tight close-up, a powerful product shot, a demonstration, a cartoon (humor always has impact) or a beautiful illustration or artwork.

Whatever the technique, though, drama must not be done for its own sake. It must have *meaning for the customer.* Unless it's tied to the catalog's positioning and speaks to the target audience, drama, by itself, holds no more intrigue than a backfiring truck.

Garnet Hill's covers, for instance, always speak to the catalog's soulful nature; Hold Everything illustrates the beauty of organization. And once customers opened that Lands' End catalog, with its shark-painted ship, they learned how the catalog tested its down parkas during an Arctic trip. That was relevance, emotion *and* drama in one great catalog cover.

SECONDARY "D" FACTOR: Differentiate

Incidentally, the letter "D" in RED could also stand for "differentiate." Successful catalog covers tell you immediately who the company is and what it stands for.

Who wouldn't, for instance, recognize a Victoria's Secret catalog, with its logo, crest and London address? It's easy to spot an L.L. Bean's cover, which always carry an unmistakable New England image. These catalogs have easy-to-read logos that customers always recognize. They carry consistent images, models and product shots from book to book. Their covers are uniquely their own, resembling no one else's.

MAKING COVERS SELL: THE COVER MESSAGE

Often, even a perfect RED cover needs a selling boost. Tough competition and tough economies today mean catalog covers must work harder than ever to give customers reason, up front, to *buy.*

Personally, I love *front-cover messages,* the ones that tell me about great offers inside, sale items or upcoming holidays. At Christmas, I want to be reminded of Federal Express shipping, and I certainly want to know, up front, about lower prices or free returns. These messages not only get me to open the book, but to shop it as well.

Here's a rundown of other message opportunities:

Holidays. Who doesn't appreciate a Sharper Image cover that shows six different products, at different prices, available for Father's Day? Fourth of July, back-to-school, Thanksgiving and other holidays give catalogers not only opportunity to be timely, but to create messages that get customers to buy.

Response-driving. Catalogers can also use cover messages to drive increased response rates or order sizes. A Clifford & Wills catalog, for instance, might advertise "50% off 90 of our best styles." J. Crew may have a cover wrap that reactivates old buyers with a $20 coupon. Victoria's Secret frequently ups order sizes by offering dollars off purchases of $75 or more.

Sales stimulation. Lower-end catalogs often stimulate sales with deferred billing cover messages, such as "Pay nothing until September." Likewise,

Fingerhut catalogs frequently offer free gifts and low payment plans on their covers, and many catalogs, like Damark, try to prod reluctant buyers with a "last catalog" message.

All of it can be effective, but only when *presented* effectively. Catalogers have as many opportunities to ruin their messages as they do opportunities to run them.

Presenting the message

Essentially, you can call on the following various techniques to execute a cover message:

- *Plain black type*
- *Devices*
- *Promotional and color type*
- *Banners and boxes*
- *Dot whacks (fake or real)*
- *Screen-backs*
- *Cover wraps*

Each one comes with its own advantages and drawbacks.

ALL-OUT PROMOTIONAL COVERS, LIKE THIS ONE FROM RELIABLE, OFFER GREAT OPPORTUNITIES FOR INK-JET PERSONALIZED MESSAGES.

1) PLAIN BLACK TYPE

Cover messages dropped in as *black type* can announce any number of offers: "Remember Mother's Day," "Look inside for new items," or "New, lower prices."

Advantages: Plain black type is easy to change on press, making it perfect for targeting different customer groups. Longtime customers can read about new items inside; prospects can learn about the catalog's low prices. Furthermore, *callouts* in black type can indicate a product's special features on the catalog cover. For its Father's Day catalog, for instance, The Sharper Image created short product descriptions and page references in black cover type.

Drawbacks. Black type lacks impact—especially if it's small. Hold Everything, for instance, often shrinks its cover messages that might otherwise "intrude" on cover art. To be effective, cover messages should not only stand out, but address what's offered on the cover, as well as what's inside.

2) DEVICES

Some catalogs create small *dingbats* to indicate items appropriate for gift-giving. Other catalogs use cover devices as quick visual shortcuts for noting special offers or services.

Advantages. Just about any message that can be put into words can be put into a visual device. Devices can indicate toll-free numbers, catalog credit, gift ideas, sale prices—just about anything that customers can then spot within the book.

Drawbacks. Busy devices, particularly promotional starbursts and the like, can cheapen a cover. Any front cover already rife with type and images probably doesn't need more fuss.

FAKE DOT WHACKS (SEE BOTTOM RIGHT CORNER) ENABLE DISCREET PROMOTIONAL MESSAGES.

3) PROMOTIONAL AND COLOR TYPE

Sometimes the front cover *is* the message. One Lew Magram book, for instance, used its entire cover to tell customers about its 10%-off sale.

Advantages. Full-cover promotions sure get noticed. Moreover, catalogs can deliver different covers to different customer segments. It's possible, for instance, that only Magram's old buyers received the "10% off" cover; regular customers possibly received an image cover.

Drawbacks. Altering entire covers is risky and expensive. Also, covers like these do nothing to promote brand image; often, they simply teach customers to expect a bargain. They're best restricted to sale books.

4) BANNERS AND BOXES

Banners are announcement "slices" put on a cover's corner. They resemble *Time* magazine's weekly announcements of featured stories. *Boxes* feature announcements in dropped-in "squares" on the cover. Either can carry a range of cover messages, from overnight shipping to sale prices to new items to deferred billing.

Advantages. Banner and box messages are easy to change (particularly if they're made up of black type on a white or light? background). This kind of flexibility lets you better target messages to specific customer groups. You can use a box or banner to promote sale items to longtime buyers; announce new resort-wear to proven bathing-suit buyers, and so on.

Drawbacks. Banners, and boxes especially, can be fairly design-intrusive. For that reason, some catalogers argue that boxes look promotional and cheap—but I've found in my experience that the more visible, the better. Boxes and banners just plain work.

5) DOT WHACKS

Dot whacks come in two styles: real and fake. Essentially, a real dot whack is a sticker affixed to a catalog cover to advertise sale items, low prices, new products or anything else that demands a "see inside." Fake dot whacks aren't stickers, but just look that way. J. Peterman, for instance, is fond of fake dot whacks for announcing sale items or sweepstakes; Frederick's of Hollywood uses them for "last catalog" cover announcements.

Advantages. Dot whacks, particularly real ones, are wonderfully flexible. Catalogers can write in any message they like for any audience they like, then glue them on in the bindery line. Moreover, dot whacks don't have to be "designed" into a catalog, as banners and boxes do. The dot whack just goes on top of what's already there. Additionally, fake dot whacks are inexpensive; they are part of the cover's artwork and won't cost you a penny more to execute.

Drawbacks. Depending on their size, dot whacks can appear one of two ways: intrusive or invisible. There's no question, for instance, that the yellow "STOP!" dot whack is the first thing you see on the Frederick's catalog. On the other hand, J. Crew's teeny dot whacks almost disappear in the catalog design.

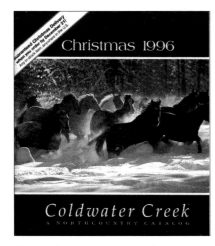

BANNERS (SEE UPPER LEFT CORNER) ARE BEST USED FOR ALERTING CUSTOMERS TO NEW ITEMS OR SERVICES.

DOT WHACKS (PARTICULARLY IN GOLD FOIL) IMMEDIATELY DRAW THE EYE TO A LILLY'S KIDS PROMOTIONAL MESSAGE.

6) SCREEN -BACKS

"Screening back" a cover means fading an image so that a photograph or background becomes a hint of an image. You can then surprint your promotional message over the screen, usually in black type.

Advantages. Screen-back covers may look less promotional than covers with banners or mortise boxes. They allow you to get across a cover message without losing the integrity of your cover. Carroll Reed, for instance, once screened back the entire front cover in order to put a reactivation message up front. The results were terrific!

Drawbacks. Screen-back covers can look busy or confusing if not executed correctly. Both the image and type must remain clear, even when printed one on top of the other. Not an easy task!

7) COVER WRAPS

Wraps are entire separate covers, usually printed on brown paper or other matte paper, and bound over the regular front and back covers. Fingerhut and Brylane, especially, are known for their cover wraps.

Advantages. Wraps can carry a lot of messages! In a typical Fingerhut wrap, you can read about payments, delivery, free gifts, and great selection—not to mention a "last catalog" threat and peel-off sticker. Moreover, wraps preserve the integrity of your "real" cover image, and they can easily be tailored for different customer segments and even individual customers. Rare, in fact, is the Fingerhut catalog wrap that does not speak personally to me, "Mrs. Jones."

Drawbacks. Wraps are pricey promotional devices. They add to the weight of a catalog (which adds postage), and they must be printed and bound separately. The only way to make them work is to make them work hard. Catalogers that go halfheartedly into wrap promotions are better off using another front-cover execution.

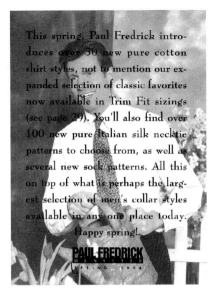

SCREEN-BACK COVERS STRESS THE PROMOTIONAL MESSAGE WHILE PRESERVING THE COVER ART.

CHECKLIST TO SUCCESS

Is your own cover at optimal selling power? Look over this checklist next time you design:

1) *Is it busy?* Front cover messages and images should be kept to minimum. Too many confuse customers and sap the catalog's selling strength.

2) *Is it organized?* Catalog covers aren't store shelves. Don't crowd them with too many products scattered willy-nilly, in hopes that customers will find at least one they like.

3) *Is it clear?* Anyone viewing your cover should know at a glance what you sell and what you're about.

4) *Is it representative?* If you run product images, make sure they speak to your main merchandise line. Don't run an image of flowers if you're a fruitcake cataloger.

5) *Is the logo prominent and easy to read?*

6) *Is the typeface clear?* Make sure type is neither too delicate nor busy, nor fighting a crowded background.

7) *Is the photography clear?* Photography should enhance products, not obscure them.

8) *Does the background complement the image?* Or do too many props and images create clutter?

9) *Does it support your positioning?* At the very least, catalog covers must relate to the company's image. Omaha Steaks, after all, does not sell cheesecake on its cover, even though it might inside.

Catalogers that get noticed are often those that break the rules.

BEWARE THE PERFECT COVER!

Now that you know the litany on cover design, here's one last piece of advice: *Don't play it too safe!*

The truth is, catalogs that get noticed are often those that break the rules. Otherwise, why would Lands' End dare run a cover with an ice-breaker ship on the cover? Why would J. Peterman run one cover (as I saw recently), with a white shirt on a white background, a white dress *turned sideways* beneath that, and a bright red fake dot whack over the whole thing?

I'm not saying these catalog covers were sales winners (though maybe they were), and that's my point. Not every catalog cover will be a winner, nor *should* they all be. Catalogers that don't stretch too far from time to time, that don't step a bit over the line, are probably playing it a little too safe. Without creative risk, there's no creative gain!

So play with your covers. Pay attention to the selling rules, but keep your covers loose and free. Instinct and imagination must combine with great research and marketing skills to produce the kinds of covers that always stand out.

THE COVER KILLERS

Let's face it: Not every catalog cover is going to be a winner. In fact, whenever a catalog lays an egg, it's probably due to one of these "cover killers." Look them over and see if any seem familiar:

Too much going on. Here's an understandable problem: A cataloger wants to mention overnight delivery, 12 new items, a super sale and free gift wrapping. Don't assault your customer! Keep this hint in mind: *Image over information.* If a cover has impact, the customer will automatically want to open the book to know more.

Not enough going on. In their quest to be "artistic," some catalogers neglect to say anything about themselves at all. Maybe they'll have a single product shot, or a lovely photograph of a sunset. Very pleasing, but hardly informative (and usually, not very impactful). Remember, covers must have relevance—and they should say something about what's inside. (Yes, yes, I know: Lands' End has its cryptic covers here and there—but they *always* relate to its product and positioning.)

Obscured logos. *Time* magazine or *Vogue* may cover up logos from time to time, but catalogers, even the best known, can't afford the risk. Logos should not be sacrificed to the art director. Customers need to know what catalog they're in. Don't make them work too hard to find out.

Unrepresentative product. Gift catalogs shouldn't put apparel shots on the cover (even if they carry it) and apparel catalogs shouldn't lead with a gift-item shot. Product covers should reflect the main merchandise mix.

Hard-to-read type. Flowery script, reverse type, obscured or strangely colored type does not belong on covers. It's imperative for customers to understand clearly what your cover is trying to say.

Out-there imagery. Some catalogers seem to confuse impact with shock value. Believe me, you gain nothing when you run bizarre photographs, whacked-out design or deconstructed creative right off the pages of the latest graphics annual. *Imagery must always relate to the catalog's product line, target audience and positioning.* Beware of turning art directors into marketers.

Undifferentiated imagery. When covers look like selling spreads—when there's no difference between cover images and what's inside—customers think they're getting an incomplete book. Nothing cues them to expect anything special.

CHAPTER 13

THE INSIDE-OUT OF YOUR CATALOG

When you think about it, Lands' End's "Inside Out" catalog (see Chapter 11) brings up a great concept. Turning any product inside out tells you a lot about its quality. After all, the $20 "Rolex" bought on a New York City street wouldn't hold up to the scrutiny given to the one that cost $2,000.

So it is with catalogs. Lots of catalogs look good, but they just don't *sell*. Good catalog marketing requires knowing each part of a catalog and how it contributes to making a sale. To get that knowledge, you have to turn a catalog inside out. You have to examine its anatomy.

Understanding your catalog's anatomy is a bit like understanding your own. No personal trainer, after all, is going to just hand you a couple of weights, or order you to do twenty military presses or fifteen reverse torso crunches. He's going to first instruct you on the muscles you're working, then show you how to move precisely for maximum benefit. Only when you know what's involved (and take the appropriate action, of course) do you start making progress.

So it is that no cataloger can blindly stick items between covers as if filling a closet. For maximum selling power, you must know the different sections of a catalog and how each contributes to the bottom line. You must know what kinds of items sell best where, and what kinds of attention customers give to each page. Only then can you take appropriate action.

In this chapter, we'll look at five different selling parts of a catalog:

1) *Opening spread*
2) *Closing spread*
3) *Hero pages*
4) *Selling spreads*
5) *Back cover*

Each part of a catalog's anatomy offers opportunities to get customers to stop, pay attention, and buy. But each opportunity is different, and they each require different marketing solutions.

THE OPENING SPREAD

In many ways, catalogs are set up like department stores. The *front cover* is the display window, pulling shoppers in from the street. *Inserts* act like sampling

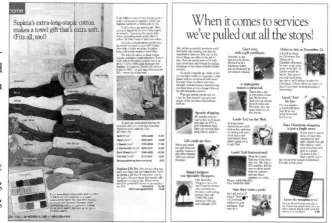

LANDS' END'S OPENING SPREAD PACKS NEW PRODUCTS, PRESIDENT'S LETTER AND A TABLE OF CONTENTS INTO ONE USER-FRIENDLY DESIGN.

booths, inviting customers to congregate. *"Hero" pages*, like retail displays, halt buyers and get them to look around. And throughout the book, *selling spreads* work like counters and store fixtures, displaying merchandise to full advantage.

The *opening spread*, then, is like the store counter near the entrance. It's part sales, part information booth. It's the place where browsers get a feel for the store and size up its merchandise, as well as pause to see what's new, what's on sale or if anything special is going on today.

Of course, an opening spread is not necessarily the first thing catalog shoppers see. After all, show me the customer who actually reads a catalog like a novel, front to back. But invariably, the opening spread is where most customers—particularly newcomers—go to get a deeper sense of what the catalog is about.

In essence, the opening spread is really the heart of *positioning*. That's why Hammacher Schlemmer, for instance, often begins here to sell its signature oddball, high-tech, high-priced goodies, like stereo chairs. J. Peterman sometimes uses the space to spread the tale of the cowboy duster. Barrie Pace indicates its different apparel styles, from Special Occasion to Summer Essentials, with photos and short descriptions. Peruvian Connection describes the sourcing and quality of its gorgeous wools, often attaching a sample. And almost all catalogers use the space to tell the consumer about service, toll-free calling, and most important, the guarantee.

The opening spread gives a bit of flavor and guidance for the catalog, like a menu for a restaurant. Regular customers glance here to see what's new. Newcomers are likely to linger. A good opening spread gives them something to look forward to in the rest of the book.

Anatomy of the opening spread

Opening spreads often (but not always) consist of up to five parts that "tell" the catalog's story:

1) *President's letter*
2) *Table of contents*
3) *Service messages*
4) *Merchandise*
5) *Positioning elements*

Each part operates by its own marketing rules.

1) President's letter

True, most people don't read much of the president's letter, which probably explains why so many of these missives, in minuscule type, are shoved into the far left corner of the spread. Nobody wants to take up selling space!

A SELECTION OF NEW PRODUCTS, COMBINED WITH A SERVICE-ORIENTED PRESIDENT'S LETTER, SPEAKS TO VETERAN LEVENGER SHOPPERS AS WELL AS NEWCOMERS.

On the other hand, president's letters *do* get read as long as they talk about customer benefits. Most customers may not care that a company was founded four score and seven years ago, or that it just moved into new Federal-style headquarters. But they might care about what's new in the book, or why certain products are perennial best-sellers. That's why the Levenger catalog, for instance, points up new products in its president's letter, as does The Sharper Image, and why catalogs like Daily Planet, an international gift book, often discourse on their latest buying trips.

President's letters also work best, naturally, when the president is part of the brand identity. No doubt, Vermont Country Store customers are always reassured that Lyman Orton, son of the founder, is still minding the register. I enjoyed how Erv Magram wished his father Lew Magram a happy birthday in his recent president's letter. And any president named Robert Redford probably justifies taking up considerable catalog space with a personal letter, even if the letter only describes the latest Sundance Film Festival.

Letters like these can bond customers with the catalog—particularly when the president ties in a customer benefit as well. I appreciate, for instance, how John McManus, president of travel catalog Magellan's, explains how he developed "basic, well-tested and dependable" travel products while working for Pan Am. I've always loved Hanna Andersson's story of finding quality clothes for children. Personal testimonials—"why I started this catalog"—can do wonders for customer confidence.

If the president treats shoppers as valued friends, they're more likely to behave that way. Once at a focus group, for instance, I was told that Eddie Smith, president of pantyhose catalog National Wholesale, was swamped by admirers when he came out to thank them for their input. These customers had gotten to know him catalog by catalog, year after year. To them, Eddie Smith was nothing less than the Tom Jones of pantyhose!

2) Table of contents

Just about every cataloger these days has debated the value of a table of contents. Frankly, debate is understandable. In a small catalog, a table of contents takes up valuable space that might be better used to sell product or emphasize services. In a larger book, it's not clear whether a contents page either helps or hinders sales. Does it aid customers in finding what they want and need, or does it keep them from leafing through the catalog for impulse buys?

There's no rule of thumb, but I suggest that catalogs of more than 64 pages—particularly those selling apparel and functional items—seriously consider listing products and page numbers. Nothing kills shopping momentum like floundering for an item. When in doubt, be generous: Give your customers a break (without discouraging them, of course, from indulging their impulses!).

THE VOYAGER COLLECTION ADDS ORGANIZATIONAL IMPACT TO ITS TABLE OF CONTENTS THROUGH THE USE OF INSET PHOTOS.

THE VERMONT COUNTRY STORE'S "CUSTOMERS' BILL OF RIGHTS" MAKES SENSE FOR THE CATALOG'S DOWN-HOME IMAGE.

COUNTRY CURTAINS' FAMILY EMPHASIS, AMPLY DEMONSTRATED IN THIS OPENING SPREAD, ASSURES CUSTOMERS THAT THEY'RE NOT DOING BUSINESS WITH STRANGERS. (NOTE DOG, GRANDCHILDREN AND VACATION PHOTOS.)

Incidentally, you can demonstrate contents in any number of ways. Barrie Pace and J. Crew use inset pictures, which makes for nice visual stimulation. Other catalogs list departments, like "Women's Accessories," with items listed beneath. Still others, of course, skip the table of contents altogether and organize the book with colored bands, headlines and banners.

We'll talk more about those elements in a later chapter focusing on organization. For now, keep in mind that if a table of contents makes sense for your customers, it would probably make sense for your bottom line. Find the balance between helping customers shop and discouraging them from just leafing through.

3) Service messages

Since the opening spread is all about positioning and customer benefits, it makes sense to start your service message here. This is where customers should find the following:

* *Toll-free order number*
* *Customer service number*
* *E-mail address or Web site*
* *Gift-wrapping, alterations or other special services*
* *Special Delivery Options*
* *Explanation of devices, such as "look for this symbol next to our wrinkleproof garments"*
* *Guarantee*

Most of these messages, of course, should also appear throughout the book and certainly on the order form. But customers in a hurry need a place to go to find out the information they want. Don't make it hard for them!

By the way, my favorite service statement has got to be The Vermont Country Store's nine-point "Customers' Bill of Rights." This no-nonsense statement (Number one: "To expect polite and courteous service.") fits perfectly with the catalog's position of old-fashioned values.

4) Merchandise

No cataloger wants an all-editorial opening spread. Bor-ing! This is valuable space: It should *sell!* Here's where you want to feature merchandise that represents your catalog and tells your story.

Lands' End, for instance, often starts off with a time-worn classic, like its mesh polo shirt. Since the polo is probably the most ubiquitous shirt in the known universe, this spread gives Lands' End a chance to tell its story on quality, and emphasize what makes it different from every other polo in the land.

Other catalogs, known for classic items, start with best-sellers, or with updated new items. Catalogers known for forward thinking, like apparel cataloger Allen Allen and high-tech gadgets cataloger Hammacher Schlemmer, use the spread to showcase what's new. This is every cataloger's opportunity to showcase its best product.

5) Positioning elements

Some catalogers use the opening spread to introduce causes or initiatives, like Vermont Country Store's support of independent store-keepers. Some speak of their environmental sensitivity. Others offer gift suggestions. Neiman Marcus historically begins its "His and Her" Christmas eye-poppers on its opening spread.

The point is, whatever appears on the opening spread must underscore the catalog's unique selling proposition. Everything here has to be *signature.* It must tell the catalog's own story, in merchandise, service messages, table of contents and president's letter.

Catalogers don't need to create wordy editorial statements about their positioning (which most customers wouldn't read anyway). That just wastes good space. But they do need to make their positioning visual and *visceral.* They need to let customers know right away what book they're in, and why they should be buying.

AN OPENING SPREAD FEATURING STANLEY MARCUS CREATES A QUALITY THEME FOR THIS LANDS' END CATALOG.

CLOSING SPREAD

For every two customers who flip a catalog front to back, I guarantee there is at least one who flips it back to front. That's why the closing spread deserves attention. It's a frequently visited space that can drive a lot of sales.

What should you sell here? For most catalogers, what works is the tried-and-true. These are the commodity goods that every good customer buys, the T-shirts, the tanks, the best-selling jeans, the cloth napkins. Bulk items and best buys balance with the opening spread, which usually features specials and new products.

If customers are on the fence about buying something different or unusual from a company, or if they're familiar with the book but looking for basics, they can usually turn to the closing spread for the comforting items they expect.

HERO PAGES

I'll always remember learning about this experiment back in psychology class. What a lesson in motivation.

Three groups of pigeons were assigned a task and rewarded one of three ways: regularly, randomly or not at all. Of course, the unrewarded birds slacked off. So, interestingly, did the birds that got regular rewards. They knew they'd be rewarded whether they worked or not, so they didn't bother working.

But the third group of pigeons worked harder, trained better and remembered tasks. They got down to business as soon as they figured out

TOP: LIFE-SIZE, NATURALLY LIT DOLLS MAKE ARRESTING HERO SPREADS FOR PLEASANT COMPANY, PARTICULARLY WITHIN THE CATALOG'S OVERSIZE FORMAT.

INSET: SOFT, WARM IMAGERY CREATES AN ENTICING HERO SPREAD FOR PLEASANT COMPANY.

that they couldn't predict when those sunflower seeds would drop down. They just knew that they had to keep working if they wanted a reward at all.

Never let it be said that customers are pigeons, *but...* the truth is, motivation works the same way with people. We like pleasant surprises. That's why we tune in to soap opera cliffhangers or go to live concerts when we could listen to CDs. That's why infrequent catalog sale books perform better than frequent ones. (Customers keep buying because they don't know when they'll have another opportunity.)

That's also why we need "hero pages." These are high-impact spreads distributed at (usually) random intervals in a catalog. They simply stand out creatively from the rest of the book. They're less dense, more impactful. They're strategically positioned to stop customers, and churn up interest. They tell readers they've tapped a new vein of something special in the book.

Of course, hero spreads often promote specific products—usually expensive ones. The Sharper Image, for instance, might create a high-impact spread for its massage chairs; Lands' End (which really puts energy into this) might use one to spell the benefits of its luggage line. Sundance catalog can stop you with heroic layouts of its $3,000 leather chair, or $1,100 ironwork bed.

Hero spreads can also introduce catalog sections. Early Winters, for instance, plasters its "Trusty Model T" sweater (with callouts and product laydowns, called "color ways") across two pages to introduce its category of "mountain" apparel. Doll cataloger Pleasant Company, with its already oversize pages, uses hero spreads beautifully to introduce each of the catalog's dolls—including the tag line, "Meet Samantha," for example. Customers, of course, can't help but "meet" a doll that's presented larger-than-life across an 11-1/2" x 17" spread.

LANDS' END'S HERO PAGES TELL THE STORY OF A PRODUCT IN WORDS AND IMAGERY.

Mostly, though, *hero spreads pace customers*. Think, for instance, about how you initially picked up this book. You might have looked at the cover, glanced at the contents, and then flipped through it—and you probably stopped where you saw graphics or an interesting headline. So, too, do we all stop flipping a catalog to get a better look at that magenta tank top, those hiking sandals, or that titanium golf club. It's not necessarily the product itself that gets us there, but the high-impact photo, the full-bleed shot or the across-the-fold presentation.

For marketing purposes, there are generally only two rules for hero pages:

1) *You need key items.* Because hero pages sport big images, you need big sales to support the space. Therefore, they should feature only key items, high-margin items, or items that support the catalog's entire selling premise. A Lands' End's hero spread for, say, cotton shirts, might tell the story of quality Egyptian cotton. J. Crew's hero pages of extended families gathered hearthside don't just sell flannel shirts, but tell you something about the catalog's warm lifestyle positioning.

2) *If you've got a big book, you need hero spreads.* It's pretty tough for customers to shop a book of, say, 72 pages without some kind of visual incen-

tive. Catalogs generous in their hero pages generally find their customers stay longer in the book.

SELLING SPREADS

As the bread-and-butter of your book, selling spreads must be fun, easy places to shop. Using the department-store analogy, think of selling spreads as the "aisles" or "racks" in your catalog, the place where you've laid out all your merchandise for browsers.

But in truth, selling spreads have to work a lot harder than most store aisles. It's best to think of them almost as little shopping plazas in themselves, complete with room to move, pleasant atmosphere, and even a helpful salesperson at the ready. In s th *they must make shopping simple.*

In a later chapter, we'll t a l k in detail about putting those spreads together. For now, keep in mind the criteria of a good selling spread.

THE TERRITORY AHEAD CREATES CRISP, BEAUTIFULLY ORGANIZED SELLING SPREADS BY MIXING SILHOUETTES AND BACKGROUNDED PRODUCT SHOTS.

Every selling spread should be...

...Designed around feature shots. Feature shots call out key items to customers. In e s s e n c e a shot is a standout presentation of the most important item on the spread. A Chadwick's spread, for instance, may sell three different blouses, a pair of pants and a blazer, but the large photograph, "color ways" p r o d u c t downs and huge, highlighted sale price headline ("Now only $29!") would tell customers that the blazer is the most important product on the spread.

Feature shots like this—along with secondary feature shots— not only help customers shop, but also pump up interest and excitement on the pages. Without feature shots, catalog products would appear the same size page after page, about as interesting as cans of soup on a grocery shelf. Customers wouldn't have a clue where to look.

...Constructed for eyeflow. Selling spreads need to give customers room t o v a r y f r o m p r o d u c t to product, *and* to rest comfortably on products they like. Too much density or thrown-about product creates a visual jumble. Too much symmetry or stylistic dullness (such as all-silhouetted product) creates visual tedium. Too much jumble or tedium, and the customer moves on.

...Easy to read. Simply put, selling spreads must follow all the usual rules of type, design and organization. Headlines must be comfortably large; copy blocks must be plainly coordinated to product; type size must be easy on the eyes. Customers should be able to make their purchase decisions without squinting, hesitating or wondering what that gizmo looks like in real life.

...Complete. Selling spreads should keep nothing from customers. Clear product shots should not be sacrificed for "artsy" ones. Complete copy descriptions should not be hewn to make

THIS SELLING SPREAD UNITES DIFFERENT TYPES OF SWEATERS AROUND THE CENTRAL THEME OF "COMFORT."

BRIGHT PRODUCT LAYDOWNS AND AN ENTHUSIASTIC SMILE ADD PUNCH TO THIS SELLING SPREAD FOR CAHDWICK'S OF BOSTON.

BARRIE PACE USES CLEAR, CONCISE TYPE TO
CROSS-REFERENCE ITS APPAREL PRODUCTS.

INK-JETTING IS AN INEXPENSIVE WAY TO
PROMOTE SERVICES OR PRODUCTS ON A
BACK COVER.

HAMMACHER SCHLEMMER'S BACK COVER
REINFORCES THE CATALOG'S INNOVATIVE
PRODUCT POSITIONING, BOTH THROUGH
MERCHANDISE AND INK-JETTING.

more room on the page. Selling spreads should anticipate questions from customers—*Is that fabric washable? How much does the travel iron weigh?*—and answer them fully. Most catalogs, after all, give a customer only one chance to see or read about a product. It's important to make the most of it.

...Service-oriented. If possible, every selling spread should carry an 800 ordering number. Service messages, such as shipping and handling, or "We answer your questions, 24 hours a day," should appear frequently. If you guarantee overnight delivery for Christmas items, be sure to emphasize that on every spread. And don't forget to include page numbers! Customers absolutely need them to shop.

Personally, I also appreciate catalogs that take the time to provide helpful information on their selling spreads, as Levenger does. Explanations on "how to buy an office chair," or what makes a Mont Blanc pen special, can definitely get a customer off the fence. Messages like these make customers believe not only that the catalog is an expert in its product, but cares enough to take the time and space to explain it.

...Cross-referenced. If you want to see frustration, have your customer try to find the great hat or pair of shoes that the model wore in a selling spread on dresses. Remember, catalogs stimulate buying impulses everywhere. Don't forget to cross-reference every product that appears on your pages.

...Brand-imaged. (You probably knew this was coming!) Selling spreads not only stand on their own, but carry the mark of the whole. In other words, each spread must carry the unmistakable stamp of your catalog's positioning. Take any page from, say, The Territory Ahead or L.L. Bean or J. Crew. You know immediately which book you're in, even if you haven't seen the logo.

See if your own catalog can pass the cover-the-logo test. Is the spread recognizably part of your catalog, or could it pass for one of a half-dozen others? If you're not sure, tune it up.

BACK COVER

A lot of the time, people pull a catalog out of a mailbox backside first. After all, that's where the address label is, so that's usually how it goes into the box.

And that means the back cover offers selling opportunity. While front covers are all about positioning, back covers are about balancing the offer, creating a complement to the front. An apparel catalog showing women's clothing on the front cover, for instance, might show men's clothes on the back. L.L. Bean might show a family camping on the front and sell "amphibious" day packs on the back. Sundance outdoor furniture might appear on a front cover; its back cover could show wall art.

For the most part, back covers tend to look like hero pages, keeping merchandise offers to one or two key items. That's partly a matter of logistics: After all, this cover needs room for an address label, customer code, and, often, shipping and express-delivery information as well. (Notice that Lands' End always puts its guarantee here.)

Moreover, hero designs are attention-grabbing. That's crucial when the back cover may be the first thing customers see. If the product here sparks interest, so will the rest of the catalog.

And don't forget: You can even use your address label for selling messages. Most labels are ink-jetted anyway, which means they enable personalization. Based on zip code or customer code, simple messages, such as "Visit our store at the Stamford Town Center," "Cookware on sale, page 25," or "This will be your only sale catalog," can add a little oomph to the cover's marketing strength. The jury is still out on how effective these messages are (and some catalogers believe they downgrade their image), but it never hurts to experiment.

The next chapter details the sixth part of a catalog's anatomy: the insert. Since that's a particularly challenging selling opportunity, it deserves discussion on its own.

EXPOSURES INCORPORATES INK-JET PERSONALIZATION RIGHT ONTO THE CATALOG'S COVER CREATIVE.

CHAPTER 14

INSERTS AND ORDER BLANKS

Any insert creates a break in a catalog, and any break, of course, creates an opportunity to sell. Inserts are the stopping points in your catalog. They get customers to slow down and look.

If you're like most catalogers, though, you're probably hesitant to use inserts—besides your order form, of course. Inserts are printed on heavier-weight paper than the rest of your catalog, so postage costs may increase. They also add printing and insertion costs, and they offer design challenges you don't face on your usual selling spreads.

But keep in mind that any change in creative is a buying stimulant. Done well, most inserts, by their look and feel, generally drive the kind of business that pays for the extra cost. Because they stand out, inserts announce a new opportunity for customers to buy. That renews a customer's shopping frame of mind.

Moreover, inserts add "buzz" to the merchandise on the surrounding pages. Merchandised correctly, these pages usually outperform other selling spreads. They drive up response for key items as well as for commodities that might otherwise get lost within the book.

So in this chapter, I'll go over the different types of inserts available, along with their creative challenges and opportunities. I'll also show you how to make the surrounding pages sell better. And, of course, you'll find everything you need to know about that largest and most ubiquitous insert, the order form.

LIKE A BARGAIN BASEMENT, INSERTS ARE GREAT FOR SALE ITEMS AND INVENTORY OVER-STOCK.

TYPES OF INSERTS

Order blanks are inserts, of course, but so are "friend-get-a-friend" cards, sale brochures, credit card offers and other special offers. Victoria's Secret, for instance, is a master at creating special brochures of sale items or other merchandise, all targeted by customer segment. J. Crew often includes inserts for gift certificates or "send a friend a catalog."

Let's look at a few examples of different types of inserts.

The sale "brochure"

Generally, these insert pages look notably different from the rest of the catalog. They're usually a narrower size, often loaded with "unde-signed" pickup art, and frequently on matte or lighter-weight paper.

COMMODITY ITEMS, LIKE PENS AND ENVELOPES, MAKE SENSE FOR A NEWSPRINT INSERT IN A BUSINESS-TO-BUSINESS CATALOG.

INSERTS AND ORDER BLANKS

BOUND-IN "FRIEND-GET-A-FRIEND" CARDS NOT
ONLY BOOST THE PROSPECTING BASE, BUT
CREATE A TERRIFIC BREAK FOR A SELLING SPREAD.

LANDS' END'S BIND-INS DON'T WASTE SPACE:
CATALOG PROMOTION ON ONE SIDE, SERVICE
PROMOTION ON THE OTHER.

TERRIFIC INSERT FROM LANDS' END: SEND IN
THE CARD TO ORDER A GIFT CERTIFICATE.

Because they're inserts, these sale brochures can be directed to any customer segment, such as top buyers or previous sale respondents. At Victoria's Secret, for instance, bathing-suit buyers may get special inserts on new suits; proven bargain hunters may receive inserts on inventory closeouts.

As a cataloger, you can also use sale brochures to better manage your inventory. (I've always admired how J. Peterman uses inserts to announce "only 242" silk blouses left in stock. Great sales stimulant!) What's more, the bargain-basement look and feel of these inserts means minimal production costs, and you can generally make up your insertion costs through the higher response rate.

"Friend-get-a-friend" cards

Some of the best prospects for your house file are probably those recommended by good customers. Friends, after all, are usually demographically and psychographically alike. That's why it's a good idea to ask customers to send in a friend's name for a free book.

Of course, most catalogers use their order blanks for "friend-get-a-friend" requests. They then complain that "nobody" ever uses them. They're right! Friend-get-a-friend requests pay off better when created on separate card inserts, which are far more convenient to drop in the mail (particularly when they're prepaid).

Not only do these card inserts offer more room for friends' addresses, they also provide room for stimulating visuals (like a catalog cover or best-selling product) *and* they create a nice break in the book. (Actually, they create two breaks, because you can fold the cards into a press signature.) That gives catalogers opportunity to merchandise those pages for higher performance.

Other card inserts

L.L. BEAN ADDS A REASSURING GUARANTEE (NOT
TO MENTION A SERVICE PROMOTION) TO ITS
"FRIEND-GET-A-FRIEND" BIND-IN CARD.

Card inserts can take myriad forms. They can be postcard-size, full-page, half-page horizontal, or even half-page vertical. They can be inserted loose and folded into the spine (so that customers pull out the card from the signature) or they can be stapled in along with the other pages, creating, in effect, two insert opportunities.

Lew Magram, for instance, once used a half-page vertical card to advertise its catalog credit card. (That vertical space enables far more information than a typical postcard.) J. Crew has used double-postcards to advertise friend-get-a-friend on one part of the insert and promote Christmas gift certificates on the other.

Cards create great sales opportunities. Creative use will give you more opportunity to do business with your customers.

Blow-ins

We're all familiar, of course, with those subscription cards that flutter out of magazines. They may annoy readers, but they work: Publishers know that readers who subcribe via a blow-in card have far better pay-up and renewal rates than those acquired through sweepstakes or direct mail.

Catalogers use fewer blow-ins than publishers, but the cards do serve a purpose, especially for credit offers and cross-promotions. Hanover Direct's Domestications catalog, for instance, recently promoted a no-fat potato-chip maker through a blow-in. The product, evidently, made sense for the catalog's demographic, but was too far afield from the catalog's merchandise mix to rate an inclusion in the book.

Blow-ins, incidentally, are cheaper to produce than other inserts. They aren't bound in on the bindery line; instead, they're shot into the already-bound catalogs with a puff of air. It's a simple, inexpensive process—but the drawback, of course, is that no one knows just whether the card ends up in pages 16-17 or 32-33. That means you can't design pages to work around the "break."

The other drawback: Bound-in inserts stay in the book until the customer removes them. Blow-ins fall out!

LIKE MANY MAGAZINE BLOW-INS, CATALOG BLOW-INS OFTEN PROMOTE "SUBSCRIPTIONS" AS A LOW-COST CIRCULATION-BUILDER.

ORDER BLANKS

Order blanks have been around since Sears sold buggy whips. And, in this day and age, it's tempting to think, "Who needs them?" After all, just about all customers now prefer dialing to mailing. Besides, it's easy to argue that order blanks add weight and expense to a catalog, look boring, and add yet another step to the bindery line. Compared to the slick glitz of the rest of the catalog, order blanks are dull stuff, like office cubicles in the middle of the Saks Fifth Avenue selling floor.

The truth is, though, we need order blanks—and so do our customers. Consider this test that CEO Alan Glazer once ran at apparel catalog Bedford Fair. In one catalog, he printed one 800 number on the order blank, and a different 800 number throughout the rest of the book, on every spread. About 80% of the catalog's phone customers, it turned out, called in using the number on the order blank.

That certainly indicates that we can't be cavalier with an order blank. Customers may not send it in to us, but they use it. It helps them locate all of a catalog's policies and services. In fact, I like to think of it as the quiet little engine at the heart of your catalog. We may not always be conscious of it, but without it, we're dead!

Here's what a good order blank accomplishes:

It answers questions. Order blanks show customers how to order, where to locate services, how to return items, whom to call for service, how to determine sizes, and a whole host of other information.

It clinches the order. It's the vehicle that moves customers from "decision" to "purchase." It also gives them space to plan and record what to buy.

IN OTHER INSTANCES, BLOW-INS CROSS-PROMOTE PRODUCT OR OTHER SERVICES THAT DON'T NAT-URALLY FIT IN THE CATALOG ITSELF.

It "breaks" the book. Because the order blank forces the book to fall open, it opens up selling opportunities on surrounding pages, particularly for impulse items.

It sells! Almost every catalog's order blank carries those last-minute, low-cost gizmos and essentials that plump up the final order.

The 10 basics

To do the job right, order blanks need to organize a lot of information in a very little space. It may not seem possible to fit it all in, but each order blank should contain the following 10 items:

1) How to order.

It doesn't matter how often you've given your toll-free number or ordering hours throughout your book. The order blank (as Alan Glazer discovered) is where customers turn when placing the actual call. It should clearly state phone, fax and mail options, as well as hours.

2) Shipping options.

Order blanks must explain not only how you'll ship merchandise and when, but what you'll charge for express services and regular delivery. They should have *clear* charts for delivery and tax charges, and, if necessary, guidelines for Canadian and international shipping as well.

3) Customer service.

Order blanks should highlight this number separately from the regular order number. Customers need to know customer-service hours and how to resolve any questions or problems.

4) Returns and exchanges.

Customers should know up front how easily they can exchange what they don't like or what doesn't fit. If you offer free pick-up, your order blank should definitely promote it.

5) Guarantee.

Critical! The best guarantees, of course, are the most concise. I particularly like Lands' End's ("Guaranteed. Period."), J. Peterman's ("Absolute Satisfaction"), and, of course, Bean's ("We do not want you to have anything from L.L. Bean that is not completely satisfactory"). Of course, not every catalog offers unconditional returns, and those that don't must *be sure to spell out* their exact guarantees.

6) Sizing.

Particularly crucial for catalogs offering specialized apparel (children's clothes, or hosiery and hats). And of course, the more you emphasize quality and fit in your catalog, the more you need to spell out sizing. Not long ago, I heard one woman say she only buys Lands' End bathing suits because, she claims, the catalog "knows" her size. That's the kind of detail that can indeed make or break not only a sale, but a customer. Order blanks must give customers confidence.

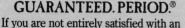

LANDS' END'S "GUARANTEED. PERIOD." BOOSTS CUSTOMER CONFIDENCE.

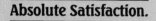

FOR PLAIN ENGLISH, J. PETERMAN'S GUARANTEE CAN'T BE BEAT.

EVEN J. PETERMAN'S FITTING INSTRUCTIONS ARE WORTH A READ. FAVORITE LINE; "DON'T CHEAT."

INSERTS AND ORDER BLANKS

7) Store locations.

While catalogs don't need to waste order-blank space with store listings, it doesn't hurt to ink-jet "visit the store nearest you" on a catalog back cover or order blank. Catalogs, after all, can be great traffic-builders.

8) Credit card options.

Order forms should always contain images of accepted credit cards, as well as names.

9) Helpful reminders.

Too often, order forms look about as user-friendly as a paper-airplane kit. It never hurts to say:

*"Please fold and seal"

*"Please tear along dotted line"

*"Have you remembered to...?"

and, of course,

*"THANK YOU for your order!"

10) Merchandise!

Since the order blank is one of the most-visited spots in your catalog, it helps to give customers a reason to go there. Order blanks, and the pages around them, commonly feature best-sellers, or items that have wide appeal to the entire audience (given that every buyer eventually gets to the order form).

Here's where most catalogers put their commodity items. Levenger, for instance, offers books on audio tape. Coach Leatherware features cleaning products. Victoria's Secret sells clearance items. The hope, of course, is that customers about to order might be tempted to add a few impulse items as well.

The options: Special services

Most catalogers these days have ramped up service to the point where *every* competitor needs to play catch-up. That's why the order blank provides great opportunity. If your catalog offers any special services, such as bridal registries or telephone-ordering for the deaf, you should spell it all out (and promote it) here.

The following are ten possible services worth mentioning on your order form:

1) Delivery options.

Most catalogs now offer one- and two-day delivery service (usually via Federal Express or another shipper). The order blank should mention all delivery options, including standard, express, and any additional charges for fast delivery. Personally, I appreciate catalogs that spell out their shipping policies as well. Next-day shipping deserves promotion.

2) Gift wrapping.

Most customers appreciate the ability to send a wrapped gift, and most seem willing to pay for the service. Catalogs like gift cataloger Wireless, for instance, charge $4.95 for a gift box, card and wrapping. The catalog highlights the service not only on the order form, but throughout the book as well.

3) Gift certificates.

Some catalogs offer certificates in set denominations; others in any amount. Those that also offer an elegant envelope or handwritten message ought to say so (prominently) on the order blank.

CREDIT CARD APPLICATIONS, LIKE THIS ONE FROM THE DISNEY CATALOG, ARE SENSIBLE ORDER-FORM FARE.

ABOVE: BEST-SELLERS, LIKE THIS CATSUIT FROM BLOOMINGDALE'S BY MAIL, MAKE GREAT ORDER-FORM MERCHANDISE.

INSET: BLOOMINGDALE'S BY MAIL ORGANIZES ITS SERVICE MESSAGES WITH "B-LINE" HEADLINES.

ROSS-SIMONS' BRIDAL REGISTRY MAKES AN EXCELLENT ORDER-FORM PROMOTION. NOTE THE SPECIAL "1-800-82- BRIDE" REGISTRY NUMBER.

GIFT SUGGESTIONS FROM CALYX & COROLLA CAN WORK WELL IN PROMPTING AN IMPULSE BUY.

BRECK'S USES THE REVERSE OF ITS ORDER FORM TO PLAY UP PROMOTIONS, LIKE CREDIT AND GUARANTEE.

4) Bridal registry.

Here's a terrific service worth promoting for certain gift catalogs. Jewelry cataloger Ross-Simons, for instance, first allows bridal customers to make their registry choices, then mails them cards that they can distribute to friends and relatives. The company also mails catalogs to lists of individuals on request.

5) Mailing-list options.

To discourage grumbling, both from privacy advocates and consumers, all catalogers should provide opt-out forms on the order blank for customers who don't want their names rented. Order blanks should also allow customers to correct their addresses and alert catalogers to duplicate mailings. After all, duplicates both annoy recipients and drain mailing budgets.

6) Special phone services.

Catalogs such as Wireless not only offer order-taking in Spanish, but special order lines for customers who have Telephone Device for the Deaf (TDD). Both services, which require separate toll-free numbers, are sure to engender loyalty among those customers who need them. Any cataloger who offers special order-taking ought to take the opportunity to promote it.

7) Corporate gifts.

Catalogs like Omaha Steaks make a big business from corporate gifts, but not every catalog needs to go to the expense of a dedicated toll-free line and 24-hour service for corporate gift-giving. Mere mention of a corporate gift program, along with a telephone number for more information, can alert interested customers.

8) Technical or advice services.

Floral cataloger Calyx & Corolla makes a "Plant Doctor" available to customers who want to know more about their flowers. Travel book TravelSmith, which supplies numerous tour companies with product, offers free travel outfitting advice ("the right rain gear for Raratonga") over a toll-free line. Any catalog that offers specialized merchandise could well benefit from sharing its expertise with customers.

9) Environmental concerns.

Though the movement waxes and wanes, environmental awareness still drives many buying and business decisions. You'll always earn applause (and, one hopes, loyalty) when you mention use of recycled paper or packing materials, or any other attempt to manufacture or source environmentally friendly product.

10) Information gathering.

The order blank is a good place to solicit names of friends (though yes, a card insert works much better) as well as other survey data, such as interest in new products. (J. Peterman, for instance, recently ran a "shopping spree" contest in which customers were asked to name the "particular thing they really, really want.")

It's always great to ask customers for information, but be warned: First, most customers won't return your order form; and second, those who do might expect you to write back! Make sure you can commit yourself to handling responses.

FINALLY, THE SURROUNDING PAGES

Creating the pages around an insert isn't quite the same as creating a spread. An insert, of course, breaks up two pages, making it impossible to create any across-the-spread presentations. It also makes it tough to present complicated presentations or wordy editorial. The insert, in and of itself, simply creates too much distraction.

So, it's a good idea to use the insert break to create hero pages with key items. Since recipients are bound to come across the image at some point (given that the catalog falls open at the insert), it makes sense to merchandise it with best-sellers or basic items, like T-shirts or towels. Complicated or esoteric product generally belongs on a different spread, where there's ample room to show and explain the goods.

In addition, the pages around the order blank work great for those last-minute commodity items. Typically, those flashlights or mini-thermometer products would not only disappear elsewhere in the book, but also consume valuable real estate. The pages around the order blank are like the store counter by the cash register. They're great for catching shoppers while they're already on the brink of buying.

SELLING PAGES AROUND INSERTS DESERVE BEST-SELLING ITEMS IN ENTICING LAYOUTS, LIKE THIS ONE FROM J. CREW.

NEXT STEP: GETTING IT ORGANIZED

Once you're familiar with dissecting a catalog, you've got to, of course, put it together. A catalog may consist of a series of parts, but it should come across as a seamless, fluid whole. The way to do it is through *organizing and pacing*, the topic of the next chapter.

EXPLICIT SIZING INFORMATION AND
GUARANTEE (NOTE "DOUBLE THE PRICE
DIFFERENCE") ADD CREDIBILITY TO
LEW MAGRAM'S ORDER FORM.

Help! How do I make it all fit? Steps for order-blank design

Between service promotions, product shots, phone numbers and the actual order area itself, most order blanks can look about as jammed as a five o'clock commuter train. Fortunately, good design can keep it in check. In fact, for any good order-blank design, catalogers need to follow one basic rule:

make it easy for the customer to work with.

Here are some guidelines on how to get it done:

1) Understand the format.
Know where the order form binds, where the ink-jetting areas are, what formats are available, and how to expand the order form if necessary. Work with your agency or order-blank supplier for lessons in getting the format right for your catalog.

2) Highlight the order-placing steps.
Use numbers or devices to call attention to all ordering information, and place the steps under a clear "How to Order" headline.

3) Give the customer some room.
Even if they're not sending in the form, customers likely will use it to write down information as they go. Make sure the lines on your order blank correspond to the average number of items per order (resist adding "wishful thinking" lines) and provide enough space for handwriting product names, SKU numbers and prices. You might want to pre-print an order example as a guide.

4) Provide address-correction space.
Leave enough room for "ship to" addresses as well, and ask for day and evening telephone numbers. If you offer gift cards, make sure your order blank carries enough room for a message.

5) Highlight methods of payment.
Credit-card information should be prominent, placed either close to or below the order grid. Provide boxes for writing down credit card numbers. That way, customers won't leave out a digit by mistake.

6) Provide shipping and tax information.
Make sure you've provided space for shipping and tax charges directly beneath the merchandise total. You might want to pre-print an across-the-board shipping charge, such as $4.50 for Federal Express.

7) Try filling it out yourself!
If you or your peers find yourselves stumbling over an order-blank mock-up, take it back to the drawing board. If it's tough for you, imagine the effect on someone who's never ordered from you!

CHAPTER 15

ADDING UP THE ELEMENTS: HOW TO PUT PACING AND ENERGY INTO YOUR BOOK

Every face has two eyes, one nose, one mouth, a chin, jaw and forehead. Yet we all know Harrison Ford is handsome and Lyle Lovett is peculiar-looking. The difference is in the details. It's the spaces and symmetries between the features that make the difference.

So it is with catalogs. Pick up a J. Crew book, and then pick up just about any other apparel catalog aimed at a younger audience. They may both use similar models, similar photography, similar clothing styles. What makes Crew so much punchier, brighter and hipper? It's in the details. Just as the lift of a brow or break of a smile can transform a face, so can the subtleties of lighting, pacing and styling transform a catalog.

In other words, any book can have terrific photography, or superb eye-flow, or dynamic models. But not every book can add everything up to make the whole stronger than the sum of its parts. It takes *pacing* and *energy* to bring about an organized, cohesive, impactful catalog.

In this chapter, I'll show you how to create impact and order using the various design elements of your catalog. No matter what your catalog's "personality," you can use pacing and energy to express its individuality.

GOING WITH THE FLOW

To pace a catalog, you have to organize it. The first step of organizing, though, isn't a matter of design. It's a matter of merchandise. Best-sellers, seasonal items, loss leaders and high-margin product all need to appear in certain sections of the catalog in order to yield the most profit. That's just basic cataloging.

The next step, however, is to create a *flow* through the book. Well-positioned catalogs not only follow a merchandising logic, but a design logic. In particular, they show a consistent *brand identity* spread after spread.

A typical L.L. Bean book, for instance, may carry scores of different merchandise categories, from fire starters to tents to women's sweaters. But each spread carries a distinctive design stamp. The typeface, styling, models and treatment of white space let readers know, page after page, that they're in an L.L. Bean book. Each spread has energy enough to stand on its own and yet still look related to each other.

So the first task in creating this kind of "flow" is to know your brand identity. If you're L.L. Bean, for instance, you build your flow around an active New England lifestyle look. If you're The Sharper Image, you build creative with lots of information and excitement about your executive toys. If you're Pottery Barn, selling merchandise that's easily found in stores, you might need a certain visual drama around your product.

The second task is to examine the parts of the catalog that you need to tie together.

SUMMARIZING THE PARTS

Each section of a catalog, of course, must connect with the other to build up the flow of a book. So it pays to practice "moving" through your book the way a customer would. Here's how it works.

First, the front cover.

As you know, here is your first (and perhaps *only*) opportunity to excite customers about what's inside. First and foremost, the cover not only has to establish the catalog's image, but *drive readers into the book.* Because you want to move customers inside fast, it's more important that your cover be interesting than obvious.

Ask yourself:

—*Is the cover intriguing? Does it offer mystery or surprise?*

—*Does the cover have relevance, emotion, drama?*

—*Does the cover set up realistic expectations about what's inside?*

—*Does the cover give a reason for opening the book?*

Next, the opening spread.

Here's the real litmus test for whether your catalog has flow. The opening spread tells customers whether you've followed up on the promise of your front cover, or whether that cover was an empty tease.

You need to ask yourself:

—*Does the opening spread sustain the drama of the cover?*

—*Does it allow breathing room for key merchandise, the president's letter and other elements?*

— *Does it spell out your catalog's positioning?*

Catalogs with a service orientation, like L.L. Bean, use the opening spread to explain their fast shipping and ironclad guarantees. Catalogs defined by a personality, like Sundance, play up that personality (Robert Redford) on the inside spread. Fashion-forward catalogs often put their newest stuff on this spread, as do hot-product catalogs like The Sharper Image. (Incidentally, catalogs also use the spread to position themselves to prospects. Usually, all it takes is a simple change of black type to create one message for prospects, another for customers.)

Finally, the selling spreads.

Lots of catalogs unfold with about as much gusto as a deck of cards. True, a selling spread doesn't have to have the same impact as an opening spread (after all, we have to sell flashlights and pencil sharpeners as well as His and Hers Hovercrafts), but they should keep customers excited, paging through for more.

So when examining your selling spreads, ask yourself:

—*Can the spread stand on its own as a strong selling vehicle?*

—*Does the spread fit stylistically with the rest of the book?*

—*Does every spread contain feature shots and secondary feature shots?*

—*Do the spreads look consistent, or merely boring? Do they look exciting and different, or merely confused?*

—*Does each spread speak to the catalog's brand identity?*

Every spread should not only be able to stand on its own, but should fit within the context of the book. The pages that come before and after each spread should make sense, both creatively and in terms of merchandising and design.

That's not easy to pull off. Take J. Crew, which alternates lifestyle shots with studio shots; laydowns with product silhouettes. For most catalogs, that melange of styles would create a stylistic mess. But Crew links everything subtly so each spread fits with the next. The sherbert colors in a laydown spread of polo shirts, for instance, echo in the cool blues of a sky in a lifestyle spread, which replays in the distressed white wall background of a softly lit studio spread.

CLOSE-UP SHOTS, ORGANIZED ON A STRONG COLOR SCHEME, PUT ENERGY INTO THESE CLIFFORD & WILLS SPREADS. NOTE THE RHYTHM CREATED BY VARIED POSES AND CLOTHING LAYDOWNS.

Most catalogers, although there are some exceptions, create this kind of flow by paginating their books *before* taking photographs. Paginating ahead of time allows them to plan backgrounds, models and proposed layouts in a way that not only reflects their positioning, but creates excitement and coordinates the spreads.

You can use paginating to space certain models evenly throughout the book, or clump certain backgrounds together in a kind of narrative. You can softly lead your customer from casual wear to career wear without a major change in mood. In short, you can turn each spread toward a coherent whole, much in the way a fashion designer can turn a single "look" into a clothing line.

ELEMENTS OF GOOD PACING

As if you couldn't tell, I'm a little biased toward J. Crew when it comes to pacing. Crew mixes up every design element, but its tone is consistent and unmistakable. Full-bleed lifestyle shots are accompanied by insets of laydown clothes; huge silhouetted laydowns are accompanied by insets of lifestyle shots. You see clothes on hangers, on mannequins, in stacks, or thrown over faded barn doors. You see models from behind, models in a blur, models covered with sand.

SELLING SPREADS SHOULD BE ORGANIZED AROUND IMPORTANT ITEMS, AS IN THIS SPREAD FROM CLIFFORD & WILLS.

What makes it all work is that, although each page may be a stylistic surprise, it always bears the Crew signature. When you see a woman wearing wool socks with her sexy underwear, you know you're looking at Crew, not Victoria's Secret. When you see socks rolled up and stacked together in a full-bleed page, you know it's Crew, not Eddie Bauer.

That's the secret of good pacing: *Keep the catalog's identity, while pushing its boundaries.*

It's tough, at times, to pinpoint the elements that make all this happen. But for energetic pacing, you need five ingredients:

1) Consistency
2) Composition
3) Styling
4) Design elements
5) Eyeflow

Let's look at each one in turn.

PACING ELEMENT #1: Consistency

Consistency fosters interest. Though it may sound contradictory, it's not.

Here's what I mean. Picture Jackie Onassis for a minute. She consistently wore the same hairstyles, the same big glasses, the same types of uncomplicated clothing. So why is it the paparazzi always followed her around and everyone wanted to know what she was wearing? Because she had established a *style* by virtue of her consistency. She knew who she was, and her elegant identity transformed whatever she wore into yet another expression of her unique personality. That consistency is far more interesting than the fashion trend of the moment or weekly hairdo makeovers.

So in catalogs, consistency doesn't mean sticking to one type of presentation, or one type of location shot. What it does mean is coordinating the elements that speak for your catalog's personality, that lend *cohesiveness* to whatever variety of presentations you choose.

Consider the following elements as tools for consistency:

Typeface. A signature type font, used headline to headline, ensures a familiar look throughout the book.

Models. Customers appreciate familiar faces. You don't need to use the same models, but the same *types* of models create consistency.

Photography. Nothing looks worse than seeing pickup photography mixed with studio and location shots. Photographs should coordinate in style and lighting for consistency.

Color. Hold Everything's gently lit backgrounds of slate, beige and ivory not only create drama for those closet coordinators and laundry bags, but also keep viewers looking at very dense pages without getting lost.

The point is, catalogers can pick any number of "signature" elements to tie pages together. To make pages interesting, a catalog's personality must be interesting—and it must be expressed through consistent design.

PACING ELEMENT #2: Composition

I'd always heard that the secret to great-looking bouquets is to arrange large blooms first, then smaller ones. It's the same with catalogs. The two largest and most critical parts of a catalog—copy and photography—must complement each other if the whole book is to going to sell.

To get the most energy from your compositions, you need two strategies:

1) *Mixing up your layouts*

2) *Innovating with product shots*

There's a lot involved in each technique. Here's how they work:

Mixing it up

Most catalogs put together copy and pictures in one of three ways: *cut and copy, columns* or a *combination* of both.

Hard-goods catalogs, such as Lillian Vernon and The Sharper Image, often prefer a *cut-and-copy* approach. Here, you simply rag copy around silhouetted or boxed product photographs. These cut-and-copy pages are simple to key, easy to read, and help the customer shop the catalog. Although they can look a little choppy, it's easy to break up the layout by using, say, a color-tinted box, or by varying the sizes of the photographs.

Columns, on the other hand, work if your catalog needs a higher level of organization or when spreads tell a story, as opposed to being item driven. Generally, column pages are less dense and more dramatic than cut-and-copy. You'll notice, for instance, that most hero pages are organized in columns, as are many spreads in fashion books, or in thinly merchandised catalogs, like J. Peterman's.

Combination layouts create the most energetic pacing. You see this in catalogs that use lots of copy, or many large and small pictures, like Lands' End. Some pages will appear dense, others light; some full of copy; others consumed by a single showstopping image. Mixing up layouts creates vitality.

While you must, of course, choose the layout design that makes sense for your merchandise (not to mention profits per square inch), you'll always benefit by combining layouts. You need to give customers something that keeps their eyes moving from page to page.

Innovating with product shots

As a cataloger, you never have to settle for the same kind of photo, again and again and again. Consider some of the following methods for varying your product shots:

Silhouettes: These photographs help break up pages. They add energy through their irregular outlines, make excellent feature shots, and create more white space. In catalogs like The Voyager Collection, a travelgoods book, mixing silhouettes with background shots keeps the book from looking staid, square and cheap.

LANDS' END ORGANIZES LOTS OF LITTLE PRODUCTS WITH A CLEAN, VERTICAL GRID.

CUT-AND-COPY LAYOUTS DON'T HAVE TO BE CUT-AND-DRY. THIS PAGE FROM THE VOYAGER'S COLLECTION KEEPS THE EYE MOVING BY FEATURING A STRONG SELLING IMAGE.

A SCREENED-BACK IMAGE LENDS A UNIFYING TOUCH TO A SPREAD OF SILHOUETTED PRODUCT IN THE DISCOVERY CATALOG.

MORE FUN STUFF FROM J. CREW. NOTE HOW CROPPING GIVES THIS SHOT FRESHNESS AND ATTITUDE.

USING REAL FOOD (IN THE REAL OUTDOORS) MAKES THE DIFFERENCE IN PROPPING THESE PICNIC ITEMS. A STUDIO SHOT WOULD HAVE DULLED THE SELLING IMPACT.

Vignettes. These photographs with blurred-out edges soften the hard outline of square, backgrounded shots. In that way, vignettes add interest to the page without sacrificing background. You can show product in context without allowing the context to take over the page.

Screened-back backgrounds can do the same thing. To juice up a product shot of tin soldiers, for instance, gift catalog Discovery added a screened-back photograph of a Civil War scene to the background. The backdrop enhanced the product without drawing attention to itself.

Angles and cropping. Photos taken from unusual angles, or cropped in unexpected ways, add energy to a catalog's pacing. In J. Crew, for instance, you'll see photos of models shot from above as they walk on the beach. Or you'll see layouts of models standing boldly on the page with the top of their heads cropped off.

Believe me, customers don't notice the details of what's going on; they don't "see" that one model is cut off from the forehead, or another from the knees. But the effect is unmistakable. Customers are immediately drawn to any image that looks a little "off"—and while I can't advocate that every catalog try shooting models from stairsteps or helicopters, I can say that any unusual product shot sparks up a page, and adds to a catalog's pacing.

PACING ELEMENT #3: Styling

For many catalogs, a good stylist is worth his or her weight in gold—or at least in order forms!

Take Harry and David. Here's a catalog that's 100% styling. After all, the catalog sells apples, pears and cakes, not sable coats or five-function alarm clocks. Since there's not much you can say about pears, nor much that keeps prospects from walking to the supermarket for them (and for a lot less money), the catalog must keep recipients hooked to the page in order to make the sale. The way it's done is through *styling.*

For good styling, keep these tips in mind:

Tip No. 1: *Don't skimp on the props.*

There's nothing that ruins a product shot faster than cheap propping. By this I mean plastic holly and fake snow, ugly wallpaper or plywood disguised as a dining-room table. If you don't think customers will "notice," the fact is, cheap props come through and affect customer perception.

Careful propping enhances product the way fine china enhances a meal. Customers may not "see" that gorgeous distressed wainscoting in a background, or "notice" that a fire in a fireplace is real. But believe me, a real fire and real stone hearth look a whole lot more appetizing in the background than a doily and a sheet of red satin. Creating a mood through great propping not only helps pace a catalog but contributes to a customer's willingness to keep "consuming."

Tip No. 2: *Be sensitive to lighting.*

Often, lighting goes hand-in-hand with propping to create the selling mood. Take a gently lit Pottery Barn display of glowing candles, for instance, surrounded by twining plaid ribbon on an antique wooden table. Maybe that warm golden lighting obscures the precise details of the candle for sale, but that gentle warmth probably sells a lot more candles than a cold, flatly lit display.

Lighting is especially critical for hard-goods catalogs. After all, linens, serving bowls, teakettles and lawn furniture are pretty much available everywhere at retail. To create the drama needed to sell them by mail, lighting usually has to do the trick. Particularly with hard goods, there's nothing more disappointing than flat, dull lighting that makes objects look as undistinguished as utensils in a drawer.

Moreover, lighting can give a catalog a signature look. Crate & Barrel, for instance, gives its spreads romantic energy with its warm lighting style. Upscale gift book Scully & Scully relies on exquisitely sharp lighting to make its objects look like museum pieces. J. Crew is often known for its tropical sun lighting in its summer books, and its overcast warmth in the fall. At times, it seems lighting can define a catalog's personality almost as well as the merchandise itself.

Tip No. 3: *Add life to your lifestyle book.*

Granted, you don't need a lot of lifestyle in most hard-goods catalogs. Customers, after all, buy crystal bowls and file cabinets based on features, practicality or aesthetic pleasure, not because they want to feel like the model in the picture.

But apparel catalogs are another story. Clothing customers need to identify in some way with the person or situation in which they see the model. Besides, models and locations can pump energy into almost any catalog—*provided they're used appropriately.*

Let's face it: People *are* dramatic. They think, they move, they emote, they react to their surroundings. Most catalogs seem to forget that, and shoot models as if they were mannequins, intent on capturing every product detail. In my opinion, it's better to push the envelope. When a catalog shoots a model in dreadlocks, for instance (as Crew has), that's sure to get people to look. And who says a model has to face forward to show off clothes? People don't always face forward in real life, and they don't in J. Crew catalogs, L.L. Bean or other lifestyle books either.

The point is, lifestyle catalogs can challenge themselves to get customers to stop and look. Don't get me wrong: It's important to take good product shots. But a catalog that radiates *energy* from a model, or from an atmospheric image (such as Garnet Hill or Smith & Hawken) can produce a lot more attention than one that has every stitch in place.

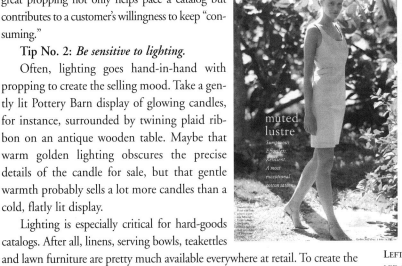

LEFT: J. CREW'S DRESS SPARKLES IN THIS SPECKLED DAYLIGHT.

RIGHT: CANDLELIGHT CREATES WARMTH IN A HOLIDAY LAYOUT FROM PLOW & HEARTH.

ABOVE: SHOW MODELS FROM BEHIND? J. CREW PROVES THAT SUCH A SHOT CAN WORK AS WELL AS ANY FORWARD-FACING POSE—MAYBE BETTER.

INSET: DREADLOCKS ADD IMPACT ON A J. CREW PAGE. THE HAIR CATCHES THE CUSTOMER'S EYE; THE SWEATER HOLDS IT THERE.

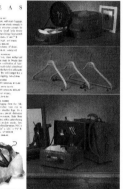

AS FAR AS LAYDOWNS GO, NOBODY DOES IT BETTER THAN J. CREW. NOTE THE APPETIZING TEXTURES AND COLORS IN THIS DARING CLOSE-UP.

HOLD EVERYTHING HOLDS EVERYTHING TOGETHER IN ITS QUIET LAYOUTS THROUGH LIGHTING AND COLOR.

L.L. BEAN VARIES ITS FAMILIAR SERIF TYPEFACE JUST ENOUGH TO CREATE INTEREST AND CONSISTENCY.

Tip No. 4: *Innovate with laydowns.*

Most catalogs aren't too imaginative when it comes to showing the six different colors of a T-shirt, or four different jeans styles, or three types of dinner plates. The usual *modus operandi* is to line everything up tin-soldier style and shoot it.

Fortunately, a little energy can make a big difference in shooting laydowns. So we'll turn again to the pacing champion, J. Crew, to point out how it's possible to use, yes, wit in clothing props, as Crew does when it shoots six polo shirts marching across a spread, looking as bright as the flag of a tropical island. Or the way it shoots underwear poking out of the top of waistbands in a jeans laydown. Or the way it invented Matisse-like cutouts for bathing-suit displays. These layouts all showed clothes in ways we hadn't seen before.

Laydowns don't have to be business as usual, the meat and potatoes of the page. In some books, like L.L. Bean, the laydowns are sometimes bigger than the lifestyle shots, bleeding across the page. A little daring and experimentation can turn a visual eyebath into a splash in the face.

PACING ELEMENT #4:
Use of Design Elements

In pacing a catalog, little things mean a lot. Type, borders, illustrative devices and other smaller elements on the page can either tie up the whole or confuse it, depending on how well they're used. Here's what to consider:

1) Color

I've already mentioned how Hold Everything and J. Crew tie their spreads together with *color*. Pick up either catalog, and right away you're hit with a color sense. Hold Everything is saturated with rich tones of earth and steel; J. Crew often pulls colors from skies and forests.

Not every catalog can afford that kind of luxurious production, but it sure helps to keep color in mind when pacing and organizing a book. Color can even become trademark. National Geographic, for instance, is defined by earth tones, as well as (of course) by its bright yellow border. The Discovery Catalog uses primary colors to reflect brand and hold its diverse product spreads together.

2) Type

In the same way, *type* can sew up a catalog's imagery, while also contributing to its diversity. A single distinctive typeface (probably L.L. Bean's serif is best known) can unify a catalog from spread to spread. No matter what the product or product category, a familiar typeface tells customers that they're in the right book and in the right place.

At the same time, though, it's good to sprinkle in opportunities to make type fun and energetic. Discovery, for instance, plays on a variety of typefaces in creating little editorial "asides" for its product. Early Winters adds "handwritten" callouts and illustrations to raise the comfort level in its ultra-organized layouts. Some kids' products catalogs add crayon letters to toy sections. And many catalogs add energy just by changing the color of their type. By switching from its usual black headline type to green, for instance, a Levenger catalog added attention to a spread of new products at the front of its book.

Type variety keeps catalogs from getting too staid and serious about themselves—and that translates into more comfortable customers. Experimentation never hurts.

3) Non-selling messages

When Warner Brothers first opened its retail stores, it aimed for entertaining as much as selling. When I first visited the store on 57th Street in New York, for instance, throngs of people packed inside as if to see a show—which they got, given the giant Bugs Bunny statues, Elmer Fudd displays and Roadrunner cartoons. Many people came in just to look—but did they end up buying? You bet!

Granted, catalogs can't afford to give up much space to cartoons and other trivia, but non-selling messages sure can add energy. Reader's Digest's HOME catalog, for instance, contains hints for working with tiles (taken from the Reader's Digest *Book of Skills and Tools*), for hanging curtains and training dogs. There's even a quote from an 1888 *Good Housekeeping*! The messages, of course, reinforce the company's positioning as the friendly, helpful home authority. More critically, they tie into the product line and give readers an opportunity to spend more time on the page.

NON-SELLING COPY, SET OFF WITH UNUSUAL TYPE, NOT ONLY HOLDS THE CUSTOMER'S EYE, BUT BUILDS CREDIBILITY FOR THE CATALOG BRAND.

It's the same with The Discovery Catalog. Every spread tells a brief story about ancient Egyptian royalty, or the history of flight, or any other encyclopedic bit that relates to the catalog's videos and products. Since The Discovery Catalog (like The Discovery Channel) positions itself as a compendium of fascinating information, it's crucial the catalog back up that positioning with related messages. It's also crucial that the catalog use those messages to pace the book and tie together product spreads. Otherwise, the catalog would seem like a jumble of unrelated product.

Catalogs, of course, shouldn't turn into magazines (after all, we're in business to make money), but they should feel free to add bits of history and knowledge. Like feature shots and hero pages, non-selling messages pace the catalog, invite customers to linger and help establish the catalog as an authority.

4) Borders and heads

As with the table of contents, there's some debate over borders and heads. Many catalogers don't believe in sectionalizing a book with borders, spread headlines and other visual markers. They prefer for customers to leaf through the book to find what they like. Others believe it's critical to let customers know where they are when they're shopping.

However, the larger the book, and the more diverse the merchandise, the more it makes sense to break it into sections. If you sell men's and women's clothing, camping gear and home-office supplies, you do the customer a favor by making it organized.

In addition, borders and heads can create a kind of visual energy in pacing the catalog. For one thing, borders keep spreads from looking disjointed or unfocused. They create little boutiques or departments within the catalog, making it easier for customers to shop.

Borders also draw the eye into a selling message, or prompt customers to look for things on the page that they might not have known they needed. For instance, a spread of exercise gizmos might not rate more than a passing glance. But that same spread, marked "Back and Neck Care" (as in the Self Care catalog) might well prompt second looks. Customers now know that these products can help solve a specific problem.

Not all borders, however, are created equal. Some disappear. Some just make the page look closed-in and boxy. A good border should act like a good picture frame: It should enhance the page without attracting unwanted notice.

I like, for instance, Early Winters' section borders, which are thick vertical stripes on the left side of the page, flanking a feature shot, and given simple text, like "Sun & Sea" and "Mountains." Reader's Digest uses small illustrations at the upper right corner of its borders to show readers the category of merchandise. Self Care uses unobtrusive blue bars to call attention to its various lines of "caring" merchandise.

Borders and headlines work as long as they contribute to the pacing and energy of a book. Like good salespeople, they should help readers out without slowing them down.

PACING ELEMENT #5: Eyeflow

We all know that it's not wise to throw lots of products on a page without some kind of eyeflow. Unrelated products, uncoordinated colors or ragged composition creates visual gridlock. The eye doesn't know where to go, so it goes nowhere.

So bear in mind that the best designed pages always have a starting point, and flow in a clockwise position. Your focal point can start anywhere on the spread—the upper-left corner, the upper right corner, the center and so on—but you need a nice circular flow to the design once the eye gets started. You don't want a feature shot on the right side of the page and another equally large in the center. You don't want to yank the eye from side to side, but rather keep it moving (and keep it resting) where your customer will be most excited.

Keep in mind, too, that hard goods usually lend themselves to a different kind of eyeflow than apparel. Apparel lends itself to vertical images,

MIXING SILHOUETTES WITH BACKGROUND-ED SHOTS CREATES PLEASING EYEFLOW IN THIS PAGE FROM THE TERRITORY AHEAD.

which creates top-to-bottom, or across-the-page eyeflow. Hard goods, on the other hand, can be better coordinated for a circular flow.

Moreover, it's not just the product shots that lend themselves to eyeflow. Typefaces, borders, illustrations, callouts, model gestures, headlines, color, secondary shots—just about every design element plays a role in the eye's movement on the page.

PUTTING IT TOGETHER

Obviously, there's a lot to consider when establishing the flow of your catalog. So I'll make it simple for you: *Just remember your brand identity.*

After all, the pacing of your catalog is really determined by your personality and positioning. If you want customers to think of you as fun, you'll probably want varied typefaces, funky product shot angles, bright colors and lots of visual devices. If you want customers to know you as hard-working, you'll probably need to increase the layout density, use functional, easy-to-read type, clear product shots, and lots of callouts.

Upscale catalogs, like Levenger, employ borders made from photographs of textured paper to slow down the pacing and convey the richness of the product line. Catalogs like home supplier Better Living prefer to show more copy and fewer visuals to bring out the workmanlike quality of their merchandise. And catalogs such as The Pleasant Company are paced as carefully as storybooks, letting little readers (and their parents) savor the wonderfully warm imagery of their dolls and accessories.

A catalog's pacing is as individual as its merchandise. And like a catalog's merchandise, it should be unique, distinctive and a plus to the bottom line.

HE ART OF STRATEGIC THINKING

LANDS' END VALUE POSITIONING EMERGES IN ITS PROMINENT USE OF CLOSE-UP SHOTS, CALL-OUTS, PROMINENT LABEL AND HISTORIC PRODUCT REFERENCES ("1994—ADDED THINSULATE TO SLEEVES; WARMS ARMS TWICE AS WELL").

HOLY PRICE POINTS! MACWAREHOUSE CLEARLY TAKES A PRICE POSITION, AS SEEN THROUGH ITS 40 COVER EXCLAMATION POINTS (MORE OR LESS) AND ITS LIBERAL USE OF THE TERMS "SLASH," "FREE" AND "AS LOW AS."

BY INVENTING ITS OWN CATALOG "BRAND," THE TJX CORPORATION DISTANCED CHADWICK'S FROM THE BRAND IMAGERY OF ITS RETAIL CHAINS, HIT OR MISS AND T.J. MAXX.

MORE THAN MOST CATALOGERS, THE DISNEY CATALOG HAS THE WHEREWITHALL TO CAPITALIZE ON BRAND.

RUE DE FRANCE CAPITALIZES ON A QUALITY POSITIONG THROUGH EVERY DETAIL OF ITS CATA-LOG, FROM THE EXQUISITE COVER IMAGE TO THE LUXURIOUS PHOTOGRAPHY AND PROPPING THROUGHOUT.

POSITIONING ITSELF ON SERVICE, VIKING CATALOG OFFERS NO LESS THAN FIVE SERVICE PROMOTIONS ON ITS COVER (NOTICE "1-800-SNAPFAX" FOR FAX ORDERS).

chapter six

TACTICAL WARFARE

VICTORIA'S SECRET
HYPES UP ITS GLAMOUR
THROUGH THE USE OF
SUPERMODELS.

EXTREME CLOSEUPS,
PARTICULARLY WITH
UNUSUAL CROPPING,
NOT ONLY STRESS
"QUALITY," BUT PROVIDE
GREAT STOPPING POINTS
IN THE CATALOG.

Lands' End and Coming Home offer different products. But both offer above-and-beyond services.

We're glad you've been a satisfied Lands' End customer for a good while. Perhaps one reason you keep dialing Dodgeville is that you appreciate Lands' End services like helpful, knowledgeable phone operators, speedy monogramming and shipping, and unusual conveniences like the temporarily tested 1-800-SHOEHORN hotline to make returning shoes easier.

If so, you should know that Coming Home, the bed-and-bath division of Lands' End, also makes shopping more enjoyable.

Selling vs. serving.
When Coming Home phone operators ask, "May I help you?" they really mean a lot more than "What can I sell you?" For starters, they know all the fine points of our goods because they've been instructed by our product managers, those globe-trotting home-textile experts. So the phone operators can answer any questions that may not be covered in our catalog copy.

The operators are also very happy to provide a number of services that'll make shopping for your home smooth home sweeter.

Free swatches.
Yes, you can send us swatches of your wallpaper or furniture fabric, like the one on our cover, so we can suggest coordinating

bedding or towels. But swatching is a two-way street here if you want a closer look at most any fabric in the catalog, just call us and we'll send out a free swatch, presto.

Monogramming.
It's a nice personal touch. And with their color boards always sure at hand, our operators can help you select the color of monogramming that will go perfectly with whatever you order, from a Claret Supima towel to a Sea Green napkin. (Remember: our speedy monogramming adds only a day or two to shipping time.)

New! Monogrammed sheets.
It's a red-letter day for the bedroom. Or any other color letters you like. Because now we'll monogram some of our solid-colored sheets, too, and ship them fast, all for a very reasonable cost. And fear not: we place your initials just as Emily Post says one should. See sheet pages for details.

New! Window experts.
Don't let all-thumbs-itis stop you from ordering curtains, shades or blinds. Just ask one of our new window experts to walk you through the job. You can call them from 8:00 AM to 6:00 PM, Monday through Saturday, at 1-800-708-4545.

Specialty Shoppers.
If you have a question that stumps our knowledgeable operators, they have a backup: our Specialty Shoppers. They're a wealth of technical and practical information, and are the ones who will suggest coordinating colors and send you product swatches when you send us samples of your wallpaper, carpeting or furniture.

Discontinued alert.
Far be it from us to mess up your decorating scheme by just dropping a pattern or color out of the blue. We give you fair warning with a special discontinued section in the catalog. And sometimes we even give you a break on the price.

Customer service chronicled.
Throughout this catalog, you'll meet several of our operators and read about some special ways they have served customers. We present them not to brag–they're the modest sort and had to be nudged in front of the camera–but to let you know what they can do for you.

So give our operators a jingle soon. You'll find that though we have a different 800 number than Lands' End, on the other end of our line you'll still find people who think providing extraordinary service is nothing unusual. Just part of their job.

© Copyright 2001 Lands' End, Inc. All rights reserved.
Prices guaranteed through July 31, 1996, unless otherwise indicated.
Cover contains a minimum of 10% post-consumer fiber.

Wallpaper from:
In Our Sanderson and Sons,
285 Grand Ave,
Englewood, NJ 07901.

TO STRESS ITS SERVICE
POSITIONING, LANDS'
END'S COMING HOME
USES A FULL PAGE TO
INTRODUCE ITS OPERA-
TORS AND SPECIALTY
SHOPPERS.

CALLOUTS, SUCH AS
THESE IN LANDS' END,
ARE AN EFFECTIVE TAC-
TIC FOR SPELLING OUT
QUALITY AND VALUE.

INFORMATIONAL TEXT
IS A FIRST-RATE TACTIC
FOR PROMOTING SER-
VICE AND QUALITY. IN
LANDS' END, THIS
QUESTION-AND-ANSWER
COPY ASSURES ANY SIZE
CUSTOMER THAT SHE
CAN FIND THE RIGHT
SUIT, WITH CONFI-
DENCE OF A GOOD FIT.

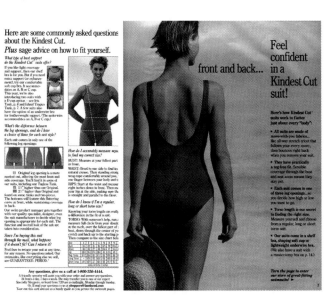

SWEEPSTAKES, LIKE THIS BIG DOG VACATION GIVEAWAY, BUILD RESPONSE RATES WHILE PROMOTING THE CATALOG'S FLAGSHIP LOCATION.

DEFERRED BILLING CAN BE A TERRIFIC TACTIC FOR RESPONSE-BUILDING, PARTICULARLY IN OFF-SEASON BOOKS.

FREE SHIPPING CAN PROVE A GOOD RESPONSE-BUILDER FOR CATALOGS THAT AREN'T POSITIONED ON PRICE, SUCH AS JOS. A. BANK.

ANOTHER RESPONSE-BUILDER: PRE-APPROVED CREDIT AND DEFERRED BILLING.

VICTORIA'S SECRET USES A TRIPLE WHAMMY FOR BUILDING RESPONSE FROM INACTIVE CUSTOMERS: $25 OFF, DEFERRED PAYMENT AND SALE OFFERS.

chapter eleven

SECRET OF MARKETING-BASED CREATIVE

EDITORIAL COPY ON CITRUS LENDS RELEVANCE TO WILLIAMS-SONOMA'S SELLING PAGES OF COOKING PRODUCTS.

ONLY PATAGONIA WOULD SHOW A BAT-WINGED SKIER TO COMMUNICATE THE AUTHENTICITY OF ITS OUTDOORS APPAREL.

"REAL" MODELS, SNAPPY HEADLINES, CHATTY COPY AND GREAT PRODUCT SHOTS MAKE LANDS' END A MASTER OF COMMUNICATION.

They dry faster than you can say, "Supplex Nylon Sport Shorts."

DENSE PAGES CAN STILL COMMUNICATE, THANKS TO LILLIAN VERNON'S ORDERLY PRESENTATION.

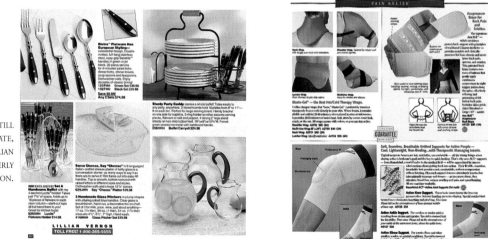

CALL-OUTS, DIAGRAMS AND SIMPLE ILLUSTRATIONS—NOT TO MENTION CLEAR HEADLINES AND BANNERS—ENHANCE SELF-CARE?'S ABILITY TO COMMUNICATE TO ITS CUSTOMERS.

ETTING THE FRONT COVER RIGHT

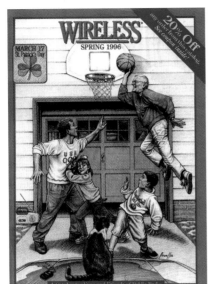

HUMOR, WARMTH, FAMILY *AND* PRODUCT PROMOTION....WIRELES S EFFORTLESSLY PACKS IT ALL INTO ONE COMPELLING COVER.

COVER WRAPS, LIKE THIS ONE ON J. CREW, ENABLE A REAL FOCUS ON THE COVER.

LEAVE IT TO LANDS' END TO "SEW" ITS PROMOTIONAL MES- SAGE ONTO ITS COVER SHOT OF A BATHROBE.

BLACK TYPE, USED EITHER IN BOXES OR STRAIGHT ON THE COVER DESIGN, ENABLES EASY-TO-SEE, EASY-TO-CHANGE PRO- MOTIONAL MESSAGES.

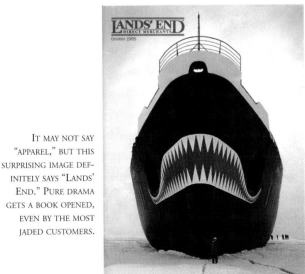

IT MAY NOT SAY "APPAREL," BUT THIS SURPRISING IMAGE DEF- INITELY SAYS "LANDS' END." PURE DRAMA GETS A BOOK OPENED, EVEN BY THE MOST JADED CUSTOMERS.

"REAL" FAMILY IMAGERY HAS THE POTENTIAL TO GENERATE AN EMOTIONAL RESPONSE.

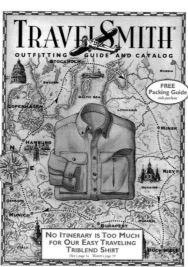

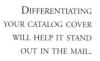

DIFFERENTIATING YOUR CATALOG COVER WILL HELP IT STAND OUT IN THE MAIL.

ANIMALS, ESPECIALLY PUPPIES AND KITTENS, ALWAYS TUG AT THE HEARTSTRINGS.

LOVE THIS COVER! THE SOLUTION-ORIENTED CATALOG CREATES A MESSAGE OF PERFECT RELEVANCE FOR BUSY, STRESSED-OUT CUSTOMERS.

FORMAT MAKES A DIFFERENCE! AN ALTERNATE SIZE OR PAPER WILL HELP YOUR CATALOG GET NOTICED.

SHOWING YOUR CUSTOMER A SCENE THEY CAN RELATE TO DEMONSTRATES THAT YOU UNDERSTAND HOW THEY LIVE.

Stanley Marcus: *On the subject of quality.*

> "Experienced merchants turn a garment or a handbag inside out to judge quality of the internal construction."

AN OPENING SPREAD FEATURING STANLEY MARCUS CREATES A QUALITY THEME FOR THIS LANDS' END CATALOG.

Fully Lined, Solid 100% Merino Wool Blazer Is the Best Buy of the ...

Buy 2, Save $20, just $... each

Buy 3, Save $45, just **$44** each

BRIGHT PRODUCT LAYDOWNS AND AN ENTHUSIASTIC SMILE ADD PUNCH TO THIS SELLING SPREAD FOR CHADWICKS OF BOSTON.

A SELECTION OF NEW PRODUCTS, COMBINED WITH A SERVICE-ORIENTED PRESIDENT'S LETTER, SPEAKS TO VETERAN LEVENGER SHOPPERS AS WELL AS NEWCOMERS.

THE INSIDE-OUT OF YOUR CATALOG

THE TERRITORY
AHEAD CREATES
CRISP, BEAUTIFULLY
ORGANIZED SELLING
SPREADS BY MIXING
SILHOUETTES AND
BACKGROUNDED
PRODUCT SHOTS.

21

LANDS' END'S
OPENING SPREAD PACKS NEW
PRODUCTS, PRESIDENT'S LET-
TER AND A TABLE OF
CONTENTS INTO ONE USER-
FRIENDLY DESIGN.

LIFE-SIZE, NATURALLY
LIT DOLLS MAKE
ARRESTING HERO
SPREADS FOR
PLEASANT COMPANY,
PARTICULARLY WITHIN
THE CATALOG'S OVER-
SIZE FORMAT.

LANDS' END'S HERO PAGES TELL
THE STORY OF A PRODUCT IN
WORDS AND IMAGERY.

INSTEAD OF MERELY
THROWING OVERSTOCK
MERCHANDISE ON A
PAGE, WIRELESS LAYS
OUT ITS ORDER-FORM
SALE ITEMS UNDER THE
"OUTLET" BANNER.

LANDS' END'S BIND-INS DON'T
WASTE SPACE: CATALOG PROMOTION
ON ONE SIDE, SERVICE PROMOTION
ON THE OTHER.

THE TERRITORY
AHEAD'S SALE
INSERT PROMOTES "
PRICE WITHOUT
SCREAMING "SALE."

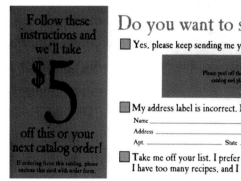

TERRIFIC MAIL-IN CARD GIVES PROSPECTS AN INCENTIVE ($5 OFF ORDER) TO KEEP GETTING
THE BLACK DOG CATALOG.

BIG DOG'S INSERT FEATURES A FALL PREVIEW OF
PRODUCTS, ACTING AS A CATALOG WITHIN A CATALOG.

ADDING UP THE ELEMENTS:
HOW TO PUT PACING AND ENERGY INTO YOUR BOOK

AS FAR AS LAYDOWNS
GO, NOBODY DOES IT
BETTER THAN J.
CREW. NOTE THE
APPETIZING TEXTURES
AND COLORS IN THIS
DARING CLOSE-UP.

INTERESTING LAYDOWNS SURROUNDI
A DRAMATICALLY CROPPED SHOT OF THE ULTIMATE SUND
MORNING CREATES FRESHNESS AND RELEVANC

ONE GREAT CROPPED
SHOT CAN GO "BOING"
IN THE CUSTOMER'S EYE.

ADDING UP THE ELEMENTS:
HOW TO PUT PACING AND ENERGY INTO YOUR BOOK

L.L. BEAN'S LIFESTYLE
IMAGERY PLAYS UP THE
FAMILIAL WARMTH OF
NEW ENGLAND. NOTE
THE USE OF "SNAPSHOTS"
TO CONVEY EMOTION.

A SCREENED IMAGE LENDS
A UNIFYING TOUCH TO A
SPREAD OF SILHOUETTED
PRODUCT IN THE
DISCOVERY CATALOG.

NON-SELLING COPY,
SET OFF WITH UNUSUAL
TYPE, NOT ONLY
HOLDS THE CUSTOMER'S
EYE, BUT BUILDS
CREDIBILITY FOR THE
CATALOG BRAND.

ADDING UP THE ELEMENTS:
HOW TO PUT PACING AND ENERGY INTO YOUR BOOK

CUT-AND-COPY LAYOUTS
DON'T HAVE TO BE
CUT-AND-DRIED. THESE
PAGES FROM VOYAGER
COLLECTION KEEPS THE
EYE MOVING BY
FEATURING A STRONG
SELLING IMAGE.

CRATE & BARREL'S
STRONG GRID LAYOUTS
ARE SOFTENED
BY THE WARMTH OF
COLOR AND LIGHTING.

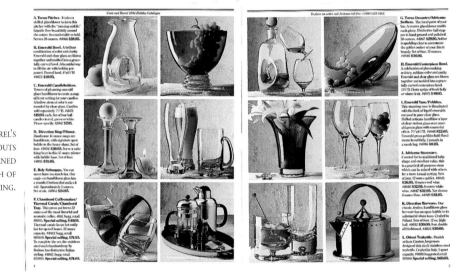

LANDS' END
ORGANIZES LOTS
OF LITTLE PRODUCTS
WITH A CLEAN,
VERTICAL GRID.

HE SUPPORTING ROLE OF GOOD DESIGN

PROMOTIONAL TYPE DOESN'T
HAVE TO SCREAM TO MAKE ITS
POINT. A PROMINENT "$30"
TELLS THE SAVINGS STORY WITH-
OUT DISTRACTING FROM THE
IMPORTANT PRODUCT SHOT.

TYPE CAN OFTEN TELL THE STORY
IN PICTURES AS WELL AS WORDS,
AS THIS "HANDSEWN" TYPE FROM
LANDS' END SHOWS.

TESTIMONIALS, ESPECIALLY WHEN
COMBINED WITH GREAT PHOTOS,
MAKE TERRIFIC SALES BOOSTERS
ON THE PAGE.

TRAVELSMITH IS A GREAT CASE STUDY
IN IMPORTANT DEVICES. ON ONE
SPREAD, NOTE EASY-TO-READ CALL-
OUTS, DIAGRAMS, DEVICES THAT INDI-
CATE WRINKLE RESISTANCE OR
ADVENTURE GEAR, TRAVEL TIPS AND
EVEN A DEMONSTRATION OF FABRIC-
STRETCHING AND WRINKLING.

THE SUPPORTING ROLE OF GOOD DESIGN

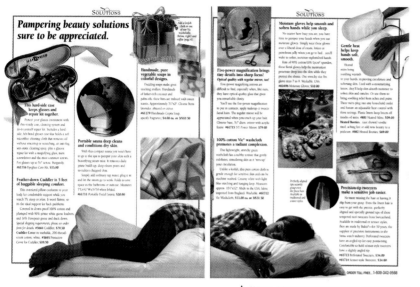

A CLEAN COLUMN DESIGN HELPS ORGANIZE MYRIAD PRODUCTS IN A USER-FRIENDLY FORMAT. A HORIZONTAL FIGURE ON THE BOTTOM CREATES IMPACT AND PULLS THE SPREAD TOGETHER.

USING A COMPANY'S LOGO THROUGHOUT A CATALOG CAN HELP BUILD BRAND; HERE CLIFFORD AND WILLS (CW) "OWNS" WOOL CORD.

New Squall Jacket now fights wind and wet 10 times better than before, for only $75.

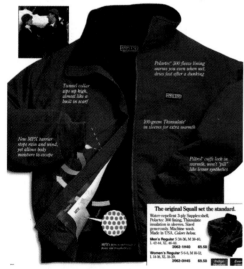

DRAMATIC PHOTOGRAPHY COUPLED WITH INSETS, CALL-OUTS AND AN UNBEATABLE HEADLINE SAY QUALITY AND INSPIRE CONFIDENCE.

COLOR TYPE LENDS APPROPRIATE BRIGHTNESS TO A HEARTHSONG CATALOG.

THIS PRODUCT HAS
BEEN A LEW MAGRAM
BEST-SELLER FOR
YEARS, THANKS
LARGELY TO THIS
GREAT MODEL SHOT.

*Brushed flannel. Weathered cord.
Discover the beguilements of soft.*

WITH ITS USE OF FILTERED SUN-
LIGHT, ELEGANT PROPPING AND
TOUCHABLE TEXTURES, RUE DE
FRANCE SELLS MORE THAN LINENS:
IT SELLS THE ROMANCE OF
PROVENCE.

GREAT LIGHTING ON A STACK OF CLOTHES NOT
ONLY BRINGS OUT COLOR, BUT TEXTURE AND VOL-
UME. YOU CAN PRACTICALLY FEEL THE SOFTNESS
IN THIS J. CREW SHOT.

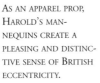

AS AN APPAREL PROP,
HAROLD'S MAN-
NEQUINS CREATE A
PLEASING AND DISTINC-
TIVE SENSE OF BRITISH
ECCENTRICITY.

TO SELL LUXURY ITEMS, YOU NEED LUXU-
RY SETTINGS, AS VICTORIA'S SECRET
DEMONSTRATES WITH ITS CHOICE OF
INDOOR LOCATIONS.

chapter eighteen

CHOOSING MODELS THAT MAKE SENSE

A CELEBRITY MODEL
AND A MILLION-DOLLAR
BRA COMBINED TO MAKE A
KILLER PRESENTATION FOR
VICTORIA'S SECRET.

LAUREN HUTTON AND
MARIEL HEMINGWAY
EXEMPLIFY THE EASY,
EAST HAMPTONESQUE
SPIRIT OF J. CREW.

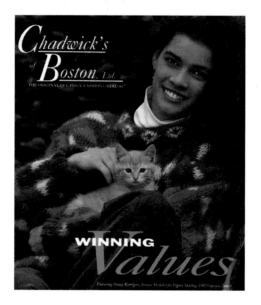

IVANA, CHRISTIE,
RACQUEL, LEEZA
AND NANCY KERRIGAN
MAY LEND
A NOTE OF INTEREST,
BUT THEY DIDN'T MUCH
BOOST SALES.

MORE "ADVICE FROM A FRIEND" THAT GETS PRODUCTS MOVING. BY EDITORIALIZING ON DRESS-DOWN FRIDAYS, LANDS' END SOLVES A COMMON CUSTOMER DILEMMA—AND AS A RESULT, SELLS A LOT OF ITS PRODUCT.

ONE SIMPLE HEADLINE IN CLIFFORD & WILLS TIES TOGETHER THREE SELLING POINTS: GIFT IDEA, PRICE AND QUALITY BENEFIT.

ONCE AGAIN, LANDS' END GOES TO THE EXTREME, THIS TIME WITH CALL-OUTS. NOTE HOW CALL-OUTS ARE LIKE THE SNACK FOOD OF CATALOG COPY: SMALL, AND HARD FOR CUSTOMERS TO STOP AT JUST ONE.

EVEN CUSTOMERS WHO DON'T HAVE TIME TO READ LONG COPY WILL STOP TO GLANCE A BULLETED LIST OF BENEFITS, AS IN THIS LAYOUT FROM JOS. A. BANK.

TALK ABOUT CREDIBILITY! LAND'S END TURNS CUSTOMER TESTIMONIALS INTO HERO PAGES, COMPLETE WITH CUSTOMERS THEMSELVES.

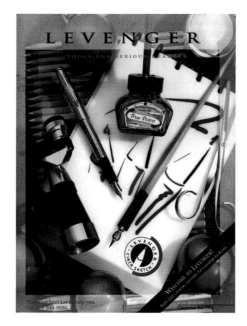

AS A KITCHEN-TABLE LAUNCH, LEVENGER'S SUCCEEDED ON ITS SELLING PROPOSITION OF FINE PRODUCTS FOR SERIOUS READERS.

FOLLOW YOUR VISION. JOHN PETERMEN CHOSE TO BE ANTIESTABLISHMENT, AND IT PAID OFF.

START-UP CATALOGS NEED TO ACQUIRE A BRAND PERSONALITY, AS PLEASANT COMPANY HAS SO ABLY DONE WITH ITS AMERICAN GIRLS CATALOG.

DAILY PLANET, WHICH STARTED OFF AS A T-SHIRT AND RUSSIAN-PRODUCTS DIRECT MARKETER, HAS EVOLVED WITH ITS UNIQUE SELLING PROPOSITION: MARKETING UNUSUAL, FUN PRODUCTS FROM AROUND THE GLOBE.

Y CURTAINS, THE SPIN-OFF FROM *UNTRY* CURTAINS, THE TYPEFACE OF HE PARENT WHILE OPTING FAR MORE MATIC PHOTOGRAPHY AND DESIGN.

VICTORIA'S SECRET COUNTRY ADOPTS THE COPY, TYPEFACE AND MODELS OF ITS PARENT (ON THE LEFT) BUT DISTINGUISHES ITSELF WITH RELAXED OUTDOOR LOCATIONS AND LARGER PRODUCT SHOTS.

THE SUNDANCE JEWELRY CATALOG CARRIES ON THE TRADE-MARK CLEAN LIGHTING AND WESTERN MOTIFS OF ITS PARENT BOOK.

IN SPINNING OFF LILLY'S KIDS, LILLAN VERNON KEPT THE DENSITY OF THE ORIGINAL BOOK, BUT ADDED BIGGER TYPE, BIGGER HEADLINES AND MORE USER-FRIENDLY ARROWS. LIKEWISE, THE LILLY'S KITCHEN SPINOFF HAS A WELL-LIT, CLEANLY-ORGANIZED LOOK STRONGLY INFLUENCED BY WILLIAMS-SONOMA.

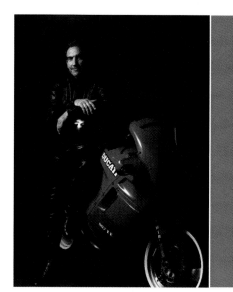

THE SHARPER IMAGE BEFORE:
LONG, BENEFIT-ORIENTED COPY;
LARGE BOXY TYPEFACE, EMPHASIS
ON EASE OF SHOPPING.
THE SHARPER IMAGE AFTER:
DARK PHOTOGRAPHY, EMPHASIS
ON BEING COOL.

CLIFFORD & WILLS
TOP: ORIGINAL CW; FRIENDLY
AND APPROACHABLE.

MIDDLE: CW IN TRANSITION
TOUGH-LOOKING MODELS, LACK
OF COPY AND SEVERE URBAN
SETTING. CLIFFORD & WILLS

BOTTOM: CURRENT CW;
SOFTER MODELS, MORE "SELL"
COPY, BRIGHTLY-LIT STUDIO AND
LOCATION SHOTS.

HE CATALOG FACE-LIFT

INTERSPERSING LIVE
MODELS WITH ITS
FAMILIAR MANNEQUIN
PROPS UPDATES THE
LOOK OF HAROLD'S
APPAREL CATALOG.

L. L. BEAN'S BADLY-NEEDED
FACELIFT KEPT FAMILIAR ELE-
MENTS, LIKE TYPEFACE AND OUT-
DOORS EMPHASIS, BUT ADDED
STRONGER, CLEANER DESIGN
AND HERO PAGES (BELOW).

THIS NEW DESIGN HAS BEEN
INCORPORATED AGGRESSIVELY
IN BEAN'S NEW WOMAN'S
CATALOG (LEFT).

Order now to continue receiving our catalog

If you act now,
you will save up to
$100
on any purchase
from this catalog.

$10 OFF A $100 PURCHASE
$25 OFF A $250 PURCHASE
$50 OFF A $500 PURCHASE
$75 OFF A $750 PURCHASE
$100 OFF A $1000 PURCHASE

Don't forget to use your
Lew Magram Credit Card

Lew Magram

A STRONG COVER EMPHASIS ON DOLLARS-OFF GIVES INACTIVE CUSTOMERS A COMPELLING REASON TO LOOK THROUGH THE CATALOG AND BUY.

A SIMPLE DOT WHACK CAN CALL ATTENTION TO A LAST-CATALOG THREAT.

ON THE OTHER HAND, DAMARK CLEARLY PREFERS THREATENING CUSTOMERS TO ENTICING THEM. IT'S A CAN'T-MISS COVER MESSAGE THAT FEW CUSTOMERS COULD IGNORE.

FINAL NOTICE

If you haven't placed an order lately, your name may be removed from our mailing list!

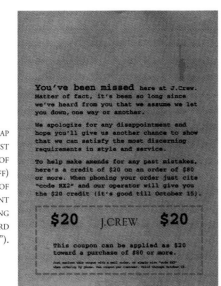

J. CREW'S COVER-WRAP MESSAGE COMBINES JUST THE RIGHT AMOUNT OF INCENTIVE ($20 OFF) WITH A TWINGE OF GUILT INDUCEMENT ("IT'S BEEN SO LONG SINCE WE'VE HEARD FROM YOU…").

A SCREEN-BACK COVER WORKS WELL IN CONVEYING REACTIVATION MESSAGES. NOTICE HOW THIS MESSAGE COMBINES THREATS ("THIS MAY BE YOUR LAST CATALOG") WITH INCENTIVES ("OUR MERCHANDISE QUALITY IS BETTER THAN EVER…MANY OF OUR PRICES ARE LOWER THAN LAST YEAR").

VICTORIA'S SECRET OFFERS A PRICE INCENTIVE TO GET PROSPECTS TO BUY.

LERNER PILES ON THE FREE-BIES TO GET A PROSPECT'S ATTENTION: FREE DELIVERY, INTRODUCTORY SAVINGS, FREE OFFERS, AND A "CALL FREE ANYTIME."

A BLACK BOX ON THE COVER ENABLES EASY-TO-SEE, EASY-TO-CHANGE PROMOTIONAL MESSAGES.

BLACK DOG'S COVER MESSAGE—"FIRST TIME BUYER/20% OFF"—GRABS ATTENTION WITHOUT DISTRACTING FROM THE COVER DESIGN.

SURPRISE! LANDS' END OFFERS NO PRICE INCENTIVES, NO FREE-BIES, NO EXTRA GOODIES: JUST A PROMISE OF "GREAT PROD-UCTS, FRIENDLY SERVICE, OUR BEST PRICE THE FIRST TIME AROUND, AND THE STRONGEST GUARANTEE IN THE BUSINESS." THE IDEA IS THAT THE CATALOG DOESN'T NEED GIMMICKS TO SELL ITSELF, AND THAT CONFI-DENCE IS INCENTIVE IN ITSELF.

chapter twenty-eight

SALE CATALOGS

CLIFFORD & WILLS, IN KEEPING WITH ITS QUIETLY ASSURED IMAGE, ADVERTISES ITS HOLIDAY SALE WITHOUT SHOUTING.

VICTORIA'S SECRET
COUNTRY SALE

Leather Anorak, WY115-106. Orig. $299. Now $219. Sweater, in natural (185) only), WY115-044. Orig. $49. Now $35. See Page 23G.

Exclusively for You:

Turn the page to discover more special price reductions not printed in the catalogue. To receive your savings, you must mention the item code and numbers printed here, i.e., WY123-456. Coupon offers are not applicable to these special price reductions.

To Order, Call Free 24 Hours: 1-800-888-8200

VICTORIA'S SECRET'S COUNTRY SALE CATALOG ENTICES WITH OFFERS "EXCLUSIVELY FOR YOU...SPECIAL PRICE REDUCTIONS NOT PRINTED IN THE CATALOGUE."

Talbots

Our store sale begins Thursday, **December 26** at 8 a.m.

OUR SALE

35-50%off
our original prices

LESS IS MORE. TALBOT'S DOES A GREAT JOB CREATING A CLEAN, SIMPLE, LOW-BUDGET SALE COVER WITH A LOT OF IMPACT.

J. PETERMAN TAKES A TYPICALLY HIGHBROW APPROACH TO THE SALE CONCEPT, LISTING BARGAINS AS IF PLANNING A MENU. THE RED BANNER, HOWEVER, IS A SUPREME ATTENTION-GETTER.

The J. Peterman Co.
Limited Quantities Sale

1996

page 2......"Man in the Linen Suit" Jacket: $150. Now $99.
page 2......"Man in the Linen Suit" Pants: $78. Now $55.
page 3......Gatsby Shirt: $83. Now $53.
page 3......'30s Suspenders: $40. Now $28.
page 5......Changing Times Pants: $48. Now $35.
page 5......Simoom Shirt: $39. Now $29.
page 5......Canvas Fishing Hat: $35. Now $24.
page 6......Double-Breasted Yachting Blazer: $225. Now $168.
page 6......Italian Yachting Sweater: $78. Now $51.
page 6......Italian Linen Bucks: $156. Now $125.
page 7......Linen Blazer: $138. Now $109.
page 8......Hooded Twill Sailing Jacket: $137. Now $129.
page 8......Russian Navy Shirt: $28. Now $22.
page 9......Double-Breasted Linen Jacket: $325. N
page 9......Double-Pleated Pants: $140. Now $22.
page 10.....Pioneer Gingham Shirt: $57.
page 10.....Isle of Wight Shirt: $56.
page 11.....Vintage Seersucker Shirt: $
page 11.....Friendship Shirt: $
page 12.....Norfolk Ja
page 13.....Washa Oxy Cotton Shirt: $54. Now $36.
page 13.....Cotton V-Neck Sweater: $66. Now $48.
page 15.....Anti-Gravity Shirt: $39. Now $24.
page 15.....Gauguin's Hat: $21. Now $15.
page 15.....Authentic Javanese Batik Camp Shirt: $35. Now $24.
page 16.....Essential Summer Shirt: $48. Now $38.
page 16.....Security Shorts: $38. Now $27.
page 16.....Surprisingly Affordable Linen Shirt: $80. Now $60.
page 17.....Exploded Piqué Shirt: $58. Now $39.
page 17.....Combat Pants: $78. Now $31.
page 18.....Horseback Pullover: $85. Now $53.
page 21.....Men's Patchwork Sweater: $198. Now $98.
page 21.....Geelong Zip-Front Sweater: $225. Now $89.
page 23.....Traditional Linen Herringbone Vest: $120. Now $89.
page 23.....Men's Classic Split-Toe Oxford: $164. Now $114.
page 24.....The J. Peterman Shirt: $37. Now $28.
page 27.....Woven Piqué Shirt: $84. Now $59.
page 30.....3-Button Jacket: $199. Now $125.
page 32.....Ravello Pullover: $56. Now $40.
page 32.....Porto Santo Stefano Springweight Pants: $125. Now $86.
page 32.....St. Andrews Argyle Vest: $67. Now $48.
page 32.....Ravello Pullover: $56. Now $40.
page 33.....Canvas Baseball Jacket: $68. Now $48.
page 33.....Roebling Pants: $67. Now $41.
page 36.....Sarong Tie Dress: $55. Now $40.
page 37.....Sleeveless Linen Blouse: $48. Now $35.
page 38.....Sheer Bush Blouse: $45. Now $28.
page 38.....19th-Century Camisole: $49. Now $39.
page 38.....Outback Skirt: $96. Now $72.
page 40.....Tea Rose Skirt: $125. Now $96.
page 41.....Scoop Neck Dress: $48. Now $36.
page 42.....Corduroy Jumper: $55. Now $35.

New Addendum following p. 48

LILLIAN VERNON, TRUE TO ITS VALUE-PRICED IMAGE, CONVEYS "SALE" IN EVERY POSSIBLE WAY: WITH PERCENTAGE-OFF, "BUY NOW, PAY LATER," TIME INCENTIVES ("SALE ENDS APRIL 11"), SPECIAL PRICES, AND EVEN A SWEEPSTAKES.

CHAPTER 16

THE SUPPORTING ROLE OF GOOD DESIGN

Like great soups and sports-car engines, great catalogs consist of small parts that are integrated into a unique whole. Type, logo, copy, photography, format, devices and other design elements combine to create the power of your catalog's brand image.

In some catalogs, of course, one element may dominate. We all recognize Victoria's Secret, for instance, by its supermodels. And when we think of J. Peterman, copy comes to mind; with Garnet Hill, it's photography.

In truth, though, Victoria's Secret models would have far less impact without the catalog's precision photography and exquisite styling. Peterman's copy is aided by supremely legible type and ample white space and Garnet Hill's photography is framed by the catalog's unusual format. Each catalog uses a complete set of design elements to support its main image.

So this chapter will examine each of these design elements—particularly type, devices and logos—and demonstrate how they contribute to a whole. Upcoming chapters will discuss photography, models and copy at greater length.

THE BUILDING BLOCK OF TYPE

Type isn't the sexiest visual element in a catalog. After all, pictures and copy do the selling job; type is the water-carrier, the pedestrian method for getting the words on the page.

At least, that's how many customers and unenlightened catalogers may see it. And it's true: Good use of type rarely calls attention to itself. Like a good picture frame, the job of type is to support and promote the word itself.

But that's exactly why the choice of type is critical. The wrong typeface can look out of place, or worse, disappear without being read. The right typeface ensures that customers will "hear" the catalog as well as see it.

Essentially, catalogers should know just two rules about type:

1) It must be readable. That gets back to the first rule of cataloging: Make sure the catalog is easy to shop. If nothing else, type must be of a size, density and color that doesn't beg squinting or translation. (One could always argue, of course, that if the customer likes what she sees, she'll overcome any inconveniences to find out about it. But why set up obstacles in the first place? Give the customer a break.)

A DESIGN DON'T: THIS ITALIC TYPE MAY LOOK ELEGANT, BUT PROVES IMPOSSIBLE TO READ.

HERE'S A TERRIFIC WAY TO SHOW A GUAR-
ANTEE: "SEW" IT RIGHT INTO THE GAR-
MENT LABEL, AS LANDS' END DOES.

HORCHOW'S CLEVER USE OF TYPE ECHOES
THE CURVE OF A PRINT FRAME.

TYPE CAN OFTEN TELL THE STORY IN PICTURES
AS WELL AS WORDS, AS THIS "HANDSEWN" TYPE
FROM LANDS' END SHOWS.

2) It must adhere to the catalog's positioning. You won't see L.L. Bean's almost clunky typeface in Barrie Pace, and you won't find the delicate serif of Levenger in the big pages of Eddie Bauer. At a basic level, type mutely acknowledges who the reader is. L.L. Bean's customers are pragmatic; Levenger's are serious readers.

Those two rules, of course, cover only the basic groundwork for choosing type. *Using* type is another matter, and most catalogers could benefit from doing it better. For optimal use of type, consider the following guidelines.

Type dos and don'ts

Do consider your customers' age group. The older your readers, the larger and more readable your typeface should be. J. Crew's young customers may not be put off by its wispy italics (personally, I am), but Lands' End's customers just might be.

Do consider serif type. Most studies suggest it's easier to read than sans serif. Newspapers use it, which means everyone's familiar with it and associates it with news and readability.

Do vary type styles. True, catalogs such as Levenger and L.L. Bean are practically all serif, but a single typeface can look stiff and pedestrian on the page. Adding sans serif headlines or prices, or switching to italics for emphasis, can break up a page enough to stop eye drift.

The Discovery Catalog, for instance, sometimes varies its type by product, using a crayon scrawl for kids' products, or an elaborate Gothic for videotapes on pharoahs and kings. The type supports both product and editorial message.

Do, however, make sure the styles integrate. If you want your book to scream "sale," then use twelve different type styles. But if you want your book to speak of integrity and brand image, coordinate your type. Make sure you use consistent body type, lead-ins and color bars throughout.

Don't use all-caps or all-lower-case, except in isolated places. Customers find it much easier to read combinations of upper- and lower-case letters.

Do use bold for key letters and prices—as long as boldface works with your design. Most customers, having located a product, want to find just two things: the description and the price. It's the catalog's job to help them find both fast. (Incidentally, a bold SKU number assists in ordering, as well.)

Don't use wide columns. Customers find it much easier to read short widths of type.

Don't use long headlines, reverse type, or type on complicated backgrounds. All of these require customers to do too much work to get the information they need. (Which brings us back to another golden rule of catalog design: *Don't* let art directors make marketing decisions!)

Do take care with color. Used well, color can enhance a headline's power, as with Hold Everything's evocative "department" headings that blend peacefully into the overall design. But color type used poorly or indiscriminately often looks cheap and promotional. Moreover, color type is difficult to change once on press, since it must be treated like a piece of four-color art.

THE NUDGE OF DEVICES

You know devices as the little symbols and logos used to announce gift-wrapping, 800 numbers, 24-hour shipping, washable fabric, "remember Mom" or a dozen other messages. To customers, devices are a whisper in the ear, a helpful "By the way." I think of them this way: "By the way, we offer large sizes on this item." "By the way, you can get that dress tomorrow." "By the way, that product won a national award."

All catalogers need devices, regardless of how pristine or luxurious the offering. Customers need reminders of upcoming events. They need helpful nudges, such as knowledge of fast shipping, overnight delivery or petite sizes. They need to quickly identify exclusive or award-winning products, and they need to know how to get in touch with the company fast.

But what they don't need are devices used poorly or in profusion, strewn about the catalog like so many pieces of graphic debris. Devices should clarify, and make shopping easier. They should add flavor and zest to a catalog, communicate its personality and promote good services. When devices confuse or annoy, they create even more problems than those they're allegedly set up to solve. Sprinkled into catalogs, devices can either have the effect of chocolate chips in cookie dough—or nails under tires.

Device dos and don'ts

Peabody Award

THE DISCOVERY CATALOG INCLUDES DEVICES THAT INDICATE CLOTHING SIZES OR AWARD-WINNERS.

Do let them communicate. Make sure your symbols are easy to understand and actually represent the message you're trying to convey. The Barrie Pace catalog, for instance, uses a tiny photo of a pincushion and tape measure to indicate its alterations services. The Discovery Catalog uses a symbol of an award to show a prize-winning product. TravelSmith devices indicate wrinkle-proof garments or tropical gear. All these make it easy for customers to grasp the products or services they need.

Don't be afraid to explain. It's not enough to describe your symbol once up front and assume customers will "get it" throughout. Most won't even bother to look it up! You need to repeat the meaning of each symbol (briefly!) wherever mentioned. A few words, such as "Petite Sizes" or "Fit Assurance" will do the job on selling spreads. More complete explanations belong up-front or in the order spread.

ANOTHER GREAT DEVICE: TRAVELSMITH'S "THE LIGHT STUFF" INDICATES WEIGHT OF TRAVEL GEAR.

Do create visuals, not just words. A symbol of a credit card, for instance, is a more potent cue than "American Express Customers Welcomed." A gift box is more noticeable than "We offer gift-wrapping." Toll-free numbers come across quicker when accompanied by a symbol or picture of a telephone. I like how Lands' End, for instance, reminded customers of Father's Day with a little cartoon, stating, "Treat Dad to something special."

PROMOTIONAL TYPE DOESN'T HAVE TO SCREAM TO MAKE ITS POINT. A PROMINENT "$30" TELLS THE SAVINGS STORY WITHOUT DISTRACTING FROM THE IMPORTANT PRODUCT SHOT.

GREAT DEVICE: A TEMPERATURE RATING INDICATES AN IMPORTANT COAT FEATURE WITH EASE AND IMMEDIACY.

TESTIMONIALS, ESPECIALLY WHEN COMBINED WITH GREAT PHOTOS, MAKE TERRIFIC SALES BOOSTERS ON THE PAGE.

TravelSmith is a great case study in important devices. On one spread, note easy-to-
read callouts, diagrams, devices that indicate wrinkle resistance or adventure gear,
travel tips and even a demonstration of
fabric-stretching and wrinkling.

Harold's "o" gives its logo the same
quirky touch that affects its overall
design and imagery.

The logo for Real Goods
expresses the catalog's
environmental sensitivity
and emphasis on solar
products.

Do use promotion devices. Sale prices, new products
and best-sellers often deserve starbursts, red type or exclamation points for emphasis.

Do use callouts. Particularly for highly technical products, callouts help customers "dissect" a product, whether it's
the inside of a sneaker sole or the components of a computer monitor. (Quality-positioned catalogs like Lands' End do
a great job with these.) Pointing out different features enables
customers to "see" a well-constructed product, which helps
build trust.

Don't make devices too large or misleading. Devices
should never be confused with the products themselves.

Don't be gratuitous. Some catalogers just aren't happy
unless their dog Sparky appears on every page. If a device doesn't add to the
catalog's communication, get rid of it.

THE CROWNING LOGO

Logos require commitment. Since they're the most recognizable part of
your catalog, they can't be redone book to book, season to season. Once you
establish a logo, your customers will expect to see it time and again. The
logo is their visual cue that they've reached the right place.

Logos are also tricky to get right. Few logos, it seems, stay fresh after years
of use (we can all think of The Gap logo, but who can picture The Limited?).
The best ones, like The New Yorker, L.L. Bean and Coke, are practically
imprinted on consumer psyches. Others are simply too bland to have holding
power (R.C. Cola), or too eccentric (Jolt) to be taken seriously.

For catalogs, logos should also sum up the feeling of what's inside. For
instance, I like Harold's eccentric squashing of the "o" in its logo, something
that gives it just enough of a British screwball flavor to complement its casual apparel. J. Crew's lower-case logo (but always large and centered) conveys
a sense of both casualness and importance. And I like how Lands' End
acquired its quirky logo by accident, when an editor mislaid the apostrophe.
What better sign of the book's humor and humanness?

Logo dos and don'ts

Don't be afraid to evolve. If a logo can't stand alone and be recognized,
it's not quite a logo. Hold Everything, for instance, is still reaching for its
logo identity, still falling to the bland side of casual and elegant. For any catalog, each successive year or season ought to allow room for just enough tin-
kering to anchor or develop a logo's meaning. But...

If necessary, *don't* be afraid to change. When a catalog repositions or
recreates itself, the logo can (and often should) change along with it.
Clifford & Wills, for instance, not long ago revamped its logo to emphasize
the "C" and "W," creating more of a lighthearted visual out of its stiff-
sounding, Brooks-Brotherish name. The logo now suits the catalog's light
and casual apparel.

Do use your logo throughout the catalog. To reinforce your name and brand, it's good to place your logo by your page number or 800 number. That's particularly critical if you've got a spin-off catalog. Customers who see the logo know they're not just shopping from any jewelry catalog, but from Sundance.

Never forget: Brands are precious commodities. Do what you can to capitalize on yours, whether through typeface, logo or any other design element.

Now that we've touched on those "supporting" elements of design, let's get to the heart of good creative: photography and copy.

A VIEW OF NORM THOMPSON'S LABEL
REINFORCES THE BRAND FOR CUSTOMERS.

CLOSE-UP SHOTS OF APPAREL CREATE
IMPORTANT HERO PAGES WITH NEAR-
TOUCHABLE TEXTURE. BEST PAYOFF:
PROMINENT DISPLAY OF THE LANDS' END
LOGO ON THE SWEATER.

CHAPTER 17

SECRETS OF PHOTOGRAPHS
THAT SELL

In most catalogs, photographs do all the heavy lifting. In a single image (particularly that cover image!), a photograph must not only display the product perfectly, but convey the catalog's mood and positioning, speak to the customer's desires and aspirations, and, of course, *sell* whatever's in the picture!

Big job, right? In fact, I've seen many books fall down because they make this mistake:

They think a product photograph is simply a representation of the item.

They think they can get away with using a manufacturer's shot (particularly inside the book) or with hiring their cousin's brother-in-law Bill, or with using someone who, say, photographs great ads or brochures.

They're wrong, of course. The job of a good catalog photograph, and good catalog photographer, is this: *to anticipate selling problems and issues and solve them.*

A photograph has to be more than flattering to merit a place in a catalog. It has to sell. And that's a lot tougher than most catalogers believe.

THE PROOF IS IN THE PHOTO

Consider the challenge home decor catalog Rue de France has in selling a $150 table linen. First of all, $150 is a lot of money for a fabric item. This cataloger knows it's tough to "prove" the linen is worth the cost. The catalog copy could explain the linen's fine stitching and thread counts, but the visual would have to get shoppers to stop and read the copy in the first place.

So what does Rue de France do? It props the linen gently on an antique table, making it look as fine and delicate as a cloud. It washes the table with natural sunlight, highlighting the perfect weave of the linen's pattern. It places the linen in a country cottage setting, indicating gracious, comfortable and European taste.

Expert photography and styling infuse this table linen with country French romance. Customers are not presented with a mere table linen, but with a memory of Provence.

All great catalogs carry photographs that can sell without a word of copy. (We'll make an exception for J. Peterman, Vermont Country Store and the like.) These photographs are as much influenced by *marketing* as by artistry

WITH ITS USE OF FILTERED SUNLIGHT, ELEGANT PROPPING AND TOUCHABLE TEXTURES, RUE DE FRANCE SELLS MORE THAN LINENS: IT SELLS THE ROMANCE OF PROVENCE.

and technical skill. They result from close cooperation of art director, stylist and photographer, with heavy input from the marketing department.

Is it any wonder that some catalogs run the same winning product shot year after year? These photographs make money. Often, it's not just the product that clinches the sale, but the look in the model's eye, the timeless setting, the slant of light illuminating the surface of the item.

Just as travel brochures know the value of palm trees to frozen New Yorkers, so do great catalogs know the value of the sheen of leather, the texture of a fabric, the crisp detail of a planter or wall-hanging. They create visuals that not only reinforce the catalog's brand image, but speak to the customer's desires, needs and wants.

STRATEGIES FOR SHOOTING HARD GOODS

Catalog pages aren't storefronts. Our customers can't pick up our products and know how great it feels or what heft it has. All we have to help them out is an inch or so of copy and a picture.

So if a still-life photograph doesn't create a sense of desire, it doesn't sell. I won't go into the details of how to build sets, set up lights or focus cameras—but I will tell you what works to create photographs that sell the following kinds of hard goods:

*Tabletop
*Food
*Jewelry
*Electronics
*Apparel
*Domestics
*Furniture

Here's the rundown on what you need:

1) Appropriate photographer

Shooting perfume bottles isn't like shooting pots and pans. So you must choose a photographer experienced in shooting precisely the kinds of products you need to sell.

Don't hire someone who shoots great portraits to do your tabletop book, and don't get a jewelry photographer to do your linens book. Above all, don't hire a general advertising or magazine photographer at all! Stick to people experienced in shooting catalogs, and in shooting your category of merchandise. They'll know best what's needed to make it sell.

2) Technical perfection

Remember, your customers use your catalog photographs to make their purchase decisions. If the product doesn't look tangible and real—if it doesn't have heft, texture, three-dimensionality and accurate color—you'll probably lose that sale.

So use appropriate focus and lighting. Go for near-reality. Products that appear "wrong" in color, fabric or style will undoubtedly end up back in your warehouse.

3) Appropriate lighting

Lighting is key to good photography—but it's also subjective. Good photographers not only light products to show detail, but also to create impact, mood, tension and emotion. Lighting alone can be a catalog's creative signature.

Commodity goods, like kitchenware and dishes, especially benefit from lighting choices. Let's take a pottery bowl. Lillian Vernon might use studio light to give the bowl a fresh, crisp, but somewhat routine image. Pottery Barn might use dramatic highlighting to surround the bowl with a romantic mood. Williams-Sonoma might try natural lighting to soften the bowl's edges and bring out richer color.

In other words, the lighting alone could show that Lillian Vernon is for value-hunting realists; Pottery Barn for would-be decorators; Williams-Sonoma for educated gourmets. Each type of customer would buy the pottery bowl for a different reason, so each cataloger needs to communicate that reason with lighting and imagery.

4) Appropriate styling

Styling is more than adjusting props. Styling essentially means creating the context for a product to come to life.

In a sense, styling sounds logical. If you're selling an expensive crystal bowl, for instance, better to place it on a mahogany surface and surround it with silver picture frames than to put it on a piece of plywood with a couple of papier-mâché roses.

But good styling, like good acting, should be invisible. The reader shouldn't "see" it. Customers shouldn't be thinking, "That's a beautifully set table." They should be thinking, "That's a beautiful bowl."

It's not easy to pull off. Some catalogs don't go far enough, throwing around fake snow for a display of boots, for instance, or shooting linens in cheesy studio "bedrooms." Others go too far, reaching for strange effects with doodads from some art director's fantasy. Imaginative props (like Harold's headless wooden mannequins) or narrative stylings (like the room settings in Peterman's Eye) can be wonderful, but catalogs that use them risk having customers look at the pictures, not the products.

The best stylists use just enough context to enhance a product, whether it's in the way Territory Ahead places polo shirts over weathered fences, or the way Levenger lays Mont Blanc pens on a surface of perfectly polished cherry. The right propping speaks not only to a catalog's image, but can make or break a product sale.

A WASH OF SIDELIGHTING TRACES THE CURVES OF FLOWERS AND VASE, CREATING A STILL-LIFE IMAGE WITH IMPACT.

Brushed flannel. Weathered cord. Discover the beguilements of soft.

GREAT LIGHTING ON A STACK OF CLOTHES NOT ONLY BRINGS OUT COLOR, BUT TEXTURE AND VOLUME. YOU CAN PRACTICALLY FEEL THE SOFTNESS IN THIS MERCHANDISE.

CUSTOMERS WON'T CONSCIOUSLY NOTICE THOSE FRESH BEDSIDE FLOWERS OR EXPENSIVE LOUVERED BLINDS, BUT QUALITY PROPS SUBTLY COMMUNICATE QUALITY PRODUCT

5) Shooting to layout

All good catalogers know in advance just what features on a product they'd like to show, and how that product should appear in the layout. So they always provide photographers with a detailed layout. It's a precise blueprint as to how products should be shot.

Without that blueprint, photographers have little guidance as to the basics of your catalog design. You could end up with product shots that don't adhere to the design of your spread. Worse, you could also end up with product shots that hide the item's selling features. Make sure your art director knows ahead of time exactly how to present each item to show it off to its best advantage.

STRATEGIES FOR FASHION PHOTOGRAPHY

The key to a good fashion shot: Never allow the customer to see how hard it was to achieve. Customers should never pick up on the fact that this "look" came only after six hours and 32 rolls of film; that the backdrop fell down four times and that an assistant 10 minutes earlier had spilled coffee down the model's back.

Believe me, fashion photography can be just that grueling. But it's worth it when our customers pick up the catalog and know that they want to look and feel just the way those models appear on the page. They want a desirable and attainable image, and that's the big challenge of fashion photography.

To get there, you need four elements:

1) Appropriate photographer

I can't stress it enough: Always hire photographers experienced in the catalog business! Annie Leibovitz may shoot great Vanity Fair spreads, but shooting catalog fashion is not like shooting a piece of journalism or an ad. A catalog photographer must shoot for both freshness and consistency, for fantasy and believability, roll after roll and page after page.

In other words, your photographer must ensure that the product is the star of the picture, not the model. The model must look great because of the way she's dressed, rather than the clothes looking great because of the model. Creating that impression is no easy achievement, and it takes a skilled and *experienced* photographer to pull it off.

2) Appropriate locations

It's less important for most hard-goods catalogs to create a sense of time or place. If you're selling computer parts or Limoges boxes, for instance, you don't need to find a sunrise on a Bermuda beach or recreate the urban grit of a city street.

Apparel catalogs, however, have a different challenge. Clothing is personal, a statement of the self. For that reason, clothing catalogers—particularly those selling casual clothes—often need to create a sense of lifestyle. They need to show customers not just how the clothes look, but how the clothes can make them *feel*.

Location can do that. Using location doesn't mean creating vacation brochures; it means finding a place that customers can identify with, fantasize about (there's nothing like a sunny locale to get customers over the hump of winter) or relate to. Of course, it also means finding the spot where the lighting flatters, the clothing looks appropriate (swimsuits don't belong on sidewalks) and the image gibes with the catalog's positioning.

That's why, for instance, Lands' End shoots clothing in park-like suburban settings (Anytown, U.S.A.). Certain apparel catalogs like Tweeds pick either downtown spots or offbeat country settings. More upscale apparel books, such as Talbots and Barrie Pace, shoot on sunny sidewalks or at well-appointed homes and offices. Each location speaks not only to the catalog's position, but creates context for the clothing.

Here's the rundown on how various locations work best:

Outdoors. Outdoor shots benefit from flattering natural light, lots of room to move, and a vitality that you just can't get indoors. Models also notice the difference in outdoor location shoots, and it often shows in their attitudes.

Indoors. Indoor locations benefit from easy mood-setting. Imagine, for instance, how Victoria's Secret might appear if it photographed its push-up bras in blank, white studios rather than in quietly luxurious bedrooms. An indoor location, whether a home, hotel lobby, office or sunroom, can lend unique personality that comes across in the photograph.

Daylight studios. Some catalogs also shoot product in "daylight" studios that use natural lighting, combining a sense of place with the convenience of a studio. Done right, a daylight studio can make an excellent substitute for a more personal indoor location.

Studios. Studio shots, of course, are the least expensive to shoot and easiest to control. However, the blank settings can sap the life out of casual wear and other lifestyle fashion. The simple, seamless backdrop of a studio usually works best for exposing the details and elegance of career wear, evening clothes or other highly styled apparel.

Mixing it up. Most successful clothing catalogs use a variety of locations to pace their books. Lands' End and J. Crew, for instance, mingle studio shots with shots of models romping in surf and snow, or wandering through kitchens or bedrooms. L.L. Bean uses studio shots to bring out the details of its shirts and shoes, then mixes in location shots of barnyards and beaches to show its clothes "at work."

So use variety. Catalogs that are all outdoors look like brochures; catalogs shot all-indoors can be static and claustrophobic. Mixing up locations will keep a customer's interest at its peak.

3) Appropriate lighting

Lighting can be just as subjective for fashion as for hard goods. Tweeds, for instance, might create moodiness with cloudy outdoors light; Saks Fifth

NOTE HOW J. CREW'S BLURRED-OUT BACKGROUND LENDS THE AUTHENTICITY OF AN OUTDOORS SETTING WITHOUT COMPETING WITH THE PRODUCT SHOT.

A DAYLIGHT STUDIO, AS IN THIS TWEEDS SHOT, COMBINES THE WARMTH OF OUT-OUTDOORS LIGHT WITH THE CLEAN, SPARE BACKDROP OF A STUDIO.

Herman Geist
Fully Lined
Twill Blazer
only
$29

WHEN A PHOTOGRAPHER "CONNECTS"
WITH A MODEL, AS IN THIS CHADWICK'S
PAGE, CHANCES ARE GOOD THAT THE CUS-
TOMER WILL, TOO.

spring essential:
cotton mock
only $24

ONE GREAT LOOK FROM A MODEL CAN
SKYROCKET SALES, AS CLIFFORD & WILLS
DISCOVERED WITH THIS WINNING SHOT.

Avenue might play up straightforward elegance with clean studio light; Neiman Marcus might set a golden holiday mood by shooting indoors. Lands' End and The Territory Ahead rely on sharp lighting of laydowns to create a hyper-real sense of "touch and feel"; J. Crew prefers the soft lighting that matches its image and clothing line.

In each catalog, lighting expresses unique positioning and personality. It places the apparel in a mood that captures the catalog's spirit.

4) Communication with models

Show me a picture that's worth a thousand words, and I'll show you one that was a winner—in sales revenues. Clifford & Wills for many years has run a single incomparable photograph of a model wearing a ribbed mock-turtleneck sweater. The model's "dare me" expression, crossed arms and just-tossed hair make her look as if she'd just turned down a date with Richard Gere in order to spend the night working on her dissertation. Customers just ate it up.

Good photographers know how to get that kind of assuredness from models. They also know how to elicit elegance, down-to-earth realness, intelligence or anything else that a catalog needs to express its brand identity.

In other words, these photographers know how to get models to look just as *customers* want to look, whether that means approachable and confident, or ethereal and introspective. They can draw out a model's strengths and make her feel she's the best in the world—and pretty soon, she starts looking like it.

I believe photographers should take at least one "safe" roll of film, where the model stands fairly still and it's easy to get a clean shot of the product. After that, they should let loose. They can let a model pretend she's walking along the Riviera next to Tom Cruise. They can tell her the guy across the street just blew her a kiss. They can have her pretend she's just won a million dollars, or that her baby has taken its first steps.

I'll talk more about choosing models in the next chapter. But remember, just as great actors show their stuff with the right director, so do great models come into their own with the right photographer. When the communication (and camera) clicks, you've got that million-dollar shot.

PHOTOGRAPHY
DOS AND DON'TS

Once you know the kind of photography that works for your book, make sure you don't blow it with poor technique or dull pacing. Keep these tips in mind:

Don't use backlighting unless you're sure of its effects. Products lit from behind can produce harsh lines on the page.

Don't shoot "artsy" or out-of-focus. The product must always be cleanly lit to give customers as much touch-and-feel experience as a page allows. Exception: In location shots, throwing the background or foreground out of focus can enhance the product while still creating a sense of place.

Don't over or underexpose. In still-life photography, make sure photographers provide three or four different exposures of the same shot.

Do light for color. Capturing a product's exact color is extremely important, particularly for apparel. Skin tones must also look true to life to cue consumers that other colors are accurate.

Do find novel ways of styling still-life shots and color ways. (*Color ways* are the color choices available for apparel and linens.) J. Crew, for instance, layers its clothing in laydown shots, and shoots stacks of sweaters and mazes of rolled-up socks. Lands' End uses "invisible man" techniques for styling its empty clothes, putting "hands" in pockets and making ties blow in the breeze. As a result, the clothes look energetic enough to walk off the page.

Don't use supplied photography. You'll never get a photograph that carries the stylistic signature of your book.

Don't make postcards. Maybe you had a great time on that Jamaica shoot, but you don't need steel drums and fishing boats to create a sense of place. Too many distractions keep customers from looking at the product.

Do pace your catalog with different photographic effects. All-location spreads look busy; all-silhouette pages look empty and cheap. A catalog's photographs should seem made by the same hand, but not necessarily made in the same place on the same day.

CHAPTER 18

CHOOSING MODELS THAT MAKE SENSE

Photographs may sell, but models (particularly in an apparel book) give your catalog *relevance*. In a sense, they're the physical embodiment of a catalog's position and imagery.

That's why the right face and body are only part of what's important in choosing models. Although models first and foremost have to look good in what they're wearing, just as critical are their non-physical attributes: attitude, poise, style, and communication with the customer. In other words, the right model makes your customer say, *I relate to this person. I could look like that and feel the way she does if I dressed that way.*

KNOW YOUR POSITIONING

As with every other creative element in your catalog, here's the rule: If you're not clear about your catalog's positioning, you'll never pick good models. It's as simple as that.

So before you go looking for models, ask yourself what your catalog stands for and what you need to convey to customers. Is your catalog approachable? Is it aspirational? Is it elite? Friendly? Whatever describes your catalog's identity also describes what you need your models to convey. (Review Chapter 4 if you need a boost of self-knowledge.)

Beyond that, you need to know your customers' aspirations and needs. Do your models fit your customer's idea of herself? It may be that your models look friendly and approachable, but they might be too young for your audience's comfort. Or they may be too thin or exotic-looking to promote believability. Or, they may have the right physical appearance for your audience, but lack the approachability you're looking for.

Models and catalogs should look made for each other. Some catalogs, for instance, benefit from models who look real, down to earth, like approachable neighbors. Lands' End, for instance, frequently uses models with gray hair or imperfect figures. They may look a little better than the folks next door, but they certainly wouldn't look out of place in the local supermarket.

Other catalogs need models who look fresh from the golf course. Some, like Lew Magram, require more of a nightclub look. Some catalogs need identifiable homemakers and moms; others need confident career executives.

In short, model choice springs from every other element in your catalog. Let's say, for instance, that two catalogs sell the same bra. One catalog is directed to the college crowd; another to aspirational young homemakers.

What might their models look like? It's easy to the picture the first catalog featuring a somewhat modest model with little makeup and short hair, or a braid. The one directed to aspirational homemakers might take a sexier point of view in order to inject a little fantasy into the image.

Or take two catalogs selling the same polo shirt. J. Crew might show a pouting young college guy. Lands' End might show a suburban Little League coach. Each would have a very different definition of "casual," and would need a different model to make it work.

THE MODEL CHASE

I'm always amazed that out of the thousands of models available today, most catalogers keep chasing the same hundred or so. Then again, there's a good reason why we see so many of the same models again and again (and why they cost so much!). These models know how to communicate with readers. They're adaptable for different "looks," which means they can create scrubbed collegiate innocence in one book, and sexy allure in another. And, of course, they simply make clothes look great!

Finding fresh talent is a challenge. If you've got a new or repositioned catalog, you'll probably need quite a few "go-sees" (interviews with models) to choose who's best for your book. Here's what you should ask yourself when considering a model:

Do the clothes look right? Never pick a model without having her try on your garments. Some models have broad shoulders and look great in turtlenecks; others have chunky legs and look lousy in skirts. Some might have the easy look suitable for casual wear; others have the more angular and polished appearance that works for career clothes or fashion-forward.

Not every model can wear your catalog's "look." (Ever notice that you never see Elle Macpherson in Victoria's Secret lingerie—but you always see her in sportswear? Not that her figure isn't perfect—it's just that her "look" is too sporty for lace.)

Is the model cooperative? Go-sees also help you find out if the model is approachable and cooperative—both critical factors, at $1,000 and up per day.

How does she photograph? At go-sees, it's important to not only shoot Polaroids, but 35mm film as well. That way you can find out how the model looks from the front and side, how she smiles (some models are superior pouters) and how she comes across to the camera.

Most models look completely different on film than in person. With a practice shoot, you can find out exactly how the model will come across in your book. Experienced models with good attitude not only produce more shots, but better ones as well.

DEVELOPING A COLLECTION

Most customers don't consciously look for certain models in your catalog. But loyal customers, at some level, like the assurance of familiar faces and images. If they identify with your models, the models in turn become like friends. Customers want to see them around.

That's why it's important to develop your own group, or stable, of models. You need an assortment of faces who can support your catalog's "look," and who can reassure customers that they're in familiar territory.

The trick to forming your own group of models is to keep aware of who's new and who might fit your image. Do you need hip and aloof? Natural and wholesome? Coiffed and polished? Sophisticated and mature? Set up your go-sees on a regular basis, not just when your next catalog is due. The more models you see, the better you can establish who fits in your book and who doesn't.

Remember, models don't necessarily represent your customer, but rather who your customers aspire to be. It's important to follow the law of consistency, and to keep recognizable faces from book to book. But since your customer is always evolving, it's also important to infuse new faces from time to time. That discourages boredom.

LEW MAGRAM'S MODELS (INSET) MAY NEVER HAVE A HAIR OUT OF PLACE, WHEREAS TWEEDS MODELS (ABOVE) RARELY HAVE A HAIR IN PLACE. EACH CATALOG CHOOSES THE MODELS THAT HAVE RELEVANCE FOR ITS CUSTOMERS.

THE ART OF PRESENTATION

Ever notice how similar clothes and similar models can look utterly dissimilar in different catalogs? That's due to presentation.

J. Crew may have the broadcloth shirts and khaki shorts of Lands' End, and perhaps even hire the same freckle-faced model. But in J. Crew's presentation, this model, unshaved, might be loading a wood stove in his dirty wool socks. In Lands' End, he might be standing neat and self-consciously with a smiling young woman, his after-shave practically wafting off the page. J. Crew's presentation, obviously, is loose, almost sloppy; Lands' End's is practical and put-together. Each reflects the different lifestyles their customers either have or want to have.

Presentation, in short, can keep a model—even one with an overexposed, familiar face—from looking the same from one catalog brand to another. Customers who keep seeing the same model presented the same way in Catalogs A, B and C start to lose track of which catalog they're in. (*Did I see her in Chadwick's or Newport News?*)

So make sure your catalog's presentation gives your model individuality. A good model can assume your catalog's unique imprint in her smile, expression and poise. Varied presentations give catalogers more mileage from overly familiar faces.

LOVING DAD IN ONE CATALOG, RELAXED EXECUTIVE IN ANOTHER: GOOD MODELS MUST BE VERSATILE TO REFLECT A CATALOG'S NEEDS.

OUTDOORS FRESH OR INDOORS FASHIONABLE: GOOD CATALOG MODELS EFFORTLESSLY REFLECT THE IMAGERY OF THE CATALOG'S BRAND. (HERE, THE SAME MODEL POSES FOR E STYLE AND J. CREW.)

CHOOSING MODELS THAT MAKE SENSE

IN THE END: THE MODEL ANALYSIS

GIVEN THAT VICTORIA'S SECRET SELLS FANTASY AS MUCH AS LINGERIE, SUPERMODELS LEND THE CAPTIVATING FINAL TOUCH.

A CELEBRITY MODEL AND A MILLION-DOLLAR BRA COMBINED TO MAKE A KILLER PRESENTATION FOR VICTORIA'S SECRET.

EVEN BUSINESS BOOKS GET THEIR CELEBS. RELIABLE BUSINESS ELECTRONICS TRADED ON THE CELEBRITY OF RAY-O-VAC ENDORSER MICHAEL JORDAN.

Once you've chosen the perfect model, there's just one way to confirm whether she really works for your book. You have to perform a *model analysis.*

Just as we all do a square-inch analysis of our catalog pages to learn how each spread performed, so should we all do model analyses to find out how each of our models performed. The fact is, some models sell beautifully and others don't. Until you sit down and calculate how much apparel you've sold *per model,* you don't really know how "perfect" your perfect model is.

Granted, presentation, photography and styling—as well as the product itself, of course—have a lot to do with why an item becomes a best-seller. But if different clothes sell *consistently* well on the same model, that means you not only have winning items, but also a winning model.

Incidentally, all clothing catalogers analyze each other's models as well. They figure, often rightly, that a model who keeps popping up from book to book is a model who makes money. That also explains why the same models turn up again and again in different catalogs: Hot performers are often subject to raids.

CASE STUDY

▼

IVANA AND THE MILLION-DOLLAR BRA

It seemed a match made in marketing heaven. When Erv Magram, president of Lew Magram, called Ivana Trump to ask if she'd like to sell her line in his book, she not only agreed to sell her clothes but to model them as well.

So it was that she appeared on the cover for the 1996 spring book. "Everyone who looked at that book—friends of mine, business associates—everyone was talking about what a terrific idea this is," says Magram. Even "Entertainment Tonight" came out to do a segment on the big news.

Magram tested Ivana against a typical merchandise cover and waited for the big lift. "To our complete and total astonishment," he says, "there was no change in response. The book did well, but the celebrity cover did not add to the overall response rates."

To be sure, Magram has had some star power in his catalog's history. In its old incarnation (pre-1975) Lew Magram was "Shirtmaker to the Stars," featuring Telly Savalas, Tony Bennett and other celeb customers in its catalog. Today, however, he admits that celebrity models may elicit lots of attention, but proper merchandising still determines response.

So what cover gimmick *does* Magram admire? Victoria's Secret's "Million-dollar Miracle Bra," which graced that catalog's cover last year. "We understand that promotion was very successful," he says. "I thought it was brilliant."

CHOOSING MODELS THAT MAKE SENSE

THE CELEBRITY MODEL

So why is it that Cindy Crawford endorses Pepsi, Michael Jordan puts on Nikes and Fran Drescher speaks of pantyhose—and none of these people model in catalogs?

Aside from the fact that they cost the world to hire, celebrity models, even minor ones, have seldom posed on catalog pages.

For one thing, catalog advertising is quite different from general advertising. Catalogers don't want customers looking at celebrities. They want them looking over product features, establishing desire, and placing an order *now.* General advertisers, on the other hand, want buyers to pay attention and get a brand fixed in their minds, ready to recall when it's time to buy.

For attention-getting, general advertisers need celebrities. But for selling, catalogers need models who have relevance for the customer. They need friendly faces, not idols.

So it is that most celebrity deals have proven a mixed bag for catalogers. "Entertainment Tonight" hostess Leeza Gibbons appeared in Ross-Simons; Christie Brinkley was on the cover of Chadwick's; The Sharper Image once had the latest James Bond actor stalking through its book. Those celebrities were attention-getters, all right, but it wasn't clear that the increase in response rate or sales (if any) made up for the price of hiring. In fact, a 1996 Ross-Simons book featuring Racquel Welch and a diamond-and-pearl necklace did nothing to lift sales, according to a source there.

Which is not to say, however, that certain celebrities don't make sense for catalogers. We can only assume, for instance, that the supermodels of Victoria's Secret more than make up for their day rates!

CELEBRITIES AS APPAREL MODELS: LAUREN HUTTON AND MARIEL HEMINGWAY EXEMPLIFY THE EASY, EAST HAMPTONESQUE SPIRIT OF J. CREW.

CELEBRITIES ON CATALOG COVERS: IVANA, CHRISTIE, NANCY KERRIGAN, RACQUEL AND LEEZA, MAY LEND A NOTE OF INTEREST, BUT THEY DIDN'T BOOST SALES.

CHAPTER 19

FINDING YOUR CATALOG'S SELLING VOICE

I have seen at least a dozen how-to books on copywriting. Any one of them could probably teach you sentence rhythm, benefit headlines, stylistic tips, action words, the whole copywriting enchilada.

What none of them can tell you, though, is how to write copy *unique to your own catalog.* The truth is, good copy is only good as long as it relates to your brand, image and positioning.

Granted, every cataloger can benefit from good copywriting tips. All good catalog copy must be economical, complete, benefit-oriented and, in a sense, somewhat seductive. If we're fishing for customers, after all, then the product is our bait, the visual is the hook, and the copy is the reel that brings the sale in.

But copy is more than mere product description. Copy is the voice and personality of your catalog, as unique as any human's. You see how catalogs like J. Peterman wind romance and adventure into palatable tales for intellectuals. Vermont Country Store copy sensibly admonishes like a well-meaning parent. Copy can tease with gentle humor (as Lands' End's does) or sink all its selling power into pithy headlines (as with J. Crew). In each case, the copy flows inevitably from the rest of the catalog's image.

Once you learn to speak your customer's unique language, you'll find that the right copy is the final, and crucial, element in developing your catalog's unique brand identity.

MAKE IT FIT

In a sense, copy finishes a catalog the way a pair of shoes finishes an outfit. When the copy "fits," it's like adding black patent leather loafers to a Bill Blass tux. Customers don't "notice" they're being sold. But when the copy doesn't fit, it can wreck the whole image as fast as a pair of pink cowboy boots.

Take, for instance, a Sunglass Hut catalog I came across not long ago. An oversize format showed off full-bleed, dramatically lit faces of Dennis Rodman and Michael Jordan in wraparound sunglasses. Submerged in deep shadow, these sports heroes were the coolest thing in Ray Bans since Jack Nicholson.

And then came the copy: "There's brand new Predator sunglasses on the scene. Seven in fact, that exemplify a young, carefree lifestyle with just the right amount of attitude."

Never mind the bad grammar: This limp copy deflated the catalog's hipness.

Copy, then, is critical to get right. While no one can slip you a magic formula for putting it together, all catalog copy must follow the four laws of selling:

1) *Believability*
2) *Complete selling information*
3) *Benefits*
4) *Speaking the customer's language*

Here's how these work.

THE LAWS OF COPY

It's true that "good" copy can take just about as many forms as "good" food. Who's to say, for instance, that homemade apple pie is better or worse than Lobster Newburg, or for that matter, a single, ripe strawberry? Much of what makes food good is a matter of taste and appetite. But at the same time, all good food adheres to the same basic laws: freshness, preparation and quality.

In the same way, all good copy can be a matter of taste and appetite as well (shopping for Mont Blanc pens, after all, involves more copy hunger than shopping for hinges). Like good food, too, all good copy also follows certain laws.

LAW #1: Believability

We're all familiar with lathered-up copy. "Most incredible candlestick ever!" "Fill your bathroom with joy and whimsy!" It's the kind of thing that makes customers turn and run.

Good copy is sincere. It has no inflated or misleading sense of importance. It states why a product is worth buying in honest, clear-eyed terms.

Consider this copy from Early Winters: "This is one smart pack. Ingenious clamshell design is a snap to pack and unpack, and allows instant access to items inside (without having to dump everything else out.) ...Zip-off "Bullet Pack" is sized to hold plenty (2-qt. water bottle, a fleece pullover, energy bars and headlamp) but to stay out of your way."

It's not hard to work believability into catalogs that sell functional products. What's tougher is creating believability in, say, apparel and gift catalogs. Since they have nothing "practical" to say, many of these catalogs blow hot air and empty adjectives, like "wonderful," "whimsical," and "fabulous."

That's why I like the description of this Frequent Flyer Jacket in the apparel catalog Departures: "Security and style mile after mile! This soft, drapable jacket is a blend of rayon and silk in an elegant herringbone weave. It simply shimmers with subtle texture! Seven specially designed pockets, including two inside zipper pockets, hold valuables securely." While "specially designed" is a mumble, the rest of the copy sells believability both on style and function.

For my money, a master of believability is Levenger. Consider this copy for leather desk accessories: "These fine leather desk tools are made for us by an American factory that has been creating superb desk products for the Supreme Court, Congress and the White House since the days of Franklin Roosevelt." But that isn't the whole selling inducement. "What makes [the product] special is the quality of the leather and the writing surface," which the catalog then goes on to describe in loving, informed detail.

Four elements of believable copy

1) Specifics. References to Roosevelt, or to the fact that a pack can hold a 2-quart water bottle, headlamp and energy bars, build credibility. They show the copywriter's familiarity with the product, as in this copy for a carved box from gift cataloger Gump's: "Originally used for storing tobacco during Japan's Edo and Meiji periods, this handcarved collectible replica is a diminutive *objet d'art.*"

2) Research. A product's history or significance enhances believability, particularly for expensive items. Using research, you can state specifically why sheets of Egyptian cotton are worth more than other sheets, or why a bookstand from the '20s makes sense for today's readers.

3) Testimonials. It's always great when customers testify to a product's importance. But you can also call on outside authorities, or your own research and experience, to toot your product's horn. When Sundance explains that its leather prairie shoes are "the most popular shoes we've ever offered," it's telling customers that those shoes have stood the test of satisfaction.

4) Language. Believable copy isn't filled with hype and come-ons. Granted, The Sharper Image introduces its $2,795 Quad Roller Massage Chair with the breathless: "You've never felt anything like it before!" But when it goes on to explain the virtues of its new four-roller system ("like the trained hands of *two* skilled masseurs") along with nineteen other benefits (I counted), you're ready to find that lead-in completely credible. Good copy backs off from empty adjectives and backs up its superlatives with facts.

LAW #2: Complete selling information

Good copy doesn't leave customers guessing about the quality, substance, durability or materials of what they're buying.

Take this copy for a hammock sold in the Sundance catalog: "... a subtly shaded Native American pattern ... create[s] a smooth, breathable surface that resists mildew, rot, fading and stretching; brass grommets resist rust. At 52" wide x 80" long, it's plenty big enough for two. Spreaders are hand bent southern oak. Plump cotton pillow attaches with Velcro® straps. Set up your hammock wherever you wish, using this stable tubular steel frame with a powder coated finish. Easy to assemble, without tools."

That's complete information. And complete information is especially critical for catalogs that sell functional items, where a photograph can't make the sale.

Consider this copy for telephone-equipment catalog Hello Direct: "Cordless phone users! The 1-line machine with remote control (#3808) lets you screen and intercept calls *from your cordless phone*. You can also play back messages, change greetings, and even turn the machine off or on remotely. You can record 3 greetings to switch between, and store incoming messages in up to 3 separate mailboxes. It gives you 13 minutes of recording."

Such copy is short, but complete. Copy that leaves out key facts either frustrates customers or ties up customer-service lines. Either way, that puts the sale at risk.

Five elements of complete selling information

1) Size. We all know size information is critical for apparel catalogs. But don't neglect size when it comes to hard goods. Customers need to know how much space that wall hanging will take up, or whether that clock will fit on a desktop. Be sure to let them know.

2) Colors. Along with color laydowns, it's important to write out the names of colors available for your items. Show customers how "magenta" differs from "claret," or "celery" from "celedon."

3) Workmanship. Whether you sell hard goods or apparel, be sure to address how your products are put together. Do those pants button or zip? Will that material shrink? Must that shirt be dry cleaned? Is that table veneer or hardwood? How durable is that "leather-like" material?

4) SKU numbers. Make sure your stock-keeping numbers are clear and easy for customers to find. Nothing frustrates like a search for tiny, unreadable numbers.

5) Price. How you present price may vary, dependent on your positioning. But one thing for sure, price should be clear, easy to read, and preferably at the very end of a copy block, where the customer is used to finding it.

LAW #3: Benefits

All copy, naturally, should note the *features* of a product, such as the size, shape and number of buttons or quarts of water it can hold. But features mean nothing without *benefits*. Benefits, in essence, answer the customer's unspoken question: "So what? What's in it for me?"

Let's go back to that Sharper Image massage chair for a moment. The copy indicates scores of features, including fixed rollers, spherical nodes, a push-button control panel with ten massage functions, and a two-speed oscillator. But by itself, a list of features like this means about as much as a sticker on a new car.

To carry it forward, the copy must push benefits. Those fixed rollers "multiply the massaging action." The nodes "massage the full length of your back with a range of motions—kneading, tapping and rolling." The control panel commands "three Shiatsu massages at your fingertips." The oscillator "restores tired calf muscles."

Every catalog needs benefits—not just those selling functional products. True, apparel shoppers may be drawn to a sweater because of its great color, or consider a piece of jewelry because it matches their jacket. Gift buyers might fall in love with that glass centerpiece or carved elephant just because of its winsome look.

But to seal the sale, you need to offer more than good looks. You need to cite benefits, which can push the customer from "just looking" to "sold."

Consider, for instance, how a Gump's floor lamp "spans centuries of decorating styles." That implies the piece is timeless, and will fit comfortably with any decor. Or think of how Sundance's jewel-drop earrings "glow in sunlight or candlelight." The benefit: You can wear them day or night.

Just look at the benefits in this Sundance copy for a sweater: "Pima cotton...is hand harvested to eliminate impurities. When spun, this yarn has unsurpassed softness and purity and takes to dyes like no other cotton." Or this simple T-shirt from Early Winters, "pigment-dyed in the dusty colors of Oregon's high desert and prewashed for the weathered look of an old favorite. A generous cut ensures an easy fit. Double-stitching prevents blowouts."

When you match features ("a generous cut") to benefits ("ensures an easy fit"), you've done the selling job.

Two elements of benefit copy

1) Focus on feelings. We all know that customers often don't buy a product for what it does, but for how it makes them feel. That red dress, for instance, may make one buyer feel sexy. This walnut desk clock may make another feel important and tasteful. That set of flannel sheets may make a third feel cozy and cared for.

Benefit copy often needs to strike that emotional chord. J. Peterman, of course, is a master at this ("Italian cut. Reminds me of his courtly, half-amused shrug."), but any cataloger can speak to a customer's heart as well as head.

2) Focus on solutions. Most benefit copy addresses a customer's unmet needs and desires. Implied in the description (usually) are one or more of the following common reasons to buy:

—*The product solves a problem.* "When sunlight's hard to come by, try basking in this state-of-the-art, radiation-shielded, full-spectrum bright light." (health-products catalog Self Care)

—*The product saves time/space/makes a task easier:* "No more clearing a path across your desk every time you need the mouse...." (office-supply catalog Reliable Home Office)

—*The product offers quality/durability:* "Thirty-one miles of cotton yarn create a three-ply rope so strong, it will never sag or give way." (home-and-garden catalog Frontgate)

—*The product offers versatility:* "It's the first genuine Panama straw hat we've seen that you can actually fold or roll." (travel catalog TravelSmith)

—*The product organizes:* "Free up work space while you keep your most frequently used computer literature and materials within easy reach." (Reliable Home Office)

—*The product makes you look better:* "Designed in a revolutionary soft microfiber that conforms to your shape without panty lines." (Victoria's Secret)

—The product makes you more comfortable: "Its thousands of tiny pores allow air to circulate through the fabric, cooling your skin without clinging to it." (TravelSmith)

—The product improves your home: "A drift of subtly shaded maple leaves handpainted across the top of this oval table gives it a one-of-a-kind distinction." (Gump's)

In short, benefits can be as varied and individual as customers. Once you know what your customers need and how they want to feel, your copy should ensure that they get what they want.

LAW #4: Speaking the customer's language

I'm sure only a handful of J. Peterman customers have breakfasted at La Repaire in Gustavia, or even know where Gustavia is. But that's not Peterman's point. What the catalog understands—and shows in its copy—is that Peterman customers like to think of themselves as worldly, different and somewhat exotic. If they've never been to Gustavia, they might still see themselves as belonging there. Peterman's copy makes them feel part of an exclusive club.

Good catalog copy, like Peterman's, neither talks over readers' heads nor condescends to them. It understands the customer the way a good friend does.

Moreover, good copy is consistent with the catalog's overall brand image. Peterman customers want intellectual seduction. Lands' End customers want humor and intelligence. Early Winters' customers relate to gutsy travel messages; Victoria's Secret buyers look for romance; and Gump's shoppers want sophistication and taste. (Conversely, Sunglass Hut customers want hipness and attitude, which is why the catalog's doddering copy seems so out of place.)

Catalog "language," then, can take just about as many forms as there are catalogs. The best way to illustrate that is with examples. That's why the next chapter will discuss which catalogs speak "their" language best, weaving benefits, selling information and believability into their copy.

THREE TIPS FOR GOOD COPY

1) *Be grammatical!* Don't undercut your carefully hewn image, your fabulous photography and gorgeous design. Bad grammar ("There's brand-new Predator sunglasses") insults a reader's intelligence.

All customers expect us to be smarter than they are—after all, we're trying to sell them something we think they need! You can't let them down. Double- and triple-check your copy.

2) *Fit the image.* Let your copywriters work with the finished layouts. Let them match copy to the mood, stylization and imagery of your visual. You don't want a warm, cozy kitchen image flanked by copy that says, "This knife is sharper than your boss' tongue!" Keep the words as close to the imagery as possible.

3) *Don't waste anyone's time.* Abraham Lincoln was once asked how long his legs were. His reply: "Long enough to reach the ground." It's the same way with copy. Make sure it's long enough to give benefits and complete selling information, but short enough not to tax your reader's patience.

That doesn't mean you should never use long copy. Believe me, you'll need it if you're selling certain new or complicated products, if you're romancing your product, or if you're establishing rapport with your reader.

But long copy is tough to do well. If it isn't a complete pleasure—if it doesn't pull the reader from paragraph to paragraph—it's a waste of space.

BEYOND CATALOG TEXT

A mere copy block shouldn't carry the whole weight of your catalog's selling job. Think of the following copy elements as your trustworthy sales assistants:

Headlines

Naturally, the purpose of a headline is to grab someone's attention and get them to read—or at least look—further. Many catalogs, however (particularly apparel), don't seem to bother. They either trot out clichés ("The Great Outdoors") or do away with headlines altogether.

Good catalogers, however, use headlines to speak to both the product and to the customer. Their headlines reinforce one or more of the following:

Benefits: "Carry a complete rainsuit in your coat pocket"

Price/value: "Save $20 when you buy the complete set"

Image: For Patagonia's adventure image: "Hydrophobia"; for J. Crew's irreverent image: "Boxer Boost"

Product groupings: "Indulge in silk's luxury"

Whether you use headlines or not is your choice. But if you do, *don't write headlines simply for the sake of writing them.* Make sure your headlines help the customer and fit the brand. Otherwise, leave them out.

Lead-ins

As step-siblings to headlines, lead-ins get customers right into the copy block. They're the bold-faced words ("Our English garden fork" or "Holiday sweater dressing") that a customer usually looks for when trying to locate the description of an item.

For that reason, most lead-ins are simply "identifiers." Their job is to eliminate confusion; they tell the customer that yes, she's looking at the right copy block for that gardening fork.

The best lead-ins, however, manage to squeeze a benefit in as well: "Vintage era baseball jersey" (Hammacher Schlemmer) or "Handknit Peruvian sweater" (Sundance) add just a touch of selling power to the product name. Some lead-ins also reemphasize the price promotion from the headline.

Lead-ins, however, shouldn't stray too far from the point. When Victoria's Secret leads a product description with "So pretty in pointelle knit," it's tough for customers to know which product they're looking at.

Non-selling editorial

Granted, you probably think you can't afford to give precious page space to an essay. But consider: Editorial copy helps establish authority, and that can spell credibility and sales.

ONE SIMPLE HEADLINE IN CLIFFORD & WILLS TIES TOGETHER THREE SELLING POINTS: GIFT IDEA, PRICE AND QUALITY BENEFIT.

EVEN CUSTOMERS WHO DON'T HAVE TIME TO READ LONG COPY WILL STOP TO GLANCE AT A BULLETED LIST OF BENEFITS, AS IN THIS LAYOUT FROM JOS. A. BANK.

NOTHING LIKE "PERSONAL ADVICE ON PENS" TO GET PROSPECTS HOOKED ON THE VALUE OF OWNING A QUALITY PEN. HERE, LEVENGER FOUNDER STEVE LEVEEN EXPRESSES THE CUSTOMER'S UNSTATED NEED (TO BE DISTINCTIVE) AND PROVIDES THE SOLUTION (A FOUNTAIN PEN).

Proving that it's more than a mere catalog of high-tech "stuff," Hammacher Schlemmer devotes one inside spread to telling the story of its company, and demonstrates how it chooses its "best" products. Result: instant credibility.

Talk about credibility! Lands' End turns customer testimonials into hero pages, complete with the customers themselves.

Damark excels at bringing customers right to the value messages, through use of strong price callouts, arrows, slashed prices and "compare at" headlines.

For instance, it's tough to sell fountain pens in this information age. So Levenger created a tribute to "The Ritual of Writing," ending with, "You may become known for your handwritten notes, like some recent presidents. Ignore your e-mail. Life is good."

The Black Dog clothing catalog, similarly, ran a page-long epistle from a customer who led the Antarctica Search for Meteorites field team. Patagonia published an eerie paean to ice-climbing. Such editorial not only props a catalog's unique selling proposition, but also tells customers that the catalog values knowledge as much as sales.

Testimonials

If you need credibility in a hurry, call on testimonials. They can emanate either from customers or outside authorities, and can emphasize product, service, price or anything else you like.

Overuse of testimonials, of course, can sound somewhat desperate. But properly used, testimonials can give credence to words that might otherwise sound like hype.

Health products catalog Self Care, for instance, used a customer testimonial to attest to the effectiveness of its "white noise" machine. It also included an article from *The New York Times* on the topic of using full-spectrum light to dispel seasonal depression. Both helped promote the benefits of products that would otherwise stretch a customer's credibility.

Captions and callouts

Particularly for functional products, such as electronics or all-weather apparel, photo captions and callouts emphasize specific benefits that might be tough to squeeze into a copy block.

Clearly, you don't need callouts if you're selling fine gifts or fashion apparel. But they work great for products whose story can't be told in a photograph. Catalogs such as Hello Direct and The Sharper Image are champs at putting benefits into these easy-to-read nuggets.

CHAPTER 20

PUTTING IT TOGETHER: POSITIONING AND COPY

Copy speaks for your catalog the way a salesperson speaks for a store. Just as you expect an athletic footwear salesman to know something about running and aerobics, so do your customers expect your catalog to "talk" with knowledge and understanding of your offer.

Poor copy can spoil a sale the way an ignorant or pushy sales rep can chase off buyers. So let's look at some examples of catalogs that do copy well. These are the ones whose voice most clearly matches their positioning.

THE LONG-COPY CONNOISSEURS

It's not hard to tell a good one-line joke. Stand-up comics do it all the time, shooting out punch lines and hoping one or two of them will stick.

But you've got to admire the stand-up who saves his punch line for the end of a long story. He's the one who will hold you in his grasp for five or 10 minutes, building slowly, inexorably and determinedly to the punch line. Bill Cosby can do it; just about anyone else risks putting the audience to sleep.

So it is that long copy takes a certain amount of guts, and a lot of talent. Pioneered by Joe Sugarman (the first to sell calculators by mail), long copy works best when you need to load on benefits or differentiate your product from competitors. But there's a big gap between copy that bores and copy that holds readers in its sway. Here are the catalogs that do it best:

Lands' End

I've said before that "quality" and "value" are the most overused words in catalog copy. That's why I love Lands' End. It's clearly positioned itself on quality, but its copy never whispers the word. Instead, it uses long copy to tell stories about its product, and it uses warm humor to make those stories worth reading. For instance:

"It's okay to say it: the inside of this blazer looks kind of funny. Fact is, we probably wouldn't point it out to you—if it weren't so important. To the drape and durability of the coat, as well as your comfort.

"Take the chest piece. In many blazers it's made from a stiff material and actually glued in place. (So it feels even stiffer.) By contrast, ours is woven from cotton and canvas, so it's soft. And on top of that, we <u>sew</u> it in place—for extra flexibility."

Lands' End buys into the importance of good copy. By running half a page on blazer anatomy, it tells customers that it cares less about square-inch analysis than about making them feel good about their purchases.

The Sharper Image

As one of the first long-copy catalogs, The Sharper Image (before its 1996 redesign) was all about benefits. Using callouts, long headlines, even long captions (try to find another catalog with captions!), The Sharper Image spelled out every advantage of its latest gizmos, with an encouraging lack of empty adjectives, like "state of the art." For instance, here's copy for a Voice Organizer:

"Thanks to voice-recognition technology that trains quickly to the way you speak, entering important information is as easy as saying it. To review a day's schedule, simply speak the date. To make a call, just say the name. ...You can even add, subtract, multiply and divide by voice!"

Three callouts, three photographs and three captions rounded out the selling story. These varied bits of copy gave the verisimilitude of a real salesperson pointing up selling points as you "examined" the product. For me, shopping at The Sharper Image stores was almost a disappointment after reading this kind of catalog copy!

J. Peterman

Granted, this cocktails-at-the-Pierre copy is not for everybody, and, thankfully, is nearly inimitable anyway. (Like bad Hemingway, you now see bad Peterman everywhere, like this line from a catalog I won't name: "Skimming along the Seine in a little bateau mouche...") Sometimes even Peterman itself stretches too far ("Blue as a campanula, green as the River Stour..."). But when Peterman copy is on, it's unbeatable. Compare these two descriptions of 1940s-style dresses.

"You see them in old 1940s photographs, lovely women turned out in hats and gloves, wearing those classic button front dresses printed with gardens of spring flowers."

Not bad. That was The Territory Ahead. Now Peterman:

Paris, 1947.

Butter, wine, and laughter have made a comeback.

Now, French couture does a little something to reward the women (and men) who stuck it out through the dark years.

The New Look. The most flattering, frankly romantic style of the century.

Bosoms, hips, and waist reappear, along with gloriously full, sweeping skirts.

(France wants deliverance from the boxy, skimpy look of an era obsessed with ration books and clothing coupons.)"

Not much about product features—but the mood and sideways-stated benefits ("the most flattering, frankly romantic style...Bosoms, hips, and waist reappear...") make a far more satisfying sell.

Honorable mentions

Hello Direct, for friendly, palatable explanations of complicated products that, to a novice, look virtually indistinguishable. Long, benefit-oriented heads ("This home office 'attendant' is so smart, it does just about everything but make coffee remotely") lots of callouts and subheads help break copy into tidy, readable bites.

Electronics catalog *Lifestyle Fascinator,* for Sharper Image-style ease of explaining electronic products. Headlines are loaded with benefits ("Add a phone jack anywhere without running wire—or an expensive installation bill!") and copy is warmly promotional. "The RCA Phone Jack System is the easiest, most affordable way to do it right. All you have to do is plug it in! No drilling. No wiring, No tools. It's that easy!"

THE BARE-BONES BENEFACTORS

At the other end of the copy spectrum, bare-bones copy gives "just the facts, ma'am." That's entirely appropriate for many apparel catalogs, where customers are more inclined to look than to read. It also works for dense product catalogs, where there's simply no room to plant details.

But the best bare-bones books are those whose copy isn't merely short, but minimalist. These catalogs know how to pack big meaning into a few words.

Victoria's Secret

With careful phrases and affected spelling ("pyjama," "colour") this Columbus, Ohio-based cataloger intones British sophistication and languor. A skin-tight chartreuse suit is denoted as "vivid in colour, and sculpted to your shape." Cotton boxer "pyjamas feel so heavenly in the summer months."

It would be easy to make this copy as lavish as its lingerie. But these few words, elegantly chosen, amply create the catalog's luxurious mood.

Lillian Vernon

Bright, punchy copy with a pragmatic undertone perfectly suits the catalog's friendly nature and dense layouts. Here's the copy for a trivet: "New! Fancy Scrolled Trivet Is Solid Iron—and will protect forever! Set down your biggest, hottest pots and this openwork design stays strong and beautiful—safeguards counters and furniture from heat marks and scratches. Great in kitchen or dining room."

That's six benefits in 40 words, for a mere everyday piece of kitchenware (and the "New!" in red type adds even more appeal). Few catalogers can match that efficiency.

Honorable mentions

J. Crew, for its headlines and subheads. The copy itself is fairly uneven, wavering between sentence fragments ("A weathered heavyweight. Fit is somewhat trim.") and sentence rambles ("Tape-lined placket, and an impression of appreciable wear and fading lend a marked, individual character to this one."). But the headlines are little bursts of cryptic hipness: "Just your standard stuff" and "Just fine points? Maybe." They work perfectly with the catalog's relaxed attitude.

THE DOWN-HOME WINNERS

"Down-home" catalogs sell on a combination of warmth, nostalgia and practicality. Customers look forward to them like a visit to the country.

Vermont Country Store

There aren't many catalogs that could emulate this sensible, commanding voice, nor would many want to. Vermont Country Store assumes its customers are as level-headed and hard-working as the catalog is. Frankly, that's the secret of its appeal.

Consider this neighborly advice: "We all know that hard, compacted soil does not make for a healthy lawn...." Or this: "If you've ever put up fence posts, you know you don't want to have to go out and replace them any time soon. Same thing with your lawn furniture." I doubt one in a thousand Country Store buyers have ever sunk a fence post, but I'm sure none of them mind the compliment, nor the nostalgic intimation.

It's no wonder Vermont Country Store single-handedly kept the Olivetti company manufacturing manual typewriters for their customers. The catalog sold them to people who prefer to "slow down to think." No other catalog captures hardheaded Yankeeness quite so well, especially for Yankee wannabes.

Norm Thompson

This catalog always seems a bit like a visit from a friendly, slightly eccentric aunt. Product-wise, you never know what tricks Norm Thompson might have up its sleeve, whether Meadow in a Can or the world's best skipping rocks. Its copy—particularly in its headlines—carries out that warm, slightly batty tone, but it's always grounded in realism and fact. A harmonica, for instance, is introduced as "The only stocking stuffer tuned to the key of C." A "soccer robot" is billed as "He's got six legs and more moves than Pele!" Teapot copy goes like this: "Sip a bit of *dolce vita* in our dappled flowers tea for one."

Honorable Mention

Plow & Hearth, for down-to-earth, believable copy that doesn't try to whitewash product or turn its readers into romantic dreamers. For its

Microlight rain suits, the copy reads, "We have three Microlight suits in our closet which we (and guests) use all the time because they're bright, light, and so easy to fit in a pocket, suitcase, golf bag or briefcase." Right away, you can picture that any cataloger who boasts a closet filled with rain suits (and an influx of guests) is probably about as easygoing as you can get.

Harry and David, for its unself-conscious way of making customers care about fruit. In speaking of Royal Riviera pears, for instance, the catalog states, "We envy anyone their first taste." Calling on words like "creamy and luxurious," "lush juiciness and melting texture," or "full of natural sass and flavor," Harry and David can still conjure up an old-timey sense of pretty orchards and magical flavors.

THE STORY TELLERS

Using words like "we" and "you," story-telling catalogs make readers feel personally involved with the book. They tend toward long copy with a distinctive narrating voice. That means these catalogs actually get customers to *read*, if only to catch up on the latest news and product discoveries.

Rent Mother Nature

With its long, chatty copy, Rent Mother Nature makes you feel as if the company owner were in the room, helping you become "part of the process," as the catalog puts it, in creating your own catalog product. Whether they rent a pecan tree or a Dorset sheep for a season (yield: one blanket), customers are invited to assume their own part in the "story," contemplating "their" sheep peacefully nibbling away in the field.

The catalog tells them, for instance, "March or April is the time for shearing, when we gently help the sheep off with their winter coats. Your wool is then rushed to the mill to be made into blankets...." Reading about it stirs the customer fantasy, and the fantasy stirs the sales.

The Territory Ahead

Though a bit purple at times, this catalog wins kudos for setting up an atmosphere as crisp as its photography. Consider this copy for a jacket: "The aspen leaves have turned the ground gold, and the last of the cattle meander down the mountain. At night the wind blows raw and cold, and the clear, moonless sky rains stars. This is the season for the Wind River Leather Jacket...."

Honorable Mention

Gift catalog *Myakka River Trading Company,* for selling its gift product with knowledgeable historical associations and the occasional story. Describing its exclusive photograph of deer on a Nebraska prairie, the catalog's copy reads, "For the next hour or so we watched as stately white tail bucks and a small group of does grazed, while their fawns frolicked with several burrowing owls, all to the utter dismay of the resident prairie dogs, who set up a constant chatter." When you buy the product, the catalog implies, you buy your part in a wonderful tale.

THE ADVENTURE/LIFESTYLE BOOKS

To a true adventurer, few things are less action-oriented than picking up and leafing through a catalog. Adventurers aren't contemplative sorts, so the copy in these catalogs must either be compelling enough to get attention, or quick and pragmatic enough to show benefits, fast.

Moreover, "adventure" catalog copy must be authentic enough to speak to real travelers, while simultaneously tickling the fancy of the adventurous wannabe. After all, adventure product is as much about image and aspiration as practicality. Think of those ubiquitous print and TV ads for four-wheel drive vehicles. Maybe one in a thousand of these overly rugged cars actually end up outside the suburbs, but the ads sell through a fantasy of wilderness, dirt roads and escape.

Patagonia

Patagonia's copy is not for the faint-hearted. The catalog will devote an entire page, for instance, to a 400-word essay on climbing a frozen waterfall named "Hydrophobia," ("Shards of snow drove headlong into my eyes, forcing tears, blinding me. Ice welded my lashes shut...") and follow up with a second page devoted to selling the $775 "Gridman suit," a snowsuit that will "protect you from the most heinous weather."

This copy isn't written by a nerd with glasses, but by someone actually out on the rock faces. Heavy use of callouts and attention to "Patagonia quality details," like zippers that run from elbow to mid-torso, establish this catalog as a wise and experienced adventure authority.

TravelSmith

For kinder, gentler adventuring, TravelSmith takes its travel mission seriously, but not too seriously. On the one hand, the catalog announces, "These are the poles famous mountaineers such as Reinhold Messner and Peter Habeler used to conquer the world's great summits..." On the other hand, it states, trekking poles "do for your body what four-wheel drive does for a car," and "Take it from the Swiss Army: Life is too short to wear cheap socks." Ample copy and benefit-oriented headlines, such as "Tiny Travel Alarm Packs A Big Display," make TravelSmith a great tour guide for those who enjoy a pleasant ride.

Honorable Mention

Early Winters, for zippy copy in which adventure knowledge mixes easily with benefits. "There's no excuse to jog/skate/bike/shoot hoops/work out in soggy old cotton sweats anymore. Not with a technical fabric like ButterFleece around."

Apparel catalog *Black Dog,* or imbuing copy with somewhat cheeky references to Martha's Vineyard, from its weather (often bad) to its pubs (always great). For Wind Pants: "Pull these over jeans or bare knees, and escape that harsh wind when the weather is turning contrary to your plans." For Duffle Bags: "The smallest carries your sunglasses, sunscreen and some cash or your little ones' shell collection, the mid-size holds a stack of T's or whatever and the largest will take towels or rope or...and still have space."

THE ROMANTICS

In essence, romantic catalog copy spins fantasies of the way customers would like life to be. The implied "benefits" are usually about a peaceful, more serene or luxurious way of life, and the copy holds forth on the realities of a product without sacrificing imagination.

Smith & Hawken

If it is possible to be romantically pragmatic, Smith & Hawken manages just that attitude. Its smart, literate copy, with its historic and geographic allusions, has the sturdy charm of a Cape Cod cottage. Consider: "A day bed is a destination. Mounded up with pillows—a hybrid of couch and settee—it offers a respite from the confines of a desk..." Or, "Cathedral windows reach peaked points to suggest heavenly ascension; in echoing the form, this trellis urges vines to climb skyward." If Martha Stewart crafted copy instead of cookie dough, this would be it.

Garnet Hill

While Garnet Hill's softly-lit photographs convey the catalog's delicately romantic mood, the copy fits as perfectly as a lace shawl over a silk gown. A blanket, for instance, is described as "lovely, cloudlike." Curtains of "fine translucent Irish handkerchief linen create a softly diffused light." With slippers, "only soft pure wool touches the feet." The words flow to the reader like a warm breeze.

THE CHEST-BEATERS

Promotional catalog copy screams "price" as loud as "product." Many catalogs can cough up value and price promotions when they have to, but true promotional catalogs hammer home the price message in an inspired number of ways.

MicroWarehouse

On its own, a 15" color monitor does little to inspire excitement, but watch how computer products catalog MicroWarehouse keeps you glued to the page. First, there's the huge yellow type at the top of the page: "Radius 15" Color! Display BLOWOUT!" Then a big red checkmark next to the subhead, "You won't find a better value!" Then a second subhead: "Don't miss your chance to get a high-quality 15" display for only $399!" Then a yellow starburst: "Only $399!" And finally, a paragraph of sales copy and an impressive list of features.

So that's price promotion times four—before the customer even gets to a single word of product description! Given that most of this catalog's customers already know the value of a 15" color monitor, MicroWarehouse rightly assumes that it can win them to a sale with price.

Chadwick's of Boston

Pick just about any block of Chadwick's copy, and I bet you'll find three or four tiers of price emphasis. The headline for a T-shirt, for instance, might state, "100% cotton, two for $30." The copy block might tell you, "Compare at retail price of $18.95." A subhead might then further point out, "Save $5 when you buy two," as well as "Special! Three or more, $10 apiece."

In short, Chadwick's can slice a price any way conceivable. That ends up convincing customers of terrific bargains.

Damark

When it comes to selling complex electronics products, Damark combines effective, knowledgeable (and brief!) copy blocks with strong emphasis on price. Copy is minimal, but complete, giving customers the sense that they're hearing the whole story: "....this all-digital cordless speakerphone features the much talked-about 900MHz technology. That's the technology that allows signals to travel farther, penetrate walls and provide overall clearer conversations."

The catalog then splashes price in large type next to the product, adding such deal-making subheads as, "Great deal price!", "Mfr. Sugg. Retail," or "WAS" accompanied by a slashed-out old price. Along with frequent mention of rebates and low-price service plans, Damark uses every promotional device to tell readers they're getting great stuff at a great deal.

THE PROBLEM SOLVERS

Years ago, *Mad* magazine ran a satire of an advertising person trying to market "elbow deodorant." The hapless executive, first, of course, had to create an ad that made people worry about their possibly smelly elbows. He could then sell the deodorant as the "solution."

To a certain degree, problem-solving catalogs have the same challenge. They have to tell customers why they need a product they may not have even known they needed! In other words, they often have to first convince customers that they *have* a problem—and then convince them that they've got the solution at hand. The best ones manage do it with believability and humor (if possible).

Better Living

With its serviceable photos and onslaught of gray type, Better Living isn't a beautiful catalog, but its unfussiness is refreshing. Consider the benefits in this headline: "Lifetime Night Light—Costs Only 2 cents Per Year To Operate". Or this one: "When Nothing Else Works, Blast Away Stubborn Weeds or Ice With Power Flame!" The illustrations may look hokey, but the catalog's function-over-form attitude perfectly matches the practicality of its product line.

Self Care

I like how this catalog solves "problems" I never knew I had! It starts with long benefit headlines ("White Noise masks disturbing sounds so you can sleep!"), adding on easy-to-read benefit-laden copy. All of it makes a compelling case for such tough-to-explain products as accupressure sleep aids and "natural" alarm clocks that wake you with light.

Even better, Self Care uses testimonials to buttress its case. One customer, for instance, wrote to say how she used the white noise machine to mask a neighbor's barking dog. The director of a mental-health program was quoted as an advocate of bright-light therapy for seasonal depression. The catalog seems to imply: Don't take our word for it. Listen to people you know and trust!

THE AUTHORITIES

Regardless of category, "authority" catalogs excel at creating the impression that they are *the* source for product. They underscore their credibility with well-researched, well-examined copy that always reads as if uttered by experts.

L.L. Bean

L.L. Bean's copy is utterly brief, no-nonsense yet packed with benefits. The catalog deals in short sentences, action verbs and sentence fragments, intuitively acknowledging the customer's intelligence. Consider this copy for a backpack: "Made from Bean Tested packcloth, tested in our lab for superior abrasion and puncture resistance. Double urethane coatings give complete water repellency. All seams are lockstitched with a special dual-cord thread, then bound with durable nylon fabric for exceptional strength—no fraying or "blowouts.""

It's easy to picture the Bean copywriter checking and rechecking every word for communication and accuracy. In that sense, the copy perfectly mirrors the catalog's own legendary fussiness over its merchandise.

Gump's

Sell a $2,300 rug in only 35 words? It's possible, given that Gump's manages copy as graceful and sophisticated as its products. "Traditional William Morris patterns and ancient Persian motifs combine in this luxuriously thick pile carpet, colored in soothing shades. Woven of pure wool with a durable cotton warp, it's marvelously soft underfoot. Handcrafted in India."

No empty adjectives, no excessive preening, and the copy assumes (rightly, I'm sure) that its customers—as well as the copywriter—know a William Morris pattern from a Persian motif.

Levenger

I don't personally know Levengers founders Steve and Lori Leveen, but I'm inclined to think they've personally converted thousands (at least!) of consumers into pen fanciers. Their palpable passion and expertise for writing and reading implements is always evident in their copy: "We commissioned one of Italy's master pen makers to design a new pen faithful to the qualities of the 1920s but using modern materials." Or, "At Levenger, we are connoisseurs of bookstands, but one thing we had never seen was an inexpensive bookstand that was attractive, so we created one."

Reading this catalog gives you the sense that the Leveens do nothing but indulge a private passion with education and research. They invite the customer into sharing that contagion, and we're always willing to go along.

Williams-Sonoma

It's said that Chuck Williams once threw out cover photographs of a quiche because the quiche didn't *taste* right—even though it photographed just fine. Such stickler behavior reflects well in the catalog's copy, which always indicates expert sourcing and knowledge of product.

section five

SOLVING YOUR CATALOG'S IDENTITY CRISIS

CHAPTER 21
Meeting the Marketing Challenge

CHAPTER 22
The Challenge of Start-ups

CHAPTER 23
The Spin-off Catalog

CHAPTER 24
Should You Reposition?

CHAPTER 25
The Catalog Face-lift

CHAPTER 26
Bringing Back Your Inactives

CHAPTER 27
Prospecting Catalogs

CHAPTER 28
Sale Catalogs

CHAPTER 29
Identity: The Foundation of Your Catalog

MEETING THE MARKETING CHALLENGE

Chances are, you first picked up this book while you faced some kind of marketing challenge.

After all, most catalogers spend their careers chasing one marketing dilemma or another. At one point, they might debate launching a spin-off. At another, they might decide to reposition to a different audience. Or they might find that the book they'd launched isn't performing to expectation. Or perhaps the "honeymoon" phase of business is over and they haven't decided how to reach the next level.

Essentially, you can address almost any marketing challenge with marketing-driven creative. Usually, those challenges occur in the following areas:

—*Start-up catalogs*

—*Spin-off catalogs*

—*Repositions*

—*Facelifts*

—*Reactivation catalogs*

—*Prospecting catalogs*

—*Sale books*

Granted, creative alone can't solve every marketing dilemma. Start-up books, for example, need circulation, merchandising, operations and financial strategies, in addition to creative. Successful prospecting catalogs depend on the right rental lists. Repositionings usually need to scrutinize their product offers.

In fact, for *any* catalog to succeed, the formula boils down to *reaching the right audience with the right product at the right price and at the right time.* If any of those elements are off, even the best creative won't get the catalog back on track.

On the other hand, marketing-driven creative has a critical role in solving marketing problems. Its job is to *make every other marketing strategy stronger and more effective.* After all, the perfect offer for the perfect list goes nowhere if the catalog doesn't get opened. If a catalog doesn't *sell,* a prospect doesn't buy.

Moreover, each marketing challenge requires a different creative approach. Repositioning a book isn't the same as giving it a facelift, and catalog spin-offs require different solutions from start-ups. So in this section, I'll not only point out the best approach to each of these challenges (and others), but share some case studies with you as well. Often the best way to solve a problem is to learn what others have done when faced with the same challenge.

CHAPTER 22

THE CHALLENGE
OF START-UPS

If I had a dollar for every person who told me he possessed the ultimate and greatest catalog idea, I could close my business and retire now. The truth is (as every experienced cataloger knows), the average guy on the street thinks putting out a catalog is as easy as filling up a photo album, and will make him as rich as Richard Thalheimer or Lillian Vernon.

But as those in the business know, Richard Thalheimer and Lillian Vernon are marketing and creative geniuses (who also possess an exquisite sense of timing). For the rest of us, starting up and spinning off catalogs requires a more pragmatic skill set. We have to know and understand our target markets, our merchandising niche, and support our catalog concepts with the right positioning and brand image.

In this chapter you'll learn about the differences between start-ups and spin-offs, and the marketing challenges each faces. You'll also discover where your own launch plans might fit in the marketplace. A strong identity, with the right marketing-driven creative, can carry just about any launch concept to success.

THE START-UP CATALOG

True start-up catalogs launch as unique books in the marketplace. They aren't spun off from a parent catalog, and they aren't (one hopes) a knock-off of an original book already in the marketplace. They make unique offers to unique target markets.

For that reason, they also run the creative gamut. Some start-ups are little more than flimsy price sheets with pick-up photography manufactured on a PC in someone's garage. Others are thick, glossy tomes put out by agencies well financed with corporate dollars.

The good news is looks and dollars alone don't determine a start-up's success. A slick, expensive book can fail just as miserably as an inexpensive book can succeed. It all comes down to *offer, image* and *positioning*. If an inexpensive book presents the right offer to the right audience in the right way, it's a winner.

Since this is a marketing book, I'm not going to delve into the financial aspects of launching a catalog (which could be a book in itself). Nor will I help you evaluate catalog concepts. No book, in fact, can tell you how to

CORPORATE START-UPS, LIKE THIS DISCOVERY CATALOG, CALL ON AS MANY IDENTIFIABLE CORPORATE CHARACTERISTICS AS POSSIBLE. NOTE NUMEROUS REFERENCES TO "THE LEOPARD SON," A DISCOVERY CHANNEL THEATRICAL RELEASE.

SUNDANCE WISELY PLAYS UP ITS ROBERT REDFORD CONNECTION IN EVERY ISSUE. THOUGH REDFORD DOESN'T SPECIFICALLY DISCUSS MERCHANDISE, HIS FACE AND WORDS CREATE AN ENVIABLE CONTEXT FOR SELLING PRODUCT.

find the right audience for that fresh-pasta catalog start-up, or whether a catalog of parenting products will be a winner.

But I will point out the *marketing and creative strategies* that start-up catalogers must consider to have the best shot at making it in a crowded market.

LAUNCH # 1: The corporate start-up

Financially blessed at birth, corporate start-ups are those born with a silver spoon in their pages, thanks to a parent company that's usually in a non-cataloging business. The Discovery Catalog, for instance, launched by the The Discovery Channel, is an example of a corporate start-up. So is the Disney catalog, National Geographic catalog, even the Sundance catalog, launched from Robert Redford's Sundance ranch.

Besides financial blessing, most of these start-ups have another advantage as well: a ready-made *brand*, and, in most cases, a brand image. In other words, these catalogs can mail out the door with a recognizable name. Prospects know something about them before they even open the book.

Truthfully, you can't buy that kind of value. Brand is the single most important motivator in customer purchase behavior. Buying brand name, after all, is a safe consumer choice. If a customer has two catalogs selling kids' backpacks at the same price, chances are good she'll go for the one with the Disney name behind it.

The creative approach

Because most corporate launches depend so heavily on brand, that's generally the creative path they have to take. Every bit of their brand identity, for better or worse, comes from the parent. It's up to the cataloger to see what works to attract mail order shoppers, and what doesn't. So...

1) Try to capitalize on brand. Some brands, for instance, have no positive associations; others have so little connection to product marketing that they don't translate well into catalogs. It's unlikely, for instance, that the Geritol brand could produce a successful catalog of women's apparel, or that Funk & Wagnall's could market kids' toys. Even *Cosmopolitan* magazine bombed when trying to create a catalog of women's merchandise. Its readers—mostly college-age women—hadn't proven themselves as catalog shoppers, and most catalog shoppers hadn't proven themselves as *Cosmo* readers.

On the other hand, some brand names translate beautifully. *National Geographic*, for instance, has been revered for years as a travel and world knowledge authority, even among those who don't read the magazine or watch its programming. Who wouldn't buy maps, books and travel videos with the *Geographic* name? Same with *Reader's Digest,* a world leader in how-to. Or Disney, entertainment colossus. Each of these brands has been in a good position to sell to catalog audiences.

2) Find the brand imagery. Name alone isn't enough to cue catalog customers into "knowing" a brand. Most customers need visual cues, as well. The National Geographic catalog, for instance, borrows the famed logo and yellow border of the parent magazine. Disney's logo is plastered all over its catalog, as are the little animated creatures that lend the brand its warmth and fuzz. The Reader's Digest catalog borrows the logo, easy-to-read typeface and family-oriented product line from the original.

Granted, not every brand image translates onto catalog pages. Discovery catalog, for instance, can't exactly duplicate the television visual of a snake hunting a rabbit, or a jet fighter screaming out of the sky. Likewise, you can't take a song from "Pocahontas" and insert it into a Disney catalog (unless it's online).

But you can transfer color, typefaces and other elements from one medium to another. The Discovery Catalog customers, for instance, can find editorial "snapshots" of Discovery channel programming on each spread. Sundance conveys the rugged imagery of its ranch with landscape covers and rustic earth tones throughout its catalog. Reader's Digest carries brief editorial tips and pull-quotes from its books, carrying on the Digest's neighborly image.

3) If the brand doesn't fit, invent another. Some catalog start-ups, for one reason or another, need to stand apart from the parent company's established brand. In Chapter 5, for instance, I mentioned how TJX Corp. wanted its catalog positioned to young career women rather than to its college-age retail customers. The result was Chadwick's of Boston, whose name eventually became a brand in its own right.

If you need to separate your catalog's brand from its corporate parent, you might have to treat it as if it were a kitchen-table launch (Launch #3, below).

AN EMPHASIS ON FAMILY VALUES IN READER'S DIGEST'S "HOME" CATALOG MIRRORS THE COMPANY'S POSITIONING.

LAUNCH #2: The retail start-up

We all know of successful catalogs that launched store chains to capture the "touch-and-feel" shopper (Eddie Bauer and San Francisco Music Box, to name just two). Sometimes, however, store chains launch catalogs to reach the convenience shopper.

When that happens, a true retail catalog does not become a store traffic-builder. Instead, it becomes a selling device in its own right, often even carrying a product mix designed especially for the mail customer. Crate & Barrel, Pottery Barn, Tiffany and Bloomingdale's retail catalogs all launched as separate but complementary businesses to their retail store parents.

The creative approach

It's tough to capture the experience of a retail store in a catalog. Stores create consumer interest by stocking hundreds or thousands of items into a space that invites wandering and browsing. Shoppers can pick up items they like, turn them around, ask questions of salespeople, and take in other sales displays through peripheral vision.

SINCE THEIR CATALOG CUSTOMERS CAN'T PICK UP GLASSES AND SILVERWARE, RETAIL CATALOGS, LIKE THIS ONE FROM CRATE & BARREL, OFTEN LIGHT PRODUCTS TO BRING OUT THE FULL THREE-DIMENSIONAL EXPERIENCE.

DAILY PLANET, WHICH STARTED OFF AS A T-SHIRT AND RUSSIAN-PRODUCTS DIRECT MARKETER, HAS EVOLVED WITH ITS UNIQUE SELLING PROPOSITION: MARKETING UNUSUAL, FUN PRODUCTS FROM AROUND THE GLOBE.

Catalogs, on the other hand, have only two dimensions to work with, along with a set number of pages and a limited number of items. A creative approach, then, requires catalogers to consider the following techniques:

1) Find the transferable elements. Most retail chains, like the corporate parents mentioned above, have spent years building up recognizable brand imagery and logos. Often, that imagery lends itself to a catalog's brand identity as well. It's easy for a catalog cover to pick up on a store's logo (the way Bloomingdale's or Crate & Barrel's does) or to recreate the store's ambiance. Tiffany catalog, for instance, not only uses the store's familiar serif typeface, but the sky blue color made famous from its gift boxes.

2) Light up the products. Products in retail catalogs need to pop off a page. Pottery Barn, for instance, creates drama for its dinner plates and glasses through highlights and shadows that play up the simple, elegant product lines. Tiffany's photographs each item as if it were being personally presented to each reader. Such lighting can help evoke the mood and three-dimensionality of seeing a product in the store.

3) Approximate the shopping experience. Though Bloomingdale's By Mail *could* show its outfits in office settings and hotel lobbies, it prefers the studio shots that more closely emulate the appearance of store mannequins and displays. Crate & Barrel, likewise, arranges many of its products in orderly, beautifully lit "compartments" on the page, as if presenting them on store shelves. Such displays stimulate the kind of browsing that store customers enjoy.

4) If appropriate, departmentalize. Retail catalogs often paginate merchandise almost as if by store department, so that customers know they'll find the career apparel in one area, casual wear in another and shoes in a third. Tiffany, for instance, arranges lower-priced gifts in one section of the book, but saves jewelry for separate sections where customers can savor the high-priced diamonds and gold. Just as customers can visit favorite parts of a store, so, too, can they turn to favorite parts of a catalog.

LAUNCH #3: The "kitchen-table" start-up

Kitchen-table is hardly the phrase for it anymore, but these launches are what we think of as "traditional" start-ups. In other words, they launch without benefit of a known brand name. They're the catalogs that emerge as the merchandising brainchild of an entrepreneur: Levenger, J. Peterman, The Sharper Image, Lillian Vernon, and on and on.

The creative approach

A non-branded catalog launch has it tough. Every year, it seems, more and more catalogs crowd the marketplace, while more and more entrepreneurs rise up to find their place in it. It takes intelligence and imagination to attract a viable customer base. Here's what start-ups need to consider.

1) Establish a brand identity. OK, you probably expected that one. Brand identity is key to a successful launch, and means finding your unique niche in the marketplace, not only in merchandising, but in creative. The greatest catalog concept ever means little without key creative elements to support it. By now we know how, for instance, Richard Thalheimer supported The

Sharper Image's high-tech catalog identity with tons of information and glossy photography. The Leveens, in launching Levenger, expressed their catalog's positioning ("tools for serious readers") with high-toned elegance in typeface, lush images, and even in the textured "paper" used as white space.

A new launch must establish creative uniqueness in everything from product to layouts to logo. A "me-too" catalog might attract buyers in the short term, but it will never find a long-term customer base.

2) Have a personality. Have a *real person,* whenever possible, define your book. Start-up catalogs that identify an owner or founder give themselves automatic credibility and awareness.

It certainly helps the Lew Magram catalog, for instance, that Erv Magram, son of the founder, still stands behind the catalog and in front of the customer. Tilley Endurables often uses Tilley family members both as models and product endorsers, displaying favorite luggage and clothing items and discussing their own personal travel tips. And while John Peterman never clearly identifies himself in his book, the catalog's tales of finding goodies in India or in trunks at estate sales certainly give the impression that an adventuresome merchandiser is at the helm.

I've already mentioned the old selling mantra: "People don't buy from companies. They buy from people." Catalogs that show real people standing behind their product (or better, telling why they wanted to start a catalog in the first place) create trust. Trust often translates to sales.

3) Follow your own vision. I once heard John Peterman say that if he'd paid attention to anything that anyone told him about cataloging, he wouldn't have had a business. He chose to be antiestablishment, and it paid off for him.

Contrariness can be a good marketing guide. Being "different," however, works only as long as that difference expresses the catalog's positioning. The frugal look of The Vermont Country Store, after all, works great for products like push mowers, but not so great for high fashion. Likewise, The Pleasant Company, Patagonia and Black Dog all use creative that would look extravagant or affected in another cataloger's hands.

Developing a unique image, in other words, isn't just a matter of knowing the right marketing principles we've already outlined in the book. It's a matter of applying those principles in a way that hasn't been done before, and making your catalog stand out.

4) Know your customer base. That sounds pretty basic, and frankly, it is. But it can't be stressed enough: The only way to succeed in a category is to *know* it first.

Look at any successful start-up. When a catalog uses marketing-based creative, you can practically "see" the customer. Levenger's images of luxuriously appointed desks and libraries, for instance, conjure up intelligent, monied professionals. We know Patagonia is for serious (or aspiring) outdoor sportspeople, judging from its "show-me" photographs and thorough copy. These catalogs understand not just what their customers want to buy, but what they aspire to. The mark of that understanding is in their creative.

5) Know your selling message. Do you want your catalog to sell quality? Lifestyle? Service? Product uniqueness?

In positioning a new book, it's important to know the message you want customers to receive. Each can require a different creative approach. Take Sundance, with its high-fashion Western appeal. It's strictly a lifestyle catalog, emphasized by covers that show horses racing through a field, or

As a kitchen-table launch, Levenger's succeeded on its selling proposition of fine products for serious readers.

Start-up catalogs need to acquire a brand personality, as Pleasant Company has so ably done with its American Girls catalog. Moreover, its club memberships build undeniable loyalty.

Customers "meet" Lillian Vernon in every issue. As the ultimate kitchen-table entrepreneur, Lillian has spent long years sealing her relationship with her customers, as demonstrated in the book's extensive use of "my" (as in "On my cover").

meadows of wildflowers surrounded by mountains. The catalog doesn't sell product so much as it does a slice of life. The Levenger selling message, on the other hand, is quality. MicroWarehouse, with its huge promotional type and pictures of happy order-takers, sells service and price.

NEXT STEP: SPIN-OFFS

Once a catalog launch is safely airborne, its marketing challenge doesn't end there. The next stage in growth is to find how else to expand on that hard-won brand identity. That's where spin-offs—the subject of the next chapter—come into play.

CASE STUDY

▼

THE START-UP OF SUNDANCE

Back in 1989, the Sundance resort in Utah had two "brand" assets: a well-known founder (Robert Redford), and an evocative name that connoted a well-bred ruggedness—at least among people who'd heard of the place.

That's a pretty slender framework on which to build a catalog, of course. Celebrities like Cher, for instance, have tried to put their own imprint on a catalog business, with little success. Sundance needed to create a brand that would have an appeal far beyond the Redford name.

So the catalog borrowed from the resort itself. "Sundance had a well-defined image rising from its activities," says catalog president Harry Rosenthal. "We just ran with that: the eclectic American, mountain/western look and feel, with a lot of handcrafted texture."

In short, Sundance became a lifestyle book. It chose cover imagery of mountain vistas rather than shots of merchandise. Its product choices showed an "elevated awareness of environment and art, and the role those two play in daily life." Its format size was large enough to make it stand out among standard-size books, and to give adequate space to the rich lifestyle imagery. The copy, though spare, included artist biographies and tales of finding glasswork on road trips to Mexico. Propping included stone fireplaces and views of open fields. Even the catalog's models looked as if they'd never seen the inside of an office cubicle.

Stylistically, the Sundance catalog strove for a balance between sophistication and frontier. The typeface, which has changed about four times, is currently a cleaner, bigger variation of its previous serif type, but is still based on a "chiseled, Western" font from the 1800s. Layouts and propping frequently vary, with increased use of silhouettes at times, or use of grid layouts at other times.

Redford himself remains almost back-burner. Although he's prominent in the opening spread, Redford has never been a shill for the catalog merchandise. Instead he uses the space to address Sundance activities, discuss the film festival or environmental issues. Though a little product endorsement here certainly wouldn't hurt, Redford's chosen stance does elevate the Sundance brand. Recipients who read Redford's editorials come away with the sense that Sundance is more than the mere sum of its catalog products.

Overall, then, Sundance's eight-year history has been "evolutionary," says Rosenthal. "Whenever you try to manage a brand and image, you have to walk a line between being boring and changing so radically that you throw away the goodwill you've built with the customer. We need to keep fresh and interesting, and still stay true to what brought us there."

CHAPTER 23

THE SPIN-OFF CATALOG

On its face, nothing could look simpler. You've got a great general merchandise catalog. You find one-quarter of your customers spend most of their purchase dollars on kitchenware. You've got enough kitchenware inventory to fill a catalog. So why not start a spin-off?

In truth, that's how most spin-offs get started. When novelty cataloger Oriental Trading Company, for instance, found a chunk of customers purchasing religious items, it spun off a separate catalog of Christian product. Sundance spun off a jewelry catalog, sensing that many of its customers were more interested in Southwestern bracelets and earrings than in boots and candleholders.

Each catalog identified an opportunity in the customer base. Each one discovered it had a broad enough audience to support a separate niche mailing. (Spiegel, you may recall, launched dozens of these niche spin-offs during the '80s.)

But, while many spin-off catalogs have no trouble finding an audience, they often have trouble finding an *identity*. Spin-offs are neither established catalogs, nor are they quite launches. They mail to customers familiar with the brand, but also to prospects who may or may not have heard of them. So they often don't know how much of the parent catalog's identity to assume, and how much to leave behind.

In this chapter, I'll go over the best ways to establish a spin-off catalog's identity. I'll also show you catalogs I thought did a great job creating their own spin-off personalities, and those that could use a little work.

THE CREATIVE APPROACH

Like corporate start-ups, spin-offs have the terrific advantage of *brand*. Because spin-off catalogs emerge with the name and reputation of a known parent catalog, they're born with instant credibility.

Even better, spin-offs have the advantage of *audience* as well. After all, customers "vote" for spin-offs with their purchases. Oriental Trading Company, for instance, would never have considered a religious catalog spin-off if a significant number of customers hadn't shown enough interest in the category.

VICTORIA'S SECRET COUNTRY ADOPTS THE
COPY, TYPEFACE AND MODELS OF ITS PARENT (ON
THE LEFT) BUT DISTINGUISHES ITSELF WITH
RELAXED OUTDOOR LOCATIONS AND LARGER
PRODUCT SHOTS.

HORCHOW HOME AND THE HORCHOW COOKS'
COLLECTION BOTH DISPLAY HORCHOW'S DIS-
TINCTIVELY RICH PHOTOGRAPHY AND STYLING.
THE HOME CATALOG, HOWEVER, ADOPTS A
MORE LUXURIOUS PRESENTATION; THE KITCHEN
CATALOG IS CLEAN AND ELEGANT.

So the creative approach to spin-offs resembles that of corporate start-ups. Namely:

1) Check your research. It's one thing to know from your sales figures that "somebody" is buying up all those gardening tools or religious items. But just who are those "somebodies?" How are they the same as your regular customer base? How are they different?

The only way to find out, of course, is to conduct research. If you've just found that your newly introduced shoe merchandise is moving twice as fast as any of your apparel, you can call shoppers to find out who they are and why they're interested in shoes. You can send out mail surveys asking shoppers to identify their demographics and product interests. Or you can query your customer panel (if you have one) on potential spin-off ideas that might appeal to them.

In short, unless you conduct research, you won't know how to market your prospective spin-off. You may find that your spin-off audience requires a far different creative and marketing approach than your regular audience!

Consider, for instance, bath products catalog The Sharper Image Spa. One wonders how much research The Sharper Image used to determine the viability of a spa products catalog to upscale females, even though its core buyers were generally male. The Sharper Image positioned its Spa spin-off with a distinctly elegant and feminine creative. Unfortunately, it was discontinued.

On the other hand, Lilly's Kids probably appeals to the same core customer base as its main catalog. Since Lillian Vernon shoppers are largely married females with kids or grandkids, the Lilly's Kids book rightly resembles its parent. Design, format, copy and layout all echo the familiar creative that inspires trust.

2) Capitalize on brand. Generally speaking, the spin-off "apple" should never fall too far from the tree. After all, spin-offs usually sell best among customers who already know the parent catalog.

For that reason, most spin-offs should carry over the logo, president's letter and other recognizable elements from the main catalog. Such imagery helps customers retain all the positive assumptions they already have about the brand. The Lillian Vernon logo, for instance, tells recipients of the Lilly's Kids book that they'll find a quality assortment of product at good prices. The Lands' End logo on its linens spin-off, Coming Home, tells prospects to expect high-quality merchandise at a great value.

3) But differentiate from the main book. The secret to a successful spin-off is knowing how much imagery to carry over and how much to originate. No spin-off should be mistaken for its parent. After all, what's the point? Customers should feel they're getting something new and special, not just the old book in new trappings.

Naturally, the further a catalog spins off from its parent, the more different it should look. Bath oils and loofahs, for instance, were a big departure from The Sharper Image's usual assortment of executive tools and toys. So The Sharper Image Spa catalog took little creative from its parent, except for the name and president's letter. It's clear from the look of the catalog that you didn't have to be a Sharper Image customer to enjoy The Sharper Image Spa.

On the other hand, some spin-off catalogs are born and raised to appeal to the main catalog's core customer. J. Peterman's home products spin-off, Peterman's Eye, carries a different format from the J. Peterman parent book, and (wonder of wonders) photography as well—but its copy, illustrations and product selection make it clear that the spin-off appeals to the Peterman customer.

So, too, with Green Mountain Mercantile, an apparel spin-off of Vermont Country Store, which borrows heavily from the creative Yankee practicality of its parent. Customers who aren't drawn to Vermont Country Store in the first place probably wouldn't be drawn to the Country Store spin-off either.

4) Position on your opening spread. Particularly if you've got a new spin-off, it's important to state your catalog's position on the opening spread. After all, the logo, president and possibly even the catalog's merchandise may look familiar to your core customers. But recipients are still likely to ask: *Why a new book? What can I find here that I can't get from the main catalog?*

Lands' End's Beyond Buttondowns, for instance, did a beautiful job positioning both its inheritance and separation from its parent. This finer men's clothing spin-off opened with a full spread explaining the catalog's benefits and services. By detailing why the book was created, how this line of clothing came together, and what the new catalog offered for quality and services, Buttondowns established itself as a distinct personality from the main book. Where Lands' End was friendly, Beyond Buttondowns showed itself to be, well, more buttoned down. Where Lands' End was casual, Beyond Buttondowns was more serious and business-oriented.

Clearly, however, the spin-off still shared Lands' End's devotion to quality and thorough service. That important link came through not only in the familiar Lands' End logo, but in informational callouts and copy. In the same way Lands' End would examine the minute details of a canvas briefcase, so did Beyond Buttondowns illustrate the seams and lapels of its apparel. The signature attention to detail gave Beyond Buttondowns a credibility it would have found tough to achieve on its own.

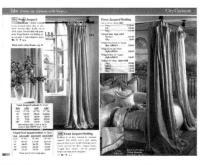

CITY CURTAINS, THE SPIN-OFF FROM COUNTRY CURTAINS, KEEPS THE TYPEFACE OF THE PARENT WHILE ADOPTING FAR MORE DRAMATIC PHOTOGRAPHY AND DESIGN.

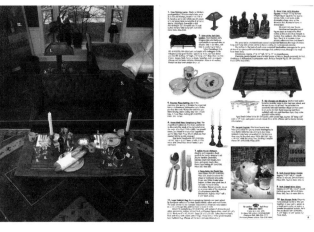

DESPITE THE LARGER-SIZE FORMAT AND USE OF PHOTOGRAPHS, PETERMAN'S EYE CARRIES THE DISTINCTIVE J. PETERMAN EARMARKS OF INSOUCIANT COPY AND WATERCOLOR ILLUSTRATIONS.

CASE STUDY

▼

SUNDANCE'S JEWELRY SPIN-OFF

Most lifestyle catalogs share a similar marketing dilemma: the product line goes broad, but not deep. It's rare, then, for a lifestyle book to accumulate enough sales in a category to actually break out a spin-off book—but that's what happened in 1996 with Sundance.

Jewelry, says catalog president Harry Rosenthal, has always been the catalog's biggest merchandise category. It made sense, then, for Sundance to try a jewelry book among known buyers in its house file. The only problem was this: How do you extend a "lifestyle" brand into a narrow product book?

Sundance's answer was to downplay the lifestyle editorial featured in its main book, and concentrate on product itself. For that reason, the Sundance name, though prominent in the spin-off, didn't dominate the "Jewelry" headline. The cover imagery switched from straight lifestyle shots to product shots. And Robert Redford's editorial, a staple in the main book, was absent from the jewelry catalog. In a targeted merchandise focus, Rosenthal explains, "There wasn't anything for Robert Redford to talk about."

Still, the jewelry spin-off did show certain traits of its parent. For instance, the catalog's photography, which initially featured jewelry laydowns on stone props, kept true to the rugged, Western mood of the main book. Moreover, future presentations, says Rosenthal, will expand the propping, and possibly the merchandise selections as well.

"It's not trying to be the main catalog," says Rosenthal. "We'll continue to vary the presentation and keep some lifestyle elements, but it will still remain a targeted offer."

THE SUNDANCE JEWELRY CATALOG CARRIES ON THE TRADEMARK CLEAN LIGHTING AND WESTERN MOTIFS OF ITS PARENT BOOK.

SHOULD YOU REPOSITION?

Every catalog can use a little creative prodding at some point. Usually, the signs of unrest are pretty clear. That's when loyal house customers stop responding the way they once did; when rental lists start pooping out, and when even your art director starts yawning at the thought of putting together yet another holiday book.

The question is, how big a push do you need? Should you do a complete overhaul of your catalog, or will a tweak here and there suffice?

A lot depends, of course, on the lifestage of your catalog, marketplace and audience. Some catalogs can go to their house file for years with the same book and never watch the well run dry. Others in crowded markets need constant updating to keep their fickle audiences afloat.

Either way, every cataloger at some point needs to look at how to freshen itself up to improve sales. Every cataloger also needs to go through the process with thought and care. Handled wrong, a repositioning can set your book back years in hard-won brand identity (remember the New Coke?). Handled well, repositioning can not only freshen your look, but draw in new prospects, revive slumbering customers and boost your competitive edge.

WHY REPOSITION?

Somewhere between a simple makeover and a complete relaunch is *repositioning*. Repositioning means shifting the imagery of your catalog. Much as Ivana Trump switched from smiling billionaire's wife to glam entrepreneur, so do repositioned catalogs reshuffle their own decks to heighten their appeal, win over new audiences and explore more profitable marketplace niches.

Repositioning happens for almost as many reasons as there are catalogs. Any shift in the following can stimulate the need to reposition:
—*Demographics*
—*Price/value orientation*
—*Competition*
—*Business strategy*
—*Market trends*

Here's how it happens:

A shift in demographics

For some catalogs, customers simply get older—or younger, or richer or poorer. Take Spiegel, which repositioned from mainstream to affluent during the '80s, and then wheeled back to a more value-oriented position in the '90s. Or The Sharper Image, whose audience went from trendy '80s yuppies to value-conscious '90s cocooners.

Conversely, some catalogs reposition, not to keep up with core buyers, but to pursue new customers entirely. Victoria's Secret, for instance, over time went from a catalog of upscale "naughties" to one of almost mass-market lingerie and clothing. The gradual repositioning greatly broadened its appeal—and its sales.

A shift in price-value orientation

Often catalogs reposition to draw bigger-spending consumers. Lillian Vernon, for instance, gradually and subtly shifted during the '80s from a mass-merchandising look to a less dense, more refined creative. The shift allowed Lillian Vernon to appeal to more upscale rental lists while keeping its old customer base.

On the other hand, some catalogs have repositioned to become more promotional. As outlet stores mushroomed and customers became more price-conscious, Spiegel, for one, gradually shifted toward a value position to keep up with consumer demand for better-priced clothing offers.

A shift in competition

Once upon a time, all catalogs looked pretty much like either digest novelty catalog Miles Kimball (cheap and small) or Sears (huge and dry). But as newer, glossier, more targeted catalogs emerged during the '80s, those catalogs were forced either to up their marketing standards or hit the road.

The same goes on today. Every time an upstart catalog or marketing position succeeds, other catalogs in the category take note. Ten years ago, for instance, few catalogers promoted anything better than a 30-day turnaround for shipping. But once catalogs like L.L. Bean started marketing faster and/or lower-priced shipping, other books had to follow suit, or lose out.

In short, competition is a major catalyst for a repositioning. (Just look at how many catalogs have tried to copy the off-price positioning originated by Chadwick's.) To hold onto core buyers, catalogers must constantly evaluate how they stand up to challengers.

A shift in business strategy

Remember "Shirtmaker to the Stars?" That was the old positioning of the Lew Magram catalog, the once-upon-a-time men's clothing catalog.

Back in the late '70s, the struggling cataloger believed that it either had to change its offer and its target market or fade away. Its repositioning as a women's apparel book clearly put it back in the running.

Business dilemmas have forced more than one catalog to reposition—or die trying. Seventh Generation, for instance, found that it could not survive on its small eco-conscious core buying audience. After a few years of business, it repositioned to appeal to a wider gift- and home-decor-buying audience.

A shift in market trends

First, we had yuppies and DINKs (double income, no kids, remember?), with all their needs for career apparel and gift items. Then we had cocooners and penny-pinchers. Next we'll have to contend with aging baby boomers. You can bet that each shift in the market has been, and will be, accompanied by repositioning on the part of catalogers.

Take catalogs like The Sharper Image. This catalog played down its luxury appeal as buyers grew more value-conscious during the '90s, then repositioned a few years later as a hard-core electronics merchandiser. Or consider how numerous apparel catalogs have repositioned from career wear to casual, given the rise of "dress-down Friday." These catalogs not only switched their merchandising, but their models, presentations, imagery and other creative as well.

TAKE TIME TO ANALYZE

First of all, repositioning is a tough call. It requires intimate knowledge of market trends, audience composition and strategic forecasting. It also requires intimate knowledge of your catalog's current positioning. Because you've undoubtedly worked hard to establish recognizable brand imagery in the first place, you have to do some deep thinking before deciding what to change, if anything.

The first step, then, is to *get a clear repositioning statement.* That means defining your current positioning, and then contrasting that with your repositioning.

To get there, you need three things:

1) *Your situation analysis.* Here, you note where your catalog now stands in the marketplace and where you intend for it to go. Ask yourself:

—What selling opportunities exist now that didn't before?

—Which selling opportunities no longer exist?

—What has changed in terms of pricing and merchandising?

—What's happening with the competition? How are competitors affecting my catalog's market share and selling opportunities?

In other words, you have to be able to define how well your catalog currently reaches its market, compared to how well it did in the past. Is a repositioning something you *need* to do, given the changing marketplace, or something you *want* to do for your own personal reasons? You may find that, even though you're bored with your catalog, it still has a valid position in the marketplace.

2) *Your audience analysis.* You know, of course, that when launching a catalog, you need to understand your customer inside and out. It's the same thing with repositioning. Ask yourself:

—What does my customer currently look like? Do I have photographs of the customer I now reach, and of those I'd like to reach?

—Where does my customer live? Suburbs? Studio apartments? Country homes?

—What is my customer's lifestyle? Does she vacation in Disney World or travel Europe with her nanny?

—Most important, *how has my customer's life situation changed?* Has my customer gone from vice president to Perfect Mom, or Perfect Mom to vice president? Is she more concerned with stock options than stocking shelves?

It pays to be as specific as possible when thinking about your customers. One apparel cataloger, for example, divides his female shoppers into 12 different categories, each based on a slightly different demographic and buying habit. He then pins up a photograph of each of these shoppers, along with a demographic and psychographic profile.

Every time he makes a marketing decision, the photographs help him visualize precisely which consumer he wants to reach. That makes it easier to choose the right message for reaching her.

Remember: Repositioning usually happens as a response to your customers. When you understand how your audience is changing, you can understand how you need to change your catalog.

3) *Your marketplace analysis.* It pays to analyze which events in the marketplace might bring about a repositioning. Ask yourself:

—Does my current positioning no longer work? (For example, if you're positioned on price, can you profit in a market of off-price retail stores and catalogs?)

—Are competitors forcing me to position my catalog with unique service, creative or merchandise?

—Am I out of step on a marketplace trend? (For instance, if everyone's buying on price and you're still pushing quality, should you change your imagery?)

Consumer trends are a big factor in repositionings. A marketplace trend toward home decor, for instance, would likely drive many books into a merchandising repositioning. A trend toward "value" might push some into seeking a price repositioning. A career-oriented apparel book might have to reposition in the wake of a casual trend.

So before attempting any repositioning, make sure you nail down all the factors—audience, situation and marketplace—that feed into current status. When you know what's behind your need to change, you're more likely to make changes that pay off.

CONDUCT RESEARCH

All too often, catalogers *know* they need to reposition, but aren't exactly sure what they need to do. All they know is that response rates are falling off, order sizes are shrinking, and outside lists just aren't working the way they used to.

To get to the bottom of what's happening, you need research. You need to understand the disease before you can know the cure. Review Chapter 9 for research help, and in the meantime, remember that self-diagnosis includes the following:

—*Surveys*, either mail or telephone, that can quantify whether your audience is aging, having children, or getting out of the career market.

—*Customer panels,* which can tell you whether buyers think your merchandising, service or product offers have been missing the boat.

—*Focus groups*, which can help you decide which positioning statements work best and what creative elements are most appealing to buyers.

Appropriate research will indicate what's happened to your marketplace and audience. More importantly, it will tell you how your customers currently feel about your catalog. You may find that the problem isn't a market trend at all—it's your own catalog's inability to communicate!

In that case, a repositioning could simply help you tell your story in a way that makes better sense for your audience. When The Sharper Image repositioned in the mid-'90s, for instance, its goal wasn't necessarily to attract a new market. It was to freshen its high-tech story with more humor and edge. The customer base hadn't changed; customer attitudes had, so The Sharper Image's attitude changed with it.

THE CREATIVE APPROACH

If you've decided to reposition, your next step is to work on your creative approach. Of course, I can't give you a list of "Ten Typefaces that say 'Quality,'" or tell you to choose Photographer X if you want more edge in your book. But I can give you important guidelines to consider when you start rejiggering:

GUIDELINE #1: Know what to keep— and what to throw away.

Repositioning is not the same as relaunching. No matter how outdated or horsey your catalog typeface or photography, it's important not to throw out the baby with the creative bathwater.

After all, thousands of customers recognize and identify with the current positioning. Most likely, those customers provide most of your revenues and profits. You can't afford to disenfranchise them.

You may recall, for instance, how Clifford & Wills once abruptly changed its creative positioning from middle-class suburban to fashion-forward urban. Instead of bright sunny backgrounds and smiling models, the catalog substituted wet city streets and tough expressions. Core buyers, namely the suburban moms and career women who identified with those sunny models, fled.

Alienated customers are tough to get back. The goal of repositioning isn't to scrap everything your catalog has and start from scratch, but to build on the strengths already present.

When choosing creative, then, *work slowly.* Consider the audience you have as well as the one you'd like to reach. Keep in mind, too, your current "message" to that audience, as you express it in typeface, photography, layouts and design. If you're going more upscale, for instance, start with less-dense page designs, more refined copy and larger photographs. If you're shifting to a younger audience, include a few younger models at first, then gradually add more with an updated look. Plot each change so that it's easily digestible to both audiences.

GUIDELINE #2: Work from a timeline

Repositioning is evolution, not revolution. For that reason, it's a good idea to plot out the pace of change. A timeline helps you decide which changes you'd like to make to your catalog's positioning, and when you'd like to make them.

Let's say, for instance, that you have a 10-year-old conservative, mid-priced women's apparel catalog. You've developed a substantial house file of loyal buyers. Your problem: The average age of these buyers is on the rise. As these women reach retirement age, you know they'll stop buying your career wear and cut back on new-clothing purchases. Moreover, you won't be able to reactivate them, no matter what promotions you try.

So you could reposition toward younger buyers—but you can't afford to let go of the customers you've already got. The last thing you want is an aggressive creative strategy that includes teenage models and spandex.

That's where the timeline comes in. Over a period of time—most catalogers prefer two to three years—you can plot out your repositioning strategy.

For the apparel catalog, which drops three times a year, the timeline might look like this:

Year One:

First drop: Begin using models in their late 30s and early 40s, along with the occasional 50-plus model.

Second drop: Modify clothing styles. Add more T-shirts and casual wear; raise skirt lengths slightly.

Third drop: Continue modified styles. Add more fashion-related words to copy.

Year Two:

First drop: Less dense pages; more "mannequin" stylings and clothing laydowns. Brighter color clothes.

CLIFFORD & WILLS BEFORE: TOUGH-LOOKING MODELS, LACK OF COPY AND SEVERE URBAN SETTING. CLIFFORD & WILLS AFTER: SOFTER MODELS, MORE "SELL" COPY, BRIGHTLY LIT STUDIO AND LOCATION SHOTS.

Second drop: More location shots; decreased typeface size.

Third drop: Begin using models in their early 30s to early 40s; drop 50-plus models. Promote overnight delivery and other services that appeal to busy, younger women.

Year Three:

First drop: Continue modified clothing styles; more hero pages with fashion-forward looks.

Second drop: Add models in their 20s; more sexy clothing and nightclub wear. Add movement to poses: smiling, running, and so on.

Third drop: Reduce copy blocks. Use more headlines. Drop models in their late 30s and 40s.

Year Four:

Transition complete.

Will you lose core customers along the way? Without a doubt. But remember: These are customers you're likely to lose anyway. Your goal is to appeal gradually to enough younger buyers to offset your losses. A slow, deliberate transition will help make it work.

Just keep Lillian Vernon in mind. Had the catalog instantly switched from downmarket to upscale, nobody would have responded. The core audience would have been confused; the upscale prospects would have been turned off by the name. As it was, a gradual trend made upscale shoppers increasingly comfortable with the Lillian Vernon brand. By the time the transition ended, higher-level buyers were hooked.

GUIDELINE #3: Use tear sheets

As you go through the timeline process, you might want to chart your progress with tear sheets. Tear out and pin up the pages of your book as it evolves. Over time, you'll get a visual sense of how you are reaching your catalog's new position.

Examine each piece of your creative carefully. Ask yourself:

—Does each image relate to my marketing and merchandising goals?

—Does each tear sheet speak to my core customers, as well as to the buyers I'd like to attract?

—Are changes happening too abruptly from catalog to catalog?

—Are images too similar from book to book?

Each issue's marketing creative should bring you closer to meeting the aspirations, needs and wants of your desired target market.

Pay attention to the pace of your progress. You might notice that the "looks" of your models aren't evolving quickly enough, or that their poses look too artificial or too animated to appeal to your potential buyers.

Done correctly, your visual timeline should show a smooth, steady transition from your old look to your repositioned look.

CASE STUDY

▼

Jos. A. Bank's research-based repositioning

For about 50 years, Jos. A. Bank maintained a modestly large retail and catalog business. But, as the '90s neared, the company knew something had to change with its catalog. By then, the catalog offered no strong brand imagery to customers. Its positioning, as a kind of off-price Brooks Brothers, no longer held sway in a world filled with better priced men's clothing outlets.

Bank had to find another, more lasting positioning. So, based on telemarketing surveys, and discussions among merchants and buyers, Bank developed three positioning concepts:

1) *The wardrobing concept.* "Jos. A. Bank specializes in head-to-toe wardrobes, demonstrating the correct tie for the correct jacket, slacks, socks and shoes."

2) *The fashion concept.* "Jos. A. Bank is traditional dressing with a fashion edge."

3) *The quality concept.* "Jos. A. Bank adheres to the highest quality-control standards, tailoring expertise and top fabrics. Customers choose Bank because of its rigorous standards."

Bank then set up focus groups of its customers from all geographic areas, divided into age groups of 25-40 and 40-55. Each group examined the three positioning statements, along with mock-ups for corresponding covers, opening spreads and product spreads. Each also gave unaided response to the question, "What do you think is important about Jos. A. Bank?"

Far and away, all groups reacted most favorably to the "quality" positioning. Bank's customers, it turned out, not only had real knowledge of clothing quality in general, but were aware of Bank's specific quality touches, such as its use of fine fabric. The customers also cited the catalog's quality services, such as its offering of pants and jackets in different sizes.

Research showed that while these customers liked Bank's wardrobing and fashion strengths, what really mattered was Bank's quality. That, of course, gave Bank a huge leg up on its repositioning. While any of its three repositioning notions *might* have worked, research proved beyond a doubt which had the best chance of success.

CASE STUDY

▼

The Sharper Image: A Tale of Two Repositionings.

We all know how The Sharper Image, the golden start-up of the 1980s, lost its Midas touch. Around 1991, core yuppie customers lost their yen for pricey gizmos. Cost-conciousness became the consumer watchword. Consumer research indicated that the catalog product was high-priced and "stuff nobody needs."

THE SHARPER IMAGE BEFORE: LONG, BENEFIT-ORIENTED COPY; LARGE BOXY TYPEFACE, EMPHASIS ON EASE OF SHOPPING.

SHOULD YOU REPOSITION?

Clearly, an overhaul was due. "The core theme of the catalog was unique product—what's new," says Sydney Klevatt, senior vice president of marketing. The catalog, however, had strayed away from unique product and into line extensions. Moreover, it featured brand-name goods, which had high recognition factor, but low margins.

So the company decided on a merchandise repositioning. It pared its product line, focused on the best and newest in a category, and switched to private-label goods with a stronger price/value relationship. "The basic design of our catalog did not really change," says Klevatt. But the new product stance paid off. "We had several good years, with sales volume coming back."

Then came 1995. Now the paper crunch started chewing at the catalog's profit margins. Worse, The Sharper Image's core customer base—high-income male professionals, age 35-55—began to age. New younger prospects (specifically, those 25-35) ignored the book. The product line earned praise in focus groups, but The Sharper Image message just wasn't getting through.

"It's always been our strategy to migrate from a product-driven company to a market-driven company," says Klevatt. So in its second repositioning, the company decided to switch from a product-driven identity to an image-driven one. "We wanted consumers to say, 'I need a gift, so I'll go to Sharper Image,'" says Klevatt. "We didn't want them to say, 'I need a gizmo, so I'll go to Sharper Image.' "

In pursuit of better brand identity, the company hired an advertising agency (Goodby Silverstein & Partners, San Francisco). A major print ad campaign was developed from focus groups and other research, and the ads ran during Holiday 1996. The catalog's redesign matched the updated image. Out went the catalog's familiar fact-laden copy and prodigious captions and callouts. In came sleeker photography, less dense pages, snappier, more insouciant copy.

THE SHARPER IMAGE AFTER: DARK PHOTOGRAPHY, EMPHASIS ON BEING COOL.

Result? Less than spectacular at first. According to Klevatt, the initial repositioned book (October 1996) beat the previous year's October book on a sales-per-thousand-pages basis. Moreover, customer comments ran three-to-one in favor of the redesign.

Some older core buyers, however, complained about the hard-to-read type, and didn't get the copy's humor. Already, however, the catalog had begun pulling back into more familiar creative territory, with an increase in product density and easier-to-read type. The Holiday 1996 catalog proved the best in three years.

Every catalog needs to walk a determined, but careful, line between appealing to new customer groups without alienating the old. If The Sharper Image can pull off its latest branding strategy, it will have forged itself a new identity into the next century. Otherwise, who knows?

CHAPTER 25

THE CATALOG
FACELIFT

As catalogers, we often follow the old saw, "No news is good news."

Let's say, for instance, we're still reaping the benefits of a successful three-year-old launch. The core audience, we believe, is healthy, wealthy and responding just fine. OK, so there *is* a new competitor in the market-place, but it hasn't stolen any of our good buyers. And OK, maybe prospect response has fallen off just a tad—but why do anything to alarm our bread-and-butter buyers? Why rock the boat?

Well, in this instance, maybe you don't need to rock the boat. But it's not a good idea to just whistle and hope those niggling little problem signs will go away. It's better to look at your catalog squarely and objectively and admit the facts: Maybe it's time for a facelift.

Every catalog needs a lift at some point in its lifecycle. If a reposition-ing is a total catalog makeover, a facelift is just that: a freshening or updat-ing of a look that already exists and already works. It doesn't require a change of positioning, and it doesn't necessarily respond to a major shift in audience or in consumer trends. Rather, it's a way to keep customers from feeling that they've seen this same old stuff a million times before.

Much as wardrobes, car styles and home decor need updating from time to time, so do catalogs. A facelift isn't an acknowledgement that something is miss-ing from or wrong with the original book. Rather, it's an action taken to pre-vent a good book from overextending its welcome by growing outdated or stale.

THE CREATIVE APPROACH

A facelift doesn't "fix" your catalog. Rather, it acknowledges what's right and keeps moving it forward.

Throughout a facelift, your catalog stays true to its positioning and brand image. It doesn't change the merchandising, logo, design or other ele-ments that customers recognize in the mail. At the same time, facelifts do help you push your catalog's creative envelope to stay fresh.

Many catalogs stay stuck in the same marketing elements year after year. Others regularly eradicate everything familiar in an attempt to stay current. It's the old Dick Clark v. Madonna syndrome: one is predictable and boring, the other unpredictable to the point of losing identity (apologies to fans).

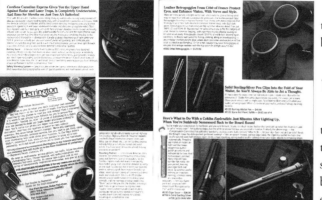

HERRINGTON'S CATALOG OF HIGH-TECH MER-
CHANDISE GAINED MORE IMPACT WHEN IT
REDESIGNED WITH A LARGER FORMAT.

INTERSPERSING LIVE MODELS WITH ITS FAMILIAR
MANNEQUIN PROPS UPDATES THE LOOK OF
HAROLD'S APPAREL CATALOG.

For catalogs, at least, neither approach works well in the long run. Instead, what's needed is to find a balance between the new and the familiar. Here's how to do it:

1) Keep the consistency...

Even after a facelift, your catalog should still be able to pass the "cover the logo" test. In other words, customers should still be able to recognize its familiar size, shape, logo, photography or type style. To maintain brand image, after all, your catalog must maintain all the elements that uniquely constitute that brand.

2) ...But push the imagery

L.L. Bean, for instance, still looks essentially like the same Bean book we've known for decades. But in the mid-'90s, it began adding more location shots, colorful laydowns and refined type style. The whole effect didn't replace what customers knew as "Bean," but it finally allowed the book to change with the times. (In fact, the Bean facelift showed that Eddie Bauer, J. Crew and Lands' End had been steadily working their creative influence!)

Each catalog needs to find its own way of moving forward. You may find all you need to do is replace pickup photography with original shots. Or you may want to have more fun with your apparel laydowns, or use more dramatic lighting and animated models. Or, you may want to use more callouts, or more helpful devices for customer service.

Anything can work, as long as it makes sense for your catalog's positioning. Dramatic lighting, for instance, may work well if you've got a catalog of home gifts and items. If you've got an outdoors/lifestyle positioning, however, you're better off pushing a different creative envelope.

3) Swipe...

Competitors almost always have great ideas you can incorporate into your own book. Creative swiping is no sin, *as long as you can translate that creative into your own catalog's marketing.*

This doesn't mean you should plagiarize the copy in Catalog X, or use the signature layouts of Catalog Y. After all, second-run designs and copycats always look second rate. But why not learn something new from the callouts in Lands' End? Why not pick up on the creative freshness from a J. Crew hero page?

You don't have to go out and employ a gangly model in dreadlocks, but a catalog's witty laydowns or adventuresome cropping can help stimulate fresh ideas in your own mind for perking up a stale design. (Just go back and look at what Bean has done with its own apparel laydowns and layouts!)

Good art directors constantly tear out print ads, catalog pages, posters, typefaces and every other kind of visual manna. All of it helps them step out of their own creative groove and learn something from the influence of others.

4) ...But keep your own creative sense

From time to time, we've all seen the results of too much copycat swiping. After a while, we can't tell catalogs apart. Look at what happened, for instance, when linens catalogs began copying the styling and promotional layouts of Domestications, or when off-price apparel catalogs started proliferating as the visual progeny of Chadwick's. Too much creative thievery leads to knock-offs, which in time leads to disappointed customers and diluted sales.

Nobody wins when everyone starts trucking in the same marketing ideas. It's important to keep integrity intact when you're tempted to follow someone else's creative lead.

5) Use care deciding what to change

Most of us have seen those "makeovers" of ordinary people in women's magazines. Half the time, I'm willing to bet those people can't wait to go home and scrub off those "improved" looks. After all, we all develop a certain look based on our core identities and life circumstances. We may want to enhance or update our looks, but we don't want to jump when we look in the mirror!

So it is with catalogs. It's important to hang on to what works for your catalog strategically, and to change what doesn't. Bean, for instance, could no more do away with its serif typeface than Liza Minnelli could go blond with curls. Customers, after all, take some of their strongest cues from that typeface. On the other hand, Bean *could* subtly lighten its dense pages, or use more animated models, and never lose its sense of self.

WITHOUT CHANGING ITS PRODUCT LINE OR TARGET MARKET, TYROL INTERNATIONAL CREATED A MORE UPSCALE LOOK FOR ITS GIFT BOOK WITH A MORE SPACIOUS LAYOUT, CLEANER DESIGN AND BETTER-QUALITY PROPPING AND PHOTOGRAPHY.

SO, WHAT CAN YOU CHANGE?

When you're considering a facelift, feel free to play with any number of elements that can enhance your communication to customers. These include the following:

Type. Bean excluded, most catalogers can do a quick, effective update by cleaning up boring type, or by freshening headlines and subheads. Simply dropping capital letters, changing point size or using color can freshen an old look.

A MORE RELAXED MODEL AND OUTDOOR
LOCATION SHOT BRINGS LEW MAGRAM
FROM THE OLD-HAT '80S TO THE FRESHER
'90S.

Talent. Catalogers rightfully like to employ dependable creative talent who give them what they want, year after year. On the other hand, a new art director, a new photographer, or at least a design consultant, can step out of the box and offer fresh thinking about old designs. Not every idea can or should stick, of course, but it's always good to hear about, or play with, new ideas.

Devices. Underscoring new services, playing up fast delivery or using new icons for toll-free numbers can spark up stale spreads. Devices allow catalogers to keep familiar elements intact while pushing forward with new marketing messages.

Opening spreads. Since the opening spread positions a catalog and plays up what's new, what better place to try something fun and fresh? Freeing up the creative here allows customers to experience something new before they head to the familiarity of the selling spreads.

Lands' End, of course, is ingenious at this. With each issue, the catalog refreshes its cover and opening spread with a new selling story. While the catalog's merchandise and selling layouts are as comfortable as old sweats, its opening spread is as fun as a pair of new sneakers.

CHANGE IS GOOD

Human beings are a superstitious lot, and catalogers, being human, are no exception. If you've used the same type of model for years, why change? If this photographer "always" does your book, why argue? If slim-jims have always pulled well, why try something different?

Well, here's why. Even if you've got good results, the fact is, you don't know how good your results *could* be—until you make a change.

Consider this story from J. Crew. For several years, the catalog offered two types of men's oxford shirts. One was an all-cotton blend, the other was 50/50 cotton/polyester. Both shirts did a combined $1 million in annual sales.

One day, J. Crew chairman Arthur Cinader decided to pull the 50/50 shirt, even though it sold equally as well as the all-cotton one. Why? Because he believed the 50/50 fabric didn't fit with the Crew brand identity.

The result? He was right. He took a risk *in favor of* the catalog's brand identity, even though it meant yanking a big seller. The move enhanced Crew's reputation as a merchandiser, and the subtle shift in product mix brought in loyal shoppers.

Try it with your own catalog. Don't be afraid to change elements that "work." If your photography, copy or paper quality simply doesn't fit with your brand identity, it needs to be examined. The payoff is in increased recognition, trust and loyalty. That means sales.

CHAPTER 26

BRINGING BACK
YOUR INACTIVES

Don't you love those first few years of a booming catalog business? It's honeymoon time. Prospects jump onto the house list as if they'd been waiting for this catalog all their lives. Customers buy small at first, then order more and more with each mailing. Every time a book hits the mail, it's celebration time.

But like every other relationship, even catalog/customer lovefests can get dull. Veteran house-file customers may get antsy, refusing to shop the book the way they once did. Response rates start to flatten out, even dip. You might have tried a facelift, but there's still something missing. How do you get these people back?

I'll be honest: inactives are tough customers. To get them going, you need more than the usual quality-and-service pitch. You need to convince those customers to change their entrenched habits.

This chapter will show you how to do that. You'll learn not just which customers to reactivate, but how to stimulate them into buying again. While I can't guarantee that a simple tweak in imagery will bring customers running (after all, the problem may be with your product mix, your price points, your customers' economic status or other factors), I can tell you that renewing your catalog's communication strengths will help your cause. You can revitalize your customers' confidence in your book.

CHANGE THE MESSAGE,
NOT THE CATALOG

A reactivation catalog isn't a whole new book. Essentially, it's a catalog that gives customers the message, explicitly or implicitly, "How can we get you back?" Some reactivation catalogs ask that question (or, similarly, "Have we done something wrong?") directly on their covers. Others offer subtle incentives to buy, like coupons or discounts.

In essence, though, most reactivation catalogs differ little from the book customers already know. The only real difference is in the message designed to get inactive customers to take another look.

FIRST, FIND THE PROBLEM

As you might imagine, there's no one "right" creative approach to reactivating customers. A lot depends on your customer base and your catalog's history with its customers.

It's important, then, to first ask the following questions:

1) Which customers are worth reactivating?

Do you want to address twelve-month inactives? Should you address eighteen-month buyers? Do you want to reactivate only apparel buyers, or gift buyers, or all types of buyers? Each customer type may require a different incentive for reactivating.

You may find too, that some customers simply can't be reactivated, no matter what you do. If your customer base is aging, for instance, you may be losing customers due to retirement or illness. Maternity and babies' catalogs, obviously, have a transient customer base, as do catalogs addressed exclusively to college-age kids or young career women. Business catalogs may address buying managers either promoted out of their jobs or transferred to other departments. None of these consumers are worth reactivating.

Sometimes, too, customers stop buying because they no longer relate to your mailings. In an economic slump, for instance, many once-loyal buyers of elegant gifts might be turning to less expensive gift sources. Or, career women who once stocked up on silk blouses may be now be shopping for cotton tees.

If your catalog offer no longer makes sense for your core customers, no coupon or incentive will bring them back. What may be needed instead is a complete merchandising overhaul, repositioning or redesign.

2) Have you done anything to lose your customers' trust?

Maybe your catalog lost customers during that service snafu, when you were setting up a new warehouse or computer system. Maybe you hit a lot of backorders because of a vendor change. Maybe your catalog just went through a new ownership change, or just pulled out of bankruptcy.

The point is, business changes can leave customers in the lurch. Frustrated by lack of service, merchandising changes or drastic redesigns, your customers may no longer enjoy or even recognize the catalog they once were loyal to. They might just stop buying, or turn to competitors. Either way, it's your problem to figure out how to win them back.

3) Is there a problem you don't know about?

Or, maybe you don't know *why* your customers left! If you haven't made drastic changes in your offering or service, you might have to take steps to find out why customers are turned off. How? Ask them!

Conduct telephone and mail surveys, and probe your customers for the reasons they haven't bought from you. Tell them that you want to understand what you've done wrong in order to make it right. (That willingness to hear out your customers can be a great sales motivator in itself!) Maybe you'll hear that your catalog was out of stock once too often, or that items didn't arrive quickly enough. Maybe you'll hear that the quality has fallen off or that the prices are too high.

Then, check your own return ratios, and check your competition in the marketplace. Are your returns running higher than usual? Are your competitors lowering prices, adding more sale books, or advertising free shipping and handling?

Decide whether you need to fix a specific problem before you start handing out customer discounts and incentives. It's important not to rush into reactivation if you don't first understand the principal causes that led you to trouble.

4) Do you have a competitive problem?

When Hanna Andersson launched its children's apparel catalog in the early 1980s, no one had seen anything like it. No other catalog offered colorful, quality children's clothing with hand-me-down durability. The catalog became a cult favorite among new yuppie parents.

The concept succeed so well, in fact, that it could hardly escape the notice of better-heeled competitors. By the early '90s, Hanna faced financial drought as Baby Gap, Gymboree and other challengers enticed its core customer base away.

And therein lies the problem for many catalogs with an eroding customer base. Customers who've been lured by the competition need special enticements to return. Ask yourself: Do your competitors offer more value for the customer's dollar? Are they in the mail more frequently? Do they have buying incentives that you haven't matched?

By recognizing your competitor's strengths and weaknesses, you can better offer your customers the price, merchandise and services they may be looking for in your own book.

THE CREATIVE APPROACH

Once you've decided on a reactivation catalog, you need to take action to bring customers back. Here's my suggested five-step program:

1) If you've had a problem, fix it.
2) Then, own up to it.
3) Decide on an approach: carrot or stick.
4) Develop a program.
5) Test your messages.

Here's how it works.

STEP ONE:
If you've had a problem, fix it.

Say a customer survey told you that your quality has fallen off, or that your prices were too high, or that customers were frustrated by service delays when your computers went down last Christmas.

Whatever the problem, address it. Don't try and reactivate customers when you haven't changed what's wrong. It won't do any good to bring a customer back if she's going to face the same disappointment.

As the saying goes, once burned, twice shy. If you "burn" your customers a second time, you'll likely lose them for good—along with their friends, family and all other potential customers they've alerted to your shortcomings.

STEP TWO: Then, own up to it.

During its early years, Chadwick's grew so fast it couldn't maintain enough inventory to meet demand. As a result, many early customers were plenty steamed, as the company soon found out with its customer research.

In response, and once the problem was addressed, Chadwick's sent a large group of its customers both an apology letter and a gift certificate. By owning up to its problem, Chadwick's showed its customers that it cared. The gift certificate, moreover, gave customers a chance to try the catalog again, practically risk-free. Given both an apology and an incentive, most shoppers proved willing to give the young catalog another shot.

If you've identified and fixed a problem with your catalog, it pays to own up to it. Regaining customer trust, after all, means regaining business.

If you've recently found new vendors who deliver better quality product, or if you've fixed a warehouse problem, tell your customers! Add a cover wrap for the message; or add comments to the president's letter, inside opening spread, or a bind-in card. Tell customers, "We're proud of what we've accomplished. We've elevated our standards, and invite you to take a look at our catalog again."

You might then want to add a discount ("Take 20% off any order"), gift certificate, free shipping and handling, or other incentive to get customers shopping your pages again.

STEP THREE: Decide on the carrot or the stick.

Many customers in an activation slump don't have disappointed customers—they've got bored ones. Their longtime customers simply may not have *noticed* the catalog of late, or may have been too distracted or busy to place an order. Because the book is so familiar, they haven't felt a sense of urgency even to pick up the catalog, never mind to order ("Oh, I'll just wait till the next catalog gets here").

These customers, of course, don't need an apology from you. After all, you haven't done anything wrong. Instead, they need a carrot and/or stick to get them moving forward. For them, it's best to develop a series of incentives and/or threats that correspond to the value they have for your business.

A STRONG COVER EMPHASIS ON DOLLARS-OFF GIVES INACTIVE CUSTOMERS A COMPELLING REASON TO LOOK THROUGH THE CATALOG AND BUY.

For instance, you certainly wouldn't want to threaten a longtime, high average order customer with, "This is your last catalog unless we hear from you now!" That wouldn't exactly come across as fine thanks for all those years of loyalty. Nor would you want to hand a $25 gift certificate to an occasional customer whose last order, for $40, came in 18 months ago.

Use common sense for reactivation, based on your type of catalog and customer. Many discount or mass-market catalogs, like Damark and Fingerhut, find that threats work well to spark casual customers into buying. (In fact, Fingerhut often combines the carrot and stick, using cover wraps that not only threaten "last catalog," but also offer free gifts "if you order now.")

On the other hand, more upscale catalogs, with a higher average order, find a softer approach works better. For them, a $20 gift certificate might make sense, especially for customers who spend $100 or more per order. Free shipping and handling might be another incentive, or 10% off the next order. Combined with a gentle "Why haven't we heard from you?," this kind of carrot-and-stick approach lets customers know they're both valued and missed.

A SIMPLE DOT WHACK CAN CALL ATTENTION TO A LAST-CATALOG THREAT.

STEP FOUR: Develop a program.

Once you've decided on your reactivation approach, you may need to enact it in stages. After all, magazine publishers often stimulate subscription renewals with a series of three to eight direct mail messages. To "renew" their own customers, catalogers might want to consider that approach.

As with magazine renewals, each message in a reactivation series can become more assertive. Let's say, for instance, that you want to reactivate 12-month to 24-month buyers who averaged $100 or more in spending. Initially, your 12-month inactives might receive a catalog with a certificate for free shipping and handling. If those customers don't buy in six more months, you might then send a $20 gift certificate and a note saying "We haven't heard from you..." Should they stay inactive for 24 months, your message could then say, "Have we done something wrong? Please take this opportunity to look over our catalog, and take 20% off any purchase." Meanwhile, your less-valuable customers might receive a "Final Catalog" notice at this point in the series.

Have patience! Generally speaking, more than half of all magazine subscription renewals come during or after the month of expiration. Likewise, your inactive customers may need some serious prodding before shopping regularly again.

STEP FIVE: Test your messages.

As with everything else in direct mail, testing is key. Try different messages and executions on different parts of your reactivation file. You might try testing, say, a screened-back cover vs. a cover wrap for a "Have we done anything wrong?" message. You might test a bind-in gift certificate vs. one on the cover wrap. You might test a stick ("We're taking you off our list") vs. a carrot ("Free gift with your next order").

Obviously, different messages work best on different parts of your file. In fact, some companies test some kind of reactivation message on almost all their mailings.

You've been missed here at J.Crew.
Matter of fact, it's been so long since
we've heard from you that we assume we let
you down, one way or another.

We apologize for any disappointment and
hope you'll give us another chance to show
that we can satisfy the most discerning
requirements in style and service.

To help make amends for any past mistakes,
here's a credit of $20 on an order of $80
or more. When phoning your order just cite
"code RX2" and our operator will give you
the $20 credit (it's good till October 15).

$20   J.CREW $20

This coupon can be applied as $20
toward a purchase of $80 or more.

J. CREW'S COVER-WRAP MESSAGE COMBINES JUST
THE RIGHT AMOUNT OF INCENTIVE ($20 OFF)
WITH A TWINGE OF GUILT INDUCEMENT ("IT'S
BEEN SO LONG SINCE WE'VE HEARD FROM YOU...").

USING THE "STICK" APPROACH FOR REACTIVA-
TION MAY BE BEST AS A LAST RESORT OR FOR
OLDEST CUSTOMERS.

J. Peterman, for instance, clearly tests incentive messages continually, ranging from sweepstakes to 20% off promotions to $25 gift certificates sent under separate envelope. While it's not clear to outsiders which messages are targeted to which groups of customers, the company obviously spends a great deal of marketing energy keeping its customers active.

CHOOSE YOUR WEAPON

Following are creative approaches worth testing for reactivation. Notice that none of them change the basic look or offer of the regular catalog mailing.

COVER WRAPS

Advantage: Easy to personalize, or to target messages to different audiences. A 12-month inactive segment could receive a gift certificate printed on the wrap, a 24-month segment might get a "Final Catalog" threat.
Disadvantage: Expensive, adds weight, hides the catalog cover.

BIND-IN OR BLOW-IN CARDS

Advantage: Easy to insert into a regular catalog to create a reactivation book.
Disadvantage: Can't be seen from the cover. If customers aren't leafing through the book in the first place, you could have a wasted promotion.

PRESIDENT'S LETTER/OPENING SPREAD

Advantage: Useful for creating messages explaining past problems or important changes to the catalog.
Disadvantage: Message not detectable from cover. A "See inside" might help.

DOT WHACKS/FAKE DOT WHACKS:

Advantage: Good for drawing attention to an incentive message ("See new products inside") or other reactivation message ("Stop! This may be your final catalog.").
Disadvantage: Message must be short. Can hide or disturb cover creative.

SCREENED-BACK COVER

Advantage: Great for explaining complicated reactivation messages, such as "We're sorry about service problems we've experienced in the past. We're proud of the changes we made and invite you to try us again."
Disadvantage: Compromises the cover creative.

SEPARATE MAILING IN ENVELOPE

Advantage: Best for lengthy explanations or apologies, particularly when enclosing a gift certificate. Will likely be taken seriously by customer.
Disadvantage: Expensive.

ALL-TYPE COVERS

Advantage: As with a screened-back cover, great for complicated messages. If you really want to get someone's attention, an all-type cover does the job.
Disadvantage: Compromises the cover creative.

MORTISE ON THE COVER

Advantage: Works for creating shorter reactivation messages, such as "20% off your next order," or "Buy now, pay later." Also allows you to test different cover messages to different customer segments, all without compromising the cover.
Disadvantage: Message must be kept relatively short.

CHAPTER 27

PROSPECTING CATALOGS

Every catalog needs prospects to grow, but I'm willing to bet only one in ten (if that) creates any kind of "prospecting" catalog.

In other words, most catalogers tend to treat their prospects the same way they treat their customers. They simply send the same book to both groups. Oh, maybe the catalog sent to prospects is a little smaller than the one that goes to the house file. And maybe it doesn't mail as frequently. But beyond that, few catalogers make much of an effort to draw in new buyers.

Frankly, it's hard to blame them. After all, it already costs you about five times the marketing effort to gain a new customer as to retain an old one. That makes it hard to justify spending even *more* money and energy creating special catalogs for buyers who have little potential of payoff. In fact, many catalogers look for ways to create a less expensive prospecting vehicle.

Besides, if you're like most catalogers, you probably believe your "house" book is compelling enough. If it works for old buyers, why shouldn't it work for new ones?

But new customers are the lifeblood of any catalog. In other words, they're worth a little effort. And that's all you really need to create a good prospecting book: a small amount of creative intelligence. That little effort, as I'll outline in this chapter, can go a long way in nabbing buyers from your rental lists.

THE CREATIVE APPROACH

Essentially, a prospecting catalog has one purpose: to pull a customer from a rental list.

In other words, its goal is not to pump a high average sale or increase the number of items per order. The idea is simply to *generate response*. You can't expect to generate profits or fat orders from your prospecting books. All you can expect is to get prospects to respond. Once you've got them on your house file, *then* you can pull out all the stops to increase their business.

So, a prospecting catalog has to do anything it can to get that first order. It has to entice someone to browse, and then move that casual browser to buying.

There are six steps for making that happen.

LERNER PILES ON THE FREEBIES TO GET A PROSPECT'S ATTENTION: FREE DELIVERY, INTRODUCTORY SAVINGS, FREE OFFERS, AND A "CALL FREE ANYTIME OFFER."

VICTORIA'S SECRET OFFERS A PRICE INCENTIVE TO GET PROSPECTS TO BUY.

A BLACK BOX ON THE COVER ALLOWS EDDIE BAUER TO CONSTRUCT OR CHANGE ITS INTRODUCTORY MESSAGE AT ANY POINT IN THE PRINT RUN.

STEP ONE:
Know whom you're prospecting.

Pay attention to the differences between your house list and your rental list. Ask yourself:

—How close is the demographic of your rental list to your customer list?

—How well does your prospecting catalog address that demographic?

Perhaps your rental list skews more male, or slightly younger, than your house file. In that case, you might modify the products you choose for the prospecting catalog, or the pagination of the book, or the cover creative. Even a slight change can get the attention of the group you mean to target.

Pay attention, as well, to the kind of customer base you're looking to build. If you're deliberately aiming for a younger audience, for instance, you might want to consider a facelift or even a repositioning of your regular catalog. In other words, you don't want to risk hooking younger customers with your prospecting book only to turn them off with your regular catalog. Ease the transition between the customer file you currently have and the one you would like to create.

STEP TWO: Welcome your prospect.

You don't have to create banners, starbursts, bells and whistles to salute your new prospects. All you really need is a black type change on your cover, perhaps combined with a welcome in the president's letter.

As long as you've got a compelling cover and offer, you've got your prospect's interest. Now to seal the deal, tell them you'll do everything in your power to make shopping with you pleasant and painless. A change in type costs very little, but can pay off well in goodwill (and orders!).

STEP THREE: Make an offer.

After welcoming recipients into your book, soften their defenses with a special offer. You might, for instance, want to offer free shipping and handling with their first order, or a free gift, or dollars off.

Anything that breaks down resistance helps motivate first-time shoppers to give the book a try. (And in my experience, incidentally, free shipping works best as an inducement, followed by dollars off.)

STEP FOUR: Give reasons to buy.

Each time you can speak reassuringly to your prospect, you open that buying window just a little bit wider. Many would-be customers need only that extra push, that extra reason, to get them to place an order.

So on your inside front cover, you might want to state "Four reasons for shopping our catalog," or "Why you won't find our products in your favorite store," or any other editorial incentive. Some catalogs also use this space to state why they started this catalog, or to give testimonials from other satisfied customers.

Think of how you might greet this new prospect in person. What would you *most* want her to understand about shopping in your catalog? Do you want to reassure her that no sale is final? That you offer the best prices she can find? That you understand her passion for gardening, or her need to get organized? That she can receive her delivery overnight?

Treat your prospect as a valued guest. Establish the trust she needs to place her order.

BLACK DOG'S COVER MESSAGE—"FIRST TIME BUYER/20% OFF"—GRABS ATTENTION WITHOUT DISTRACTING FROM THE COVER DESIGN.

STEP FIVE: Don't focus on order-building.

Because you need to pull response, you don't need to push your most expensive items on your cover. Instead, focus on your more marketable, commodity-driven items, or your known winners.

Don't risk turning off potential buyers by offering a $350 gold necklace on the cover instead of a popular set of $50 silver rings. Your customers may be used to your expensive items, but your prospects need to lower their defenses and buy.

STEP SIX: Create a smaller book.

Particularly if you've got a "big book" for your house file, you may wish to cut back to a smaller catalog for your prospects. After all, your prospects don't need as much of a product selection to make just one purchase decision.

Make it easy for them. Select your more popular items. Or, choose items targeted to your prospect group. Often catalogers find a "Best of" book works most effectively to convert prospects into buyers.

WHY NOT SALE BOOKS?

Many catalogers prefer to send sale books for prospecting. After all, it's not expensive to put sale books together (they use pickup art, primarily), and the prices can be a great incentive for someone who's considered buying from you.

Sale books, though, may not be the best first impression and may appeal primarly to bargain hunters. If you're sure your prospect has already seen your book, a sale book might work fine for getting her off the fence. But if your discounts are deep, you risk coming off as "cheap" and may not achieve the same success on future, full price offers.

Sale books can be a great tool, but you must be careful how you use them, since they can affect long-term as well as short-term performance. An important strategy in every cataloger's marketing plan, sale books are discussed in the next chapter.

CHAPTER 28

SALE CATALOGS

Try as we may, none of us can ever predict how many of those silk blouses, woolen blankets or frog-shaped water sprinklers we may sell in any given catalog. That's why most of us, at some point, need a sale catalog. When sales dip or inventory stockpiles, for whatever reason, we need a way to liquidate the merchandise.

The tricky part, of course, is doing it at the least possible cost—without sacrificing your catalog's precious image and brand identity. Sale books, in other words, have to contribute to both long-term and short-term customer performance and sales. Like every other catalog, they must attract customers, but they must do it at the lowest price to make up for those tightened product margins.

That's the first challenge for a sale catalog. The second is to ensure that a sale book *delivers a cohesive message.* That can be a tough job creatively, since sale books generally tend to feature assorted product, photography styles and copy blocks. Without a cohesive message to tie it together, a sale book can create confusion among your hard-won customers. A tangled creative approach invites customers to wonder what your company stands for in the first place.

So in this chapter, I'll show you how to do a sale catalog without losing your shirt—or your customer base!

THE CREATIVE APPROACH

First, the good news: An inexpensive sale book is actually a better customer magnet than an expensive one.

Think about it. Higher density spreads, less copy and cheaper paper stock communicate low prices—and customers love a bargain! In fact, many customers won't shop a catalog unless they feel they're getting a terrific price/value.

Sale books work best, however, if customers are already familiar and supportive of the catalog's total brand image. In other words, customers wouldn't necessarily buy a J. Crew sweater from a slim-jim sale book unless they already believed the product was a high-quality, fashionable item. How do they know that it is? By the exacting presentation and exciting creative

CLIFFORD & WILLS, IN KEEPING WITH ITS
QUIETLY ASSURED IMAGE, ADVERTISES ITS
HOLIDAY SALE WITHOUT SHOUTING.

LILLIAN VERNON, TRUE TO ITS VALUE-PRICED
IMAGE, CONVEYS "SALE" IN EVERY POSSIBLE WAY:
WITH PERCENTAGE-OFF, "BUY NOW, PAY LATER,"
TIME INCENTIVES ("SALE ENDS APRIL 11"), SPE-
CIAL PRICES, AND EVEN A SWEEPSTAKES.

LESS IS MORE. TALBOTS DOES A GREAT JOB
CREATING A CLEAN, SIMPLE, BUDGET SALE COVER
WITH A LOT OF IMPACT.

of the regular J. Crew catalog presentation. The better the brand-building effort in the regular catalog, the better performance one can expect from a sale book.

A sale book, then, can be a wonderful opportunity to try different sizes, formats and paper options. Let's look at some of them.

STEP ONE:
Experiment with size and paper

Very often, a size change alone in a sale book generates a lift in response. If you use a 7" by 9" catalog format for head-to-toe fashion shots, for instance, you could try an 8" by 8" square format to accommodate the increased density of your sale book. Or, if you normally produce an 8.5" by 11" book, you might want to go with a slim-jim or digest. The size alone would communicate a special offer.

For cost reasons too, it might also make sense to try a different trim size. If the print run of the sale book requires you to switch from gravure to off-set, for example, you'd find each type of printing process has its most efficient sizes.

Paper also contributes to the feel of a sale book. A cheaper grade of paper signals your customer that she's looking through a special-offer book. Of course, that doesn't mean you should load up on gray-toned supercalendered stock: Pick a paper grade that saves you money while at least *maintaining* your brand image.

STEP TWO: Pay attention to covers

The first rule of catalog covers is doubly important for sale books. *The cover must stand out.* You want your customer to know immediately that she's received a special offer. That means your sales message must be clear, and if possible, dramatic.

What works? Big type, starbursts, headlines ("50% off sale!") and other graphic devices do the job of communicating bargain prices. In some cases, an all-type cover can effectively announce a big sale, just as all-type department store windows do.

The task, however, is to keep it simple. Don't go overboard with wacky type elements and other bells and whistles. Keep the message clear and easy to understand: Spell out your percentage discounts, your sale categories and any time or quantity limitations. (And, of course, your toll-free number!) Then add just enough graphic elements to focus your customer right on the message.

STEP THREE:
Don't forget about back covers

As you know, your back cover has a 50/50 chance of being the first thing your customer sees. So don't neglect it! An effective back cover tells your customer she's got a special offer, even as she's taking it out of the mailbox.

Consider treating the back cover almost as a graphic extension of the front. This "wrap-around" effect can create a solid, cohesive impact for your sales message, no matter where your customer looks first. If you can, use this critical space to highlight or repeat a strong price offer from inside the book.

STEP FOUR: Keep up the momentum on the opening spread

If you've got a lot of overstock to sell, it's quite tempting to start cramming it in on every page, starting with the opening. Resist! Don't lose the precious energy you've created on the cover. Reiterate your sales message; explain (briefly!) why this is a sale book. If you don't often publish a discount book, explain that as well.

Just don't get too wordy. This isn't the place to talk about how you founded your catalog 15 years ago or what new fashion colors will appear this spring. After all, those receiving your sale book may already be familiar with your catalog and prospects should only have to scan key information. Try using bullets, highlights or other devices on the opening spread to keep your information concise and simple. If you offer products in a number of merchandise categories, you might want also to create a brief table of contents here, using graphics and photography to keep the informal touch.

Keep your best merchandise offers on this spread as well. Curious customers will look here first to check the nature of the sale. How deep are the price cuts? Are these last season's goods or "wear now" merchandise? Make sure your opening represents the tone and offer of your entire sale catalog.

We all know the importance of first impressions. Your opening spread in a sale book is your best opportunity to impress your customer and keep her moving forward.

STEP FIVE: Control your density

The average page in a sale catalog generally features twice the number of items as the average page in a regular book. What's more, these items usually appear in pickup photography from previous catalogs. That means you've got to somehow organize studio shots of evening wear with bright Caribbean location shots of outdoor wear with indoor shots of lingerie with outdoor shots of sporting goods. Translation: sale books can be a big mess.

So for maximum impact, sale book pages should have a clean and relatively simple design. Follow these hints for a unified look:

—Keep like photography on the same spreads. Try not to mix up the studio shots from the spring drop with the moody, atmospheric photographs from your fall shoot. Group like with like, wherever possible. If you need to put dissimilar shots on the page, separate them with space or rule lines.

—Try to silhouette shots that have the most disruptive backgrounds. Silhouettes not only eliminate confusing backdrops, they can also create space, interest and pacing in your book, particularly if your sale catalog is already loaded with background shots.

VICTORIA'S SECRET'S COUNTRY SALE CATALOG ENTICES WITH OFFERS "EXCLUSIVELY FOR YOU...SPECIAL PRICE REDUCTIONS NOT PRINTED IN THE CATALOGUE."

—Work with your separator to create matching backgrounds. You might find that you can match the backgrounds of simple studio shots at minimal expense. If you want to pay more, you can do almost anything with your pickup shots, from cloning to creating new backgrounds.

STEP SIX: Don't shoot the photographer!

Sometimes you need to ask yourself why your sale item didn't meet its original sales projections. You might find the problem wasn't the item or the fickle audience—it was the creative or photography that held it back.

If that's the case, don't just throw the old pickup photograph into your sale book. Correct the problem by reshooting the item. You'll find the cost of a reshoot is peanuts compared to the revenue generated by a successful photograph.

STEP SEVEN: Hone thy copy

Dense sale pages mean less room for copy. You can address the challenge in one of three ways: Edit copy to a minimum; decrease the point size or line spacing of your type (or choose another typeface); or shrink your photography.

Option three is probably the least effective. After all, the photo attracts the customer's eye. The smaller the photo, the more likely the item will pass unnoticed by your customer. Besides, most of us find we have to shrink our photographs anyway just to accommodate the smaller page size, or the increased number of items on the page.

The best option may be to whittle your copy instead. Chances are, you can find words to cut without compromising main feature and benefit information. More helpful than a yard of copy is a chance to peruse the item visually and contemplate its low price. Keep your descriptions brief, with an emphasis on value or limited quantities.

STEP EIGHT: Push the price

Fill your headlines and copy with command statements: "Order now for best selection!" "Buy now for the best prices of the year!" Call out savings, promotions and limited quantities. Personally, I love how J. Peterman's sale books emphasize "Only 115 left" beneath pictures of each item.

You can also emphasize price with bold or color type, or with red slashes through your old price, and the new price featured prominently. Choose your callouts, icons and devices with care: You want to promote price, but you don't want to contribute more confusion and density to the page. Keep your customer's eye moving toward that all-important value message.

Make sure, as well, that you keep your guarantee prominent, perhaps featuring it throughout the catalog. Give the toll-free number on every spread, including the front and back covers. Make the shopping experience as easy and reassuring as possible.

STEP NINE: Show the book around

As with any catalog, it's important that your marketing, merchandising and creative team work together to create your sale book. But why stop there? It's a good idea to pass your creative work by people who are less involved with design and might more accurately reflect the views of your customer. Show the book to other employees, warehouse staff or even informal "focus" groups of friends or relatives. Ask whether they feel the catalog looks too much like the "same old book," or whether it seems like a must-read for bargains. They'll be sure to let you know whether your sale catalog has the impact it deserves.

CHAPTER 29

IDENTITY: THE FOUNDATION OF YOUR CATALOG

There's no question about it. Establishing a unique identity for your catalog is a lengthy process, both in time and effort. It involves extensive research, customer knowledge, advance planning and a great deal of creative thought.

But it's worth it. Regardless of the stage your catalog is in, regardless of its challenges, problems or opportunities, one thing is plain: A catalog goes nowhere without a solid, unique, likable identity.

A catalog's identity is what allows its customers to know, trust and buy from it. Done well, this identity underpins every element of the catalog—every block of copy, every photograph, every choice of model, every use of color.

What's more, a "brand" catalog—a catalog with a strong, unique identity—has priceless advantages over its competitors right from the start.

It establishes a following. Because a brand catalog has relevance to its target audience, customers are drawn to it. This catalog doesn't continually need to employ discounts, coupons or other gimmicks to entice customers to buy. Its customers want to buy simply because they identify with the offering.

It becomes a leader. Because of its unique identity, a brand catalog becomes a leader, not a challenger. It establishes itself as the authentic source for its particular offer. For that reason, too, it deters knockoffs, since customers know that only *this* catalog offers the authentic experience they're looking for.

It can expand its business. Once a catalog becomes a known brand, it can choose to use its valuable name in creating spin-offs. Customers who know and trust the brand become willing to know and trust other offerings made under its name.

It can reposition painlessly. A catalog with a unique identity has the ability to "move" with its customers. Because of its strong bond with its customers, it has the wherewithal to update or shift its imagery without losing the strong resonance of its brand name.

It can ask more of its customers. Brand-loyal customers are less price-sensitive than customers of non-brand catalogs. They're willing to pay more for the experience of shopping "their" catalog. Their loyalty also makes them more willing to respond to surveys, join relationship programs, or receive frequent mailings. Brand-loyal customers are hard to wear out. Even if they receive 10 catalogs in a day, they'll be sure to shop "their" catalog first.

The bottom line, then, is that a strong, unique identity adds to a cataloger's bottom line. Establishing identity is like preventative health maintenance for your catalog. For every minute and dollar spent in creating your catalog's identity, you save ten times the amount in repairing problems that would otherwise creep up on your business.

So choose your catalog's brand identity as carefully as you choose its merchandise. A catalog with a firm brand, identity and positioning is a catalog that's around for the long haul.

ABV Acronym for Attributes, Benefits and Values. Used for analyzing and determining a catalog's brand identity.

analysis, audience The process of learning the demographics, psychographics and composition of a customer base.

analysis, competitive The process of learning the traits, price points, services, financial health, offers and other characteristics of a catalog's competition.

analysis, competitive positioning The process of learning how a cataloger's competitor creates a unique selling proposition in a marketplace.

analysis, model The process of calculating how much apparel is sold per model.

analysis, situation Financial and marketplace analysis of a catalog. Determines where a catalog currently stands in the marketplace (in market share, total sales, etc.) and where the cataloger would like it to go.

attributes The physical features of a product.

banners Graphic "bars" placed on a catalog cover to promote special messages, such as new products or lower prices.

benefits The perceived and real positives consumers receive from a product or service.

bind-in cards Inserts stapled or stitched into a catalog to draw attention to special messages. Often used for "friend-get-a-friend" cards, cross-promotion of other catalogs, or credit-card offers.

blow-in cards Inserts "shot" into an already-bound catalog with a puff of air. Like bind-in cards, used to communicate or draw attention to special messages.

borders Graphic designs in the margins of a catalog page. Often used to "announce" or separate certain sections of a catalog.

bottom line A cataloger's net profit.

boxes Graphic dropped-in squares or rectangles normally found on a catalog cover. Often used for special announcements, such as "lowest prices of the season."

brand The attributes, benefits and values associated with a formally named product or service.

brand identity A unique "personality" for a product or service that customers recognize symbolically, through logos, typefaces and so on.

brand image The visual and creative elements that make up a brand's identity, such as logo, typeface, photography and so on.

bundling Selling unrelated but like merchandise in a special offer. For instance: A cutting board and knife sold together at a price that is 10% less than if purchased separately.

business plan A report that analyzes a catalog's marketplace, audience, competition and sales opportunities, and recommends specific actions that need to be taken to meet a marketing objective.

callouts Brief, descriptive information that accompanies illustrations, charts or photographs. Often used in catalogs to "call out" the features of a complex or special product.

captions Descriptive information that appears beneath an illustration or photograph.

circulation The total number of catalogs mailed.

closing spread The final two pages in a catalog, preceding the back cover.

color ways Illustrations of color choices available for clothing, accessories and linens.

column layout See *layout, column.*

commodity items Those products that supply an ongoing, ordinary need. T-shirts, napkins, pencils, pantyhose and batteries are all examples of commodity items, typically undifferentiated in the consumer's mind.

competitive analysis See *analysis, competitive.*

competitive positioning analysis See *analysis, competitive positioning.*

consistency Indicated by the regular, ongoing use of familiar elements in a catalog. L.L. Bean's outdoor emphasis, for instance, is made *consistent* by its continual use of sporty illustrated covers and wholesome models.

continuity products Items that are purchased on a regular basis over a period of time. Books, music and collectables are sold in this manner, on an installment basis.

consumer The end user of a product.

consumer trends See *trends, market/consumer.*

corporate startups See *startups, corporate.*

coupons Promotional cut-out/mail-in devices used to grant dollars off, free shipping, discounts or other customer inducements.

cover, back Last page of a catalog.

cover, front First page of a catalog.

cover wraps Separate covers, often printed on brown or matte stock, that bind on top of the regular front and back cover of a catalog. Normally used for special messages for targeted audience segments, such as "Take 20% off any purchase over $100."

creative strategies The process of using design elements, such as photography, typeface and illustration, to create maximum selling power in a catalog.

cropping The process of editing or cutting a photograph to produce a certain graphic result.

cross-reference In a selling spread, an indication of the page number on which a non-featured item may be found.

customer code Codes that appear on a catalog indicating a specific recipient or information about that person. Customer codes are used to track response and purchase behavior.

customer panels Groups of customers selected by a cataloger to answer survey questions on a regular basis.

customer-profiling research See *research, customer-profiling.*

customer-satisfaction research See *research, customer-satisfaction.*

customer surveys See *surveys.*

cut-and-copy layouts See *layouts, cut-and-copy.*

DMA See *Direct Marketing Association.*

database Compiled information accessible by computer. In cataloging, a customer database may include name, address, sex, age and purchase history.

demographics Identifying information about a customer or group of customers. Demographic details might include job title, family size, age, income and sex.

density In cataloging, refers to the amount of product on a page. Pages with high density normally feature a great deal of product and/or type with little white space; pages with low density feature only a few products with ample breathing room.

devices Small graphic elements or symbols used in catalogs to communicate information, such as new products, important services, special sizes, exclusivity or awards.

digest A catalog of small trim size, approximately 5" X 7".

dingbats See *devices.*

Direct Marketing Association Trade association for the direct marketing industry.

discount, dollar A response-building promotion in which customers are offered a certain number of dollars off a regular price. Used in building average order size, liquidating inventory gaining new customers, etc.

discount, percentage-off A response-building promotion in which customers are offered a certain percentage off a regular price. Used in building average order size, liquidating inventory, gaining new customers, etc.

dot whacks Stickers affixed to a catalog cover to promote services, discounts, new products or other messages. Dot whacks can be either real stickers or fake (artwork).

eye-movement research Research method that measures where a customer's eye falls on a catalog layout.

eyeflow The ability of a page design to keep a customer's eye moving easily across all the items on a selling spread or page.

facelift Applied to cataloging, a freshening or updating of a catalog's design.

feature shot Standout presentation of the most important item in a selling spread.

focus-group research Research method in which a group of customers or prospects are invited to give in-person, spontaneous opinions on a chosen topic, such as a catalog repositioning.

frequency In cataloging, refers to the number of times a customer makes a purchase within a certain period of time.

friend-get-a-friend Refers to the effort to induce catalog recipients to send names of others who would like to receive the catalog.

fulfillment The act of receiving and filling a request for a product or service.

go-sees In-person interviews with models for prospective catalog shoots.

guarantee A catalog's promise of customer satisfaction.

hard goods Non-apparel merchandise.

heads, headlines Brief, descriptive information (in larger-size type) that introduces a product or block of product copy.

hero spreads See *spreads, hero.*

high-end Refers to upscale products and catalogs.

horizontal-market catalogs Catalogs that appeal to a wide range of customers within a market.

identity The image and voice of a catalog; its fundamental personality; that which communicates its specialness and uniqueness.

image, imagery Visual and creative elements in a catalog used to create or reinforce a catalog's identity.

impact The ability of a catalog image to resonate with its audience.

impulse items Commodity catalog products, usually lowered priced and often featured on or around the order form.

informational copy See *non-selling copy.*

inserts Cards or brochures bound into a catalog, usually featuring special services, offers or sale merchandise. Usually designed to break up a catalog and stop customers at a certain point in the book.

key, key code The letter or number that identifies an item on a page, used to refer to the item's accompanying copy block.

key items Products that are important sellers within a catalog.

kitchen-table startups See *startups, kitchen-table.*

knockoff Catalogs, often new, that copy the merchandising and positioning of other, established catalogs.

laydowns Photographs of apparel laid on a surface.

layouts Compositions of photographs, copy blocks and other design elements within a catalog spread.

layouts, column Layouts in which copy and photography appears in columns on the page.

layouts, combination Layouts in which cut-and-copy alternates with column design.

layouts, cut-and-copy Layouts in which blocks of type appear next to or ragged around the photographs they describe.

lead-ins Identifying words, usually in boldface, that describe an item at the beginning of a block of copy.

lifestyle catalogs Those catalogs featuring a certain psychographic attitude, behavior or way of life, to present merchandise.

lifetime value The monetary value of a single customer over the course of the average customer's lifetime.

list rental Names of other direct mail customers rented by a cataloger for the purpose of sending an offer or mailing.

logo The identifying name of a catalog displayed in its own unique, signature typeface.

loss leaders Value-priced, low-margin, best-selling products that induce prospects to try a catalog.

loyalty programs Efforts to build customer loyalty through clubs, frequency programs, regular discounts, special offers or other ongoing promotional programs.

margin, product The amount of gross profit a cataloger receives from the sale of a product. Low-margin products yield little profit relative to cost; high-margin products yield greater profit.

market, primary A cataloger's main target audience.

market, secondary/tertiary A catalog audience of lesser importance than a primary market. In selling children's apparel, for example, parents might be considered a *primary market;* grandparents and relatives might be a *secondary market.*

market share The amount of sales one cataloger has within a market, relative to the catalog's competitors.

market trends See *trends, market/consumer.*

marketing objective Measurable, specific goal to be achieved over a specified time period.

marketing, relationship The act of proactively building customer loyalty through ongoing promotional efforts, such as clubs, newsletters and special offers, in order to generate incremental sales and ensurecustomer satisfaction. See also *loyalty programs.*

mass market catalogs Catalogs that appeal to a broad-based group of consumers.

merchandising The act of product selection for a catalog.

model analysis See *analysis, model.*

mortise boxes Plain graphic boxes with borders, placed on a catalog cover, usually used for promotional messages.

niche-market catalogs See *vertical-market catalogs.*

non-selling copy Explanatory or informational editorial copy that helps enhance the perceived quality of the catalog brand and/or the merchandise.

offer The announcement of price and conditions pertaining to a product or service, to an interested consumer.

one-on-one interviews Research conducted person-to-person by a researcher asking questions of a prospect or customer.

order forms Inserts within catalogs used by customers to plan or list their purchases. These inserts also carry pertinent ordering, service, fit and delivery information.

opening spread The first two pages of a catalog, after the cover. Generally used for positioning copy, table of contents, president's letter, lists of new products and/or services, or other introductory catalog messages.

overnight shipping/delivery Services often promoted by catalogers to create a competitive edge.

POPS Acronym for Product, Organization, Person, Symbol. Used in helping specify and define a catalog's brand identity.

pacing The selling momentum of a catalog, created through the use of design, pagination and layouts.

pagination The act of creating a particular sequence for catalog pages. See also *repagination.*

parent catalog The original catalog brand or owner, from which other, more specialized catalogs may be spun off.

percentage-off discount See *discount, percentage-off.*

pickup art/photography Photography created for one catalog edition and repeated, or handed down, to another.

positioning The crystallization of a catalog's selling proposition; the way in which a catalog presents itself to its target audience. Good positioning matches the target consumers most important need(s).

positioning research A form of qualitative research in which customers are asked to give feedback on design, copy, logo and other positioning elements.

predictive modeling The act of analyzing a mailing list, using statistical analysis, to identify individuals most likely to respond.

president's letter Personal message from the cataloger to the recipient, usually used to promote merchandise, enhance catalog brand and/or develop a relationship with the customer. Normally appears on opening spread.

price points The prices for products in a catalog.

primary market See *market, primary.*

promotion In cataloging, discount, free gift or special service designed to entice customers to shop a particular catalog.

propping/props Stylistic elements and accessories used in a photography shoot, arranged to enhance the appearance of the main product.

prospect A person identified as a likely candidate to make a purchase.

prospecting The act of mailing catalogs or promotions to prospects.

psychographics Attitudinal information gleaned from studying a group of customers. Psychographic information may include political leanings, recreational interests, entertainment interests, and "how they think" in various areas.

qualitative research In depth research that explores customer opinion, feedback and attitudes, with small samples.

quantitative research Research that determines measurable customer information such as age, income and purchase history on large, statistically projectable samples.

RED Acronym for Relevance, Emotion, Drama. Used in determining the selling power of a catalog cover.

reactivation The act of bringing back lapsed or inactive customers.

relationship marketing See *marketing, relationship.*

relevance In cataloging, the use of design, copy, logo and art that has meaning and resonance for a particular target audience. Relevance involves understanding and responding to who the customer is and how she sees herself.

repagination Changing the sequence of pages or spreads in a catalog. Usually performed to create a fresh or more profitable appearance for the merchandise.

repositioning Shifting a catalog's presentation. Usually performed in order to enhance the catalog's appeal to a new or changing audience, or to explore a new marketplace niche.

research The act of exploring and understanding the behavior, attitudes, makeup, buying potential and demographics of a target market or audience. Research can be used to confirm positioning, find customer hot buttons, solve design issues and straighten out catalog emergencies.

research, customer-profiling Quantitative research, usually conducted by telephone or mail surveys, that details the demographics, attitudes and and/or purchase behaviors of customers.

research, customer-satisfaction Research, usually conducted by telephone or mail surveys, that measures how happy customers are with product mix, service and overall appeal of a catalog.

research-driven creative Catalog design and creative based on research and understanding of a customer base and marketplace. Such creative, including photography, model selection, copy, layouts, order form and logo, is designed to support the catalog's established identity and positioning in the market.

research, secondary Existing information that comes from a market-research firm or other source rather than from a cataloger's own customer base. Used to determine consumer trends or determine potential markets.

response/response rate The percentage of persons, out of the audience reached, who respond to a catalog mailing.

retail start-ups See *start-ups, retail.*

return rate The percentage of items, out of the number shipped, returned to the cataloger for refund or exchange.

SKU/SKU number Acronym for stock-keeping unit. A SKU number identifies a piece of merchandise in a catalog.

SWOT Acronym for Strengths, Weaknesses, Opportunities, Threats. Used in brand management to determine a catalog's position in the marketplace, and to determine how the catalog's strengths and assets match up with its competitors and with the catalog's customer base.

screen-back A "faded" photographic image used as a background for a product shot, copy block or promotional message.

secondary market See *market, secondary.*

secondary research See *research, secondary.*

selling spreads See *spreads, selling.*

spreads Successive two-page layouts in a catalog.

spreads, hero High-impact spreads distributed throughout a catalog, strategically positioned to stop customers on important selling spreads.

spreads, selling Two-page layouts featuring a catalog's regular, trademark merchandise.

silhouettes Photographs of products or apparel without a holding background, allowing the product's outline or "silhouette" to appear on the white space of the page.

situation analysis See *analysis, situation.*

slim jim A catalog of narrow dimension, approximately 4" X 10". Often used for sale or prospecting catalogs.

"snapshots" Photographs that capture the appearance of reality or intimacy between models. Useful for creating emotion in catalogs.

space ads Direct-response advertisements for catalogs or catalog products in magazines and newspapers.

spinoffs Catalogs that emanate from an original, or "parent," catalog. Usually created to address a large target niche within the parent catalog's market or audience.

starbursts Star-shaped graphic elements used to highlight promotional messages.

startups Newly launched catalogs.

startups, corporate Catalogs launched by an established corporate parent.

startups, kitchen-table Catalogs launched by an individual entrepreneur, or group of entrepreneurs.

startups, retail Catalogs launched by a retail chain.

still life Photographs of hard-goods products.

strategies The method(s) or the approach used to achieve a specific goal or marketing objective.

styling Creating the context for a catalog product in a photography shoot, using surfaces, backgrounds and props.

surveys Questions asked of customers that either measure customer satisfaction, or determine demographics or purchasing behavior and attitudes. Surveys can be conducted by telephone, mail or in person.

table of contents A listing of catalog-product categories, along with the pages on which they appear. Usually appears in opening spread.

tabletop Used to describe merchandise that appears on a table, such as crystal, china, silverwear, napkins and so forth.

tactics Actions and methods that support a cataloger's strategies. If a cataloger's strategy is to improve customer relationships, tactics might include creating loyalty programs and establishing regular customer surveys.

tagline A stand-alone descriptive headline or motto, usually found on a catalog cover.

target audience Those prospects that a cataloger determines would be interested in a particular catalog offer.

target market The marketplace in which a cataloger's target audience resides.

tertiary market See *market, secondary/tertiary.*

testimonials Publishable quotes or comments from customers that praise a catalog's products or services.

testing The act of mailing a certain number of catalogs to an audience segment in order to gauge response. Often used to determine the viability of new creative concepts, products or lists.

threefers See *twofers, threefers.*

trends, market/consumer Economic or sociological events (such as a recession, fad or baby-boom) that affect a cataloger's ability to sell within a certain market or to a certain group of consumers.

trim size The outer dimensions of a catalog.

twofers, threefers Promotional technique of selling certain items two-for-one or three-for-one in order to build average order size or liquidate inventory.

type, typeface The style and size of lettering used within a catalog.

unique selling proposition A catalog's single most important differentiating characteristic(s) — actual or perceived.

upscale Designed to appeal to educated, affluent consumers.

value Price and quality of a product.

values Emotional attachments or connotations that customers may associate with a brand.

vertical-market catalogs Catalogs that appeal to a group of consumers within a narrow market (i.e., young mothers), or who are defined by an interest in a particular type of product or service (i.e, Corvette-lovers).

vignettes Photographs with blurred-out edges.

A

ABV (attributes, benefits, values) analysis, 30
Address labels, 121
Appended information, *see* Demographics, research;
   Psychographics, research
Assets analysis, 22
Audience, *see also* Customers; Lists
 analysis
  for repositioning, 207–8
  for spin-off catalogs, 199
 segmentation, 24

B

Backend activities analysis, 40
Banners
 on covers, 108
Bargains
 use for improving response rates, 61
Benchmarking, 80, 86
Benefits perceived by customers, 16
Borders
 for pacing, 141–2
Boxes
 on covers, 108
Brand catalogs
 advantages of, 239–240
Brands
 capitalization
  as strategy, 42
  for corporate start-up catalogs, 192
  in spin-off catalogs, 200
  strategy, 43
  tactics, 51–2
 creation of, 49
 identity
  nature of, 9
  strategies, 37
  tactics, 37
  value of, 9–13
 image
  for corporate start-up catalogs, 193
  for traditional start-up catalogs, 194–5
 nature of, 15–20
 promotion
  strategy, 49
 value of, 43
Budget issues, 97
Bundling
 use for increasing order size, 62
Business plans, 39–40
Buying patterns analysis, 63

C

Callouts, 148
 for promoting value, 55
Carroll Reed
 prospect problems
  case study of, 64
Categories of catalogs, 29
Celebrities, *see under* Personnel, models
Chadwick's
 brand identity
  case study of, 49
Change, 103–4
Changes
 choices in
  for updating, 217–8
 value of, 218
Circulation analysis, 40
Clifford & Wills
 repositioning
  case study of, 38
Closing spreads, 117
Color
 consistency, 136
 for pacing, 140
 in type, 146

Communication

Communication
 between models and photographers, 156
 nature of, 94
 role in creative, 94
Comparisons
 for promoting price, 55
Competitors
 analysis, 26, 39, 90
 as cause for eroding customer base, 223
 as sources for ideas, 216–7
 brand name *vs.* no-name, 43
 changes
  as indication to reposition, 205–6
 understanding of
  to aid in positioning, 26
Composition
 for pacing, 137–8
Consistency
 for pacing, 136
 in choice of models, 161
 nature of, 96
 of imagery, 19
 role in creative, 96
 value of when updating, 216
Consumers, *see* Customers
Copy, 165–172, *see also* Information
 explanatory, 56
 in sale catalogs, 236
 informational, 54
 successful examples, 175–184
 wording, 20
Corporations
 start-up catalogs, 192–3
Cover wraps, 109
 in reactivation catalogs, 226
Covers, 103–110, 134
 back, 120–1
  for sale catalogs, 234–5
 for sale catalogs, 234
 in reactivation catalogs, 226
 mistakes, 110
 use for improving response rates, 60
 value of, 103
Creative
 for corporate start-up catalogs, 192–3
 for retail start-up catalogs, 193–4
 for traditional start-up catalogs, 194–6
 marketing-based, 93–98
 nature of, 94
 tactics, 93
 updating, 215–216
  for repositioning, 209–211
 uses of, 97–8
Credibility, 11
 of spin-off catalogs, 199
Cross references
 in selling spreads, 120
Customers
 ages of, 72
  relation to typography, 146
 attitudes, 81
 behavior, 81
 decisions
  timing, 11
 identification with catalog, 9
 inactive (*see* Lists, inactive customers)
 knowledge of
  for traditional start-up catalogs, 195
 level of education, 47
 loyalty (*see* Loyalty)
 motivation, 23
 needs, 23, 24
 panels (*see* Panels (customers))
 profiling, 79, 81–2
 satisfaction research (*see* Research, satisfaction)
 target, 39
 wants *vs.* needs, 24

D

Demographics, 23
  changes
    as indication to reposition, 205–6
  for customer profiling, 81
  of prospect lists, 230
  research, 88–89
Density of spreads, 54, 55, 56, 97, *see also* Design
  in hero pages, 118
  in sale catalogs, 233, 235
Design, 145–149, *see also under* various design elements,
      e.g., type, layout, banners
  for covers, 109
  for pacing, 136–143
  for promoting price, 55
  in sale catalogs, 235–6
  in selling spreads, 119
  nature of, 96–7
  order blanks, 130
  role in creative, 96–7
  value of, 96–7
Devices, 147–8
  on covers, 107
  updating, 218
Differentiation, 11, 28, *See also* Uniqueness
  analysis, 73
  from competitors, 26–7
  of customers, 13
  of products, 13
  spin-off catalogs from main catalogs, 201
  through brand names, 43
  through covers, 106
  value in positioning, 21, 29
Discounts
  in reactivation catalogs, 224
Dot whacks, 59
  in reactivation catalogs, 226
  on covers, 108
Drama
  for pacing, 139
  use in covers, 105–6

E

Ease of use, 94, 96
  in selling spreads, 119
  order blanks, 130
  type, 145
Economic trends
  effect on positioning, 23
Eddie Bauer
  positioning
    case study of, 31
Emotionality, 51
  for pacing, 139
  of customers, 23, 24
  positioning, 24
  use in covers, 104–5
Employees, *see* Personnel
Evolution of brands, 16
Eyeflow
  for pacing, 142–3
  in selling spreads, 119
  research, 88

F

Facelift, *see* Updating
Familiarity, 19
  role in creative, 96
Feedback, 57
Financial issues, 59
First catalogs, 29
Fit
  assets with customers, 22
  brand identity with strategy, 42
  brand identity with tactics, 42
  cover image with audience, 104
  positioning with model choice, 159–60
  type with product, 146

Flow (catalog), *see* Pacing
Focus
  value in positioning, 29
Focus groups, 26, 85–87
  for positioning research, 82
  use in repositioning, 209
Franchising, 11
Frequency of purchase
  increasing
    tactics, 63–4
  nature of, 62–3
Freshening, *see* Updating
Front covers, *see* Covers
Fulfillment analysis, 40

G

Goals, 38–40, *see also* Objectives
  financial, 42
Gross margins, 40

H

Headlines
  for pacing, 141–2
  in sale catalogs, 236
Hero pages, 91, 117–9
  as back covers, 120–1
House files, *see under* Lists

I

Identity of catalog, 20
  analysis, 30
  definition of, 28
  through covers, 103
  value of, 239–240
  vs. other industries, 10
Image
  as coordinated with positioning, 28
  as reflection of customer, 19
  nature of, 15–20
  through covers, 103
Imagery, 10, 19, 20, 53–4
  as indication of quality, 46
  for corporate start-up catalogs, 193
  for pacing, 137–140
  in spin-off catalogs, 200
  of brands, 15–16, 43
  updating, 216
  use in covers, 104
Impact
  nature of, 95
  of hero pages, 118
  role in creative, 95
Inclusivity
  in selling spreads, 119–120
Information, *see also* Copy
  for educating customers, 54
  history of catalog, 22–3
    in opening spreads, 117
  in closing spreads, 117
  in hero spreads, 118
  in reactivation catalogs, 221
  in reactivation programs, 225
  in sale catalogs, 233, 234, 235
  in selling spreads, 119–120
  in service messages, 116
  non-selling
    for pacing, 141
  on covers, 106–7
    presentation, 107–9
  on order blanks, 126–8, 130
  on positioning
    in opening spreads, 117
    in spin-off catalogs, 201
  president's letter, 114–5
    in reactivation catalogs, 226
    in spin-off catalogs, 200
  selling
    for traditional start-up catalogs, 195

tables of contents, 115–6
through copy, 165–172
through devices, 147–8
Inserts, 123–125
brochures, 123–4
cards, 124
bind-in
in reactivation catalogs, 226
blow-in, 125
in reactivation catalogs, 226
friend-get-a-friend, 124
placement, 129
value of, 123
Interviews
one-on-one, 85, 87
for positioning research, 82–3
use in secondary research, 89

J
Jos. A. Bank
repositioning
case study of, 212

K
Kitchen table start-up catalogs,
  see Traditional start-up catalogs
Knockoffs, 12
Knowledge of customers, 22–23, 28, 95

L
Layout
for improving response rates, 60
for pacing, 137
for promoting price, 55
use by photographers, 154
Leadership
value in positioning, 29
Lew Magram
research
case study of, 91
use of celebrity models
case study of, 162
Lifestyle
positioning, 12
use for pacing, 139
Liquidations, 233
Lists, 60
analysis, 88–89
house files, 70–1
inactive customers, 221–2
older names, 72
prospects, 64, 71, 229
use in customer profiling, 82
use in positioning research, 83
use in satisfaction research, 80–81
Logos, 19, 147–9
analysis, 73
establishment, 52
in spin-off catalogs, 200
Loyalty
analysis, 73–4
as objective, 42
creation of
as strategy, 42
strategy, 44–5
tactics, 52–3
value of, 11, 44
vs. price sensitivity, 20

M
Market
analysis, 39
for repositioning, 207–8
changes
as indication to reposition, 205, 207
growth, 25
horizontal, 24
mass, 43, 47

maturation, 25
niche, 13, 29, 43
analysis, 74
for spin-off catalogs, 199
position, 29
trends (*see* Trends)
vertical, 24
Marketing
objectives, 35–7
problems
analysis, 69–74
strategies, 35–7
tactics, 35–7
Merchandise
in opening spreads, 116
screenings, 91
Message, *see* Information
Models, *see* Personnel, models

N
Name
as identity, 10
Niche, *see* Market, niche

O
Objectives, 39
in marketing, 35–36, 40, 42
strategies, 37
tactics, 37
Opening spreads, 113–7, 134
in reactivation catalogs, 226
in sale catalogs, 235
in spin-off catalogs, 201
updating, 218
Opportunities analysis, 27
Order blanks, 125–130
placement, 129
Order size
averages
analysis, 71–2
decreases, 69–70
increasing
tactics, 61–2
nature of, 61
Order-takers, *see* Personnel, order-takers
Ownability
of brand, 17

P
Pacing, 133–143, 135–6
for repositioning, 210–211
through hero spreads, 118
value of, 143
Pagination, 135
use for increasing purchase frequency, 63–4
Panels (customers), 85, 87–8
for creating loyalty, 52
for repositioning, 209
for spin-off catalogs, 200
Paper
changes
for sale catalogs, 234
Percentage off
use for increasing order size, 62
Perception
value in positioning, 29
Personality of catalogs, 21, 30
testing, 18
traditional start-ups, 195
Personnel
art directors, 146
creative staff, 28
changing, 218
designers, 97
focus group mediators, 87
interviewers, 86, 87
models, 156, 159–163
analysis, 162

celebrities, 162–3
consistency, 136
order-takers
    role in satisfaction research, 80
    value in promoting service, 56–7
photographers, 152, 154, 156
role in customer profiling, 81
role in positioning research, 82, 83
role in satisfaction research, 80
Photography, 151–157
    closeups
        for promoting quality, 54
    consistency, 136
    fashion, 154–6
        lighting, 155–6
        locations, 154–5
    feature shots, 119
    for pacing, 137–8
    hard goods, 152–54
        lighting, 153
        props, 153
        technical details, 152–3
    in sale catalogs, 235–6
    laydowns
        for pacing, 140
    lighting
        for pacing, 139
    props
        for pacing, 138–9
    tips, 157
    updating, 216
Planning, 36–8
Point of view
    of catalog, 18
POPS (product, organization, person, symbol)
    analysis, 30
Positioning, 10, 82–3, see also Repositioning
    as coordinated with image, 28
    as guide to choosing models, 159–60
    as related to price, 20
    as related to strategy, 38
    attainability, 28
    complexity, 28
    definition of, 28
    for corporate start-up catalogs, 193
    for spin-off catalogs, 201
    how to, 21–31
    nature of, 15–20, 17–18
    of brand, 15–16
    purpose of, 31
    rational, 24
    research, 79, 82–3
    steps for, 21–2
Predictive modeling
    for increasing purchase frequency, 63
Price point execution
    for improving response rates, 61
Prices
    changes
        as indication to reposition, 205–6
    cutting
        for increasing purchase frequency, 64
    in relation to positioning, 20
    promotion, 236
        as strategy, 42
        strategy, 47–8
        tactics, 54–5
    vs. quality, 46
Pricing
    high, 11, 39
    low, 47
Products
    attributes, 16
    market research, 89
    mix, 40
    positioning, 48
Profiling, see Customers, profiling
Promotions

analysis, 73
    for increasing purchase frequency, 64
    on covers, 108
Prospect files, see Lists, prospects
Prospecting catalogs, 229–231
Psychographics
    for customer profiling, 81
    research, 88–89
Purchase frequency, see Frequency of purchase

Q
Quality
    follow-through, 28
    promotion
        strategy, 42, 46–7
        tactics, 53–4
    vs. price, 46

R
Reactivation catalogs, 221, 223–6
RED (Relevance, Emotion, Drama), 104
Relationships
    between catalog and customers, 44–45
        creation of, 53
        value of, 53
    between models and customers, 159, 161
    between models and photographers, 156
Relevancy
    nature of, 95
    role in creative, 95
    use in covers, 104, 105
Rented lists, see Lists, prospects
Repositioning, 38, 205–213
Reputation, 12
Research, 77–83, see also under various types of
        research, e.g., Focus groups, Surveys
    for repositioning, 209
    market
        for spin-off catalogs, 200
    qualitative, 82
    quantitative, 81
    satisfaction, 79–81
    secondary, 89–90
    tools, 85–91
    uses of, 77–9, 91
    value of, 77–8
Response rates
    decreases, 69–70
    improving
        tactics, 60–1
        through cover information, 106
    nature of, 59–60
Retail businesses
    start-up catalogs, 193–4
Rewards
    to create loyalty, 52
Risk
    regarding creative, 110

S
Sale catalogs, 233–237
Sales stimulation
    through cover information, 106–7
Samples
    for promoting quality, 54
Screening backs
    on covers, 109
        in reactivation catalogs, 226
Sections of a catalog, 113–4
    organization, 134–5, 142
Selling spreads, 119–120
    elements of, 113–121
    flow, 135
    pacing (see Pacing)
Services
    add-on, 25
    follow-through, 28
    promotion

strategy, 42, 48–9
  tactics, 56–7
shipping and handling, 60
value of, 45, 48, 56
Sharper Image, The
  repositioning
    case study of, 212–3
Size of catalogs
  changes
    for sale catalogs, 234
  length, 13
    of prospecting catalogs, 231
Space
  use of, 54, 56
Spin-off catalogs, 199–202
Spreads, *see* Closing spreads; Hero pages; Opening spreads;
    Selling spreads
Start-up catalogs, 191–197
Stickers, 61
Strategies, 38, 41–49
  as reflection of brand identiy, 38
  as related to positioning, 38
  assessment, 39–40
  business
    changes
      as indicators for repositioning, 205–7
  in marketing, 36–7
    nature of, 35–6
  prioritization, 42
Strengths analysis, 22, 27
Styling
  for hard goods photographs, 153
  for pacing, 138–140
Sundance
  spin-off catalog
    case study of, 202
  start-up catalog
    case study of, 196–7
Surveys
  Direct Marketing Association
    for satisfaction research, 80
  for creating loyalty, 52
  for spin-off catalogs, 200
  mail, 85–6
    for satisfaction research, 80
  questionnaires, 81
  telephone, 85, 86
    for satisfaction research, 80
  use in repositioning, 209
SWOT (strengths, weaknesses, opportunities, threats) analy-
    sis, 22, 27
Symbols, 147–8
  for promoting quality, 53–4
Syndicated media research, 89

T
Tables of contents, 115–6
Tactics, 38, 42, 49
Tag line, 28
Tear sheets
  use in repositioning, 211
Testing, 78
  sale catalogs, 237
  using reactivation messages, 225–6
Text, *see* Copy
Threats analysis, 27
Timeline
  for repositioning, 210–211
Tradition, 28
Traditional start-up catalogs, 194–6
Trends, 25
  analysis, 27
    for repositioning, 207–8
  changes
    as indication to reposition, 205, 207
  effect on positioning, 23
  societal

effect on positioning, 23
value of, 27
Trust, 9, 22
  gained through reactivation catalogs, 224
Twofers
  use for increasing order size, 62
Type, 19, 54, 145–6, *see also* Design
  consistency, 136
  for pacing, 140–1
  on covers, 107
  updating, 217

U
Uniqueness, 29, *see also* Differentiation
  lack of, 47–8
  of brand, 17
  of catalog, 18
  of product and price
    use for promoting value, 55
  of quality, 46
  positioning, 94
  through model presentation, 161
  value of, 12, 27, 45, 239–240
    in positioning, 21
Updating catalogs, 215–218, *see also* Changes
  use for increasing purchase frequency, 63

V
Value
  changes
    as indication to reposition, 205–6
  promotion
    strategy, 42, 48
    tactics, 55–6
Value-added benefits, 44
Values
  of brand, 15, 16–17
  of customers, 23
Vision
  for traditional start-up catalogs, 195
Visual nature of catalogs, 19
Visuals
  use for promoting quality, 53–4
Voice, 165–172, *see also* Copy
  of brand, 15–16
  of catalog, 19, 20
  successful examples, 175–184

W
Weakness analysis, 27